G. E. MOORE'S ETHICAL THEORY

This is the first comprehensive study of the ethics of G. E. Moore, the most important English-speaking ethicist of the 20th century. Moore's ethical project, set out in his seminal text *Principia Ethica,* is to preserve common moral insight from skepticism and, in effect, persuade his readers to accept the objective character of goodness. Brian Hutchinson explores Moore's arguments in detail and in the process relates the ethical thought to Moore's anti-skeptical epistemology. Moore was, without perhaps fully realizing it, skeptical about the very enterprise of philosophy itself, and in this regard, as Brian Hutchinson reveals, was much closer in his thinking to Wittgenstein than has been previously realized.

This book shows Moore's ethical work to be much richer and more sophisticated than his critics have acknowledged.

Brian Hutchinson teaches in the philosophy department of the University of Iowa.

G. E. MOORE'S ETHICAL THEORY

Resistance and Reconciliation

BRIAN HUTCHINSON

University of Iowa

CAMBRIDGE
UNIVERSITY PRESS

PUBLISHED BY THE PRESS SYNDICATE OF THE UNIVERSITY OF CAMBRIDGE
The Pitt Building, Trumpington Street, Cambridge, United Kingdom

CAMBRIDGE UNIVERSITY PRESS
The Edinburgh Building, Cambridge CB2 2RU, UK
40 West 20th Street, New York, NY 10011-4211, USA
10 Stamford Road, Oakleigh, VIC 3166, Australia
Ruiz de Alarcón 13, 28014 Madrid, Spain
Dock House, The Waterfront, Cape Town 8001, South Africa

http://www.cambridge.org

First published 2001

Printed in the United States of America

Typeface Baskerville 10/12 pt.   *System* QuarkXPress [AG]

A catalog record for this book is available from the British Library.

Library of Congress Cataloging in Publication Data
Hutchinson, Brian.
G.E. Moore's ethical theory: resistance and reconciliation / Brian Hutchinson. p. cm.
Includes bibliographical references (p.).
ISBN 0-521-80055-2
1. Moore, G. E. (George Edward), 1873–1958 – Ethics. 2. Ethics, Modern – 20th
century. 3. Moore, G. E. (George Edward), 1873–1958. Principia ethica. I. Title.
B1647 M74 H85 2001
171'.2 – dc21   00-064189

ISBN 0 521 80055 2 hardback

To Joyce, with love

The author wishes to thank Professor Richard A. Fumerton for his criticisms, encouragement, and advice.

Contents

Introduction: Irony, Naïveté, and Moore

There is no purer expression of the objectivity of value than G. E. Moore's in *Principia Ethica*. We can best capture the purity of Moore's vision by reaching across the ages to contrast him to the philosopher with whom he shares the deepest affinities, Plato. Plato trounces both the logic and psychology of Thrasymachus's confused and callow diatribe that the notion of objective value is based on a hoax. Still, there are times when one wonders whether he is just saying how *he* would manage the hoax were he in charge. Even if Plato's giving great lines to skeptical opponents is finally not an expression of unease, but of supreme confidence in the power of his thought and the beauty of his poetry to overwhelm the gravest of doubts, this comparison highlights the fact that in *Principia*, Moore never even *entertains* doubts about the objectivity of value. It is not outright skeptics who catch Moore's ire, but philosophers who refuse to serve objectivism straight.

J. M. Keynes points in the direction of this fact about *Principia* in his loving and clear-eyed memoir when he speaks of Moore's innocence.[1] How a man of thirty, especially one who kept the company Moore did, could have remained innocent is a mystery difficult to fathom. Perhaps it is to be savored rather than solved. Likely, it is no part of its solution but only another way of pointing to the mystery to observe that Moore seems to have been utterly lacking in irony. Because he was as he seemed, he trusted things to be as they seemed.

Irony has been part of the stock in trade of philosophers since Socrates captivated Plato and in this era irony has even greater currency than usual. We thus have trouble believing that such a work as *Principia* could be great. But its lack of irony is actually the key to *Principia*'s greatness. Because the unwarranted, debilitating doubt that haunts others is the one thing Moore is skeptical of, he is able to tell a simple and moving story about how human beings constantly jeopardize the plain awareness of objective value that is their birthright. He makes us ache at how much unhappiness we cause ourselves by letting the simple truth about goodness, which should be nothing very hard to hold on to, slip *almost* entirely away. At the same time, the simple and sophisticated philosophical con-

---

[1] J. M. Keynes, "My Early Beliefs," in *Essays and Sketches in Biography* (New York: Meridian Books, 1956), p. 250.

ception of value lying behind his story makes him as tough-minded and tenacious as Joe Frazier in stalking the doubts of others. Because the deeper view, finally, is the one that comes to grips with doubts it has itself felt, we are unlikely to agree with Keynes that Moore surpasses Plato.[2] Nevertheless, we all have moments when the profoundest truths appear to be the ones right on the surface, when the idea of *depth* seems illusory.[3] *Principia* captures this thought as beautifully as any that has the depth to defend it.

Its being an expression of the thought that wisdom lies in accepting the simple, obvious truth makes *Principia* problematic to many philosophers. Most philosophers instinctively regard themselves as challengers rather than defenders of what all people, including philosophers, instinctively believe. It is thus difficult for them to avoid concluding that even if these beliefs are not simply to be jettisoned as terminally simpleminded, in the service of offering a revelation, it is their duty to make them over so thoroughly as to leave them unrecognizable. But it may just be that the greatest of iconoclastic acts is to renounce iconoclasm and to defend or, with the thought that it is not really defending that they need, just completely and confidently articulate the simple views that even philosophers hold when they forget they are philosophers: Moore is not afraid to be a lonely philosopher and stand with the crowd.

Those not given to irony make easy targets for it and history has targeted Moore in a particularly delicious way. In very little time, it became the received view that the philosopher who claimed to have cleared the ground of the obstacles impeding the complete philosophical acceptance of objectivism inadvertently laid bare its untenableness. Within a generation, two different ways of dismissing Moore's positive views were being rehearsed by those who accepted his negative arguments against objectivist theories less robust than his own. Some, such as A. J. Ayer, while finding much to praise in his making clarity the *sine qua non* of intellectual seriousness, dismissed his positive views with a sneer. Others, like C. L. Stevenson, posing as one who would eagerly look for the needle if only Moore would tell him what it looked like, dismissed them with a shrug.[4]

The view that Moore's thought was too barren to sustain objectivist ethics became more firmly entrenched after the Second World War, even as philosophers renewed their sympathies toward objectivism. Since Moore had been responsible for scorching so much of the ground, he could hardly be expected to help reenliven it. He rather deserved op-

[2] Ibid.
[3] Ludwig Wittgenstein, *Philosophical Investigations* (New York: Macmillan and Company, 1953), p. 47.
[4] Alfred Jules Ayer, *Language, Truth and Logic,* 2nd ed. (New York: Dover Publications Inc., 1946), pp. 32, 33–4, 68. C. L. Stevenson, "The Emotive Meaning of Ethical Terms," *Mind,* Vol. 46 (1937), pp. 30–1.

probrium for steering ethics into so horribly dead an end that emotivism or some equally benighted offshoot seemed for a time to be the only way out. It is in the work of the philosopher-historian Alasdair MacIntyre, with a historical sweep and sense of Moore's importance almost matching Moore's own, that the view of Moore as destroyer achieves its ironic apotheosis. MacIntyre holds Moore to be a major figure not just in the decline of English-language ethical thought, but in the moral deterioration of Western culture that has gone on for centuries.[5] One might find there to be a rough justice in the way history has come to look at Moore. What has been done unto him is no different than what he, so melodramatically assuming the role of revolutionary, had done unto others.[6] But even if *Principia* is responsible for nothing but mischief, the least it deserves is something it has not received to this day – a careful, reasonably sympathetic, and *thorough* reading.[7]

No doubt Moore must receive some of the blame for the partial readings his work has received. His overplaying his revolutionary part has made it difficult for many to see that rather than destroying the Western ethical tradition, which after all has for the most part been objectivist, he actually sheds a light upon it that allows its objectivist outlines to stand out more sharply than ever. By his own fiery words, he directs attention to the part of *Principia* in which he is most melodramatically in opposition. This, of course, is the Open Question Argument. The attempt to understand great figures is often impeded by the overwrought praise of early adulators who only half understand them. So it is no surprise that the high repute in which so many prerevisionist admirers held that argument has abetted the overly great, far more critical attention it has received in the years following.[8] One of the aims of this book is to take that very famous argument down more than a notch so that *Principia* and the rest of Moore's ethics may be more easily read as an organically unified whole.

In this, the book employs the same strategy but a different tactic than the one employed by a book to which this book, however much it might

---

[5] Alasdair MacIntyre, *After Virtue*, 2nd ed. (South Bend: University of Notre Dame Press, 1984), pp. 14–19.

[6] For quotes from anonymous early reviewers of *Principia* who express grave reservations about the accuracy of Moore's history, see Tom Regan's *Bloomsbury's Prophet* (Philadelphia: Temple University Press, 1986), pp. 19, 196–7.

[7] Regan is a great admirer of both Moore and his work, but his work is as much a spiritual and intellectual biography as a philosophical study. Other sympathetic and more distinctly philosophical studies of Moore's ethical thought such as John Hill's *The Ethics of G. E. Moore, A New Interpretation* (Assen: The Netherlands, Van Gorcum and Co., 1976) and Robert Peter Sylvester's *The Moral Philosophy of G. E. Moore* (Philadelphia: Temple University Press, 1990), do not deal with Moore's work in its entirety.

[8] William K. Frankena, "The Naturalistic Fallacy," in *Readings in Ethical Theory*, Willfred Sellars and John Hospers, eds. (New York: Appleton-Crofts Inc., 1952), pp. 103–4, notes the early uncritical praise for the OQA.

disagree with it, acknowledges a great debt, Tom Regan's *Bloomsbury's Prophet*. Regan attempts to bring Moore back to life as a superb ethicist whose work has profound and surprising ramifications for social and political philosophy. Coincident with that, Regan also presents Moore as a figure whose personality and voice were compelling enough to dazzle a coterie of interesting artists and intellectuals. But although he considers the claim that good is an indefinable property to be of crucial importance to Moore, Regan *ignores* the argument by which he attempts to prove it. His single reference to this "particularly important argument" has to do with Virginia Woolf's vertiginous feelings of bafflement about it.[9] There is much to be said for Regan's tactic. The argument is but one small part of a grandly conceived book. The historical evidence amassed by Regan suggests that the conception drove the argument, which is the opposite of what the great critical emphasis on the argument suggests.[10] Nevertheless, this book chooses to confront the argument early on and acknowledge its weakness as an argument. Later, it suggests ways to free it from the burden of being the thing everything else depends on. Even if Moore placed great weight on the definitiveness of the OQA *for a time,* in this most ironical of ages we should be willing not to take a philosopher at his own word.[11]

One who wishes to deflate the OQA in order to revive interest in the entirety of Moore's theory faces imposing obstacles. A 1992 article on the current state of ethics commissioned by *The Philosophical Review* in celebration of its one-hundredth year may fairly be considered to represent the age's received opinion.[12] In "*Principia*'s Revenge," the very first section of that article's introduction, the authors observe that the controversy initiated by the OQA is only slightly less old than the *Review.* While celebrating the one "without reserve" they wonder whether they should be "equally happy about the continuing vitality of the other." They worry that "Moore's accident-prone deployment of his . . . argument . . . appeal[s] to a now defunct intuitionistic Platonism." Still they conclude, "However readily we now reject as antiquated his views in semantics and epistemology, it seems impossible to deny that Moore was on to something." The sad truth then is that the OQA must be separated from the rest of *Principia* because it is the one part of it time has not passed by. Al-

---

[9] *Bloomsbury's Prophet,* pp. 197–8.

[10] Thomas Baldwin notes in *G. E. Moore* (London and New York: Routledge 1990), pp. 87–8, that the section in which Moore presents the OQA is the only part of his early discussion that does not come directly from his original book-length effort, *The Elements of Ethics,* Tom Regan, ed. (Philadelphia: Temple University Press, 1991). But this seems rather tenuous evidence for his conclusion that "Moore felt that the argument . . . needed a more careful statement than he had previously given it."

[11] G. E. Moore, Preface to *Principia Ethica: Revised Edition,* Thomas Baldwin, ed. (Cambridge: Cambridge University Press, 1993), p. 3.

[12] Stephen Darwall, Allan Gibbard, Peter Railton, "Toward *Fin de siècle* Ethics: Some Trends," *Philosophical Review* (January 1992), pp. 115–89.

though it does not lead these authors to wonder with any great humility about what their own final philosophical destinations might be, the illustriousness of Moore's company in the graveyard might ease his disappointment at being found inept and outmoded. Just possibly, it might also suggest that for strong and compelling expressions of major philosophical points of view, time's sting is never quite permanent.

Much of the current age's unease with Moore has to do with its obsession with the thought that many different points of view may be taken about anything at all and that none of them can be validated as presenting the world as it really is. Any attempt to assess the adequacy of a point of view must be made from a different point of view; *that* point of view must then be assessed from another, and so on and on. The thought naturally arises that it is impossible for us ever to know that we have cognized the world as it really is. When that thought is fully absorbed, a second one naturally arises that there *is* no way the world "really is." If, from the first point of view, one considers Moore to be trying to present the world as we would all acknowledge it to be but for our letting it get sicklied o'er with philosophical thought, the response is that he actually just presents us with another *appearance* of the world. If, from the more radical point of view, one considers him without realizing it to be trying to present the *original* appearance of value upon which all other appearances are worried elaborations, the first response is that there just is no such appearance. But even if there were, no matter how ingenious and ingenuous his *re*-presentation of it would happen to be, it would, since it lies on the other side of doubt, have to be something different. So Moore makes not one, but two, failed attempts to retrieve an incontestable starting point for ethics: he gives us neither pure reality nor pure appearance.

Papers Moore allowed to gather dust show that for a time even he adhered to such lines of thought as these. But in the same year as *Principia,* he puts forward a view of consciousness that allows him to escape the perspectivalist conundrum.[13] Rather than having "contents," consciousness is directed to objects lying outside it. There can thus be present *to* consciousness (part of) the very world itself. It follows then that it is possible for one who is not benumbed by doubts of philosophical making just to *observe* how (part of) the world is. Turning to value, Moore does not then just deliver to philosophers the *perspective* on the world taken by the naïve and for that reason, clear-minded child – he delivers them the *world.* The joke turns out to be on those sophisticates who think that things must be seen through rather than just seen. Although he came to be unhappy with the particulars of it,[14] once Moore offered his refutation of idealism,

---

[13] "The Refutation of Idealism," in *Philosophical Studies* (Totowa, New Jersey: Littlefield and Adams, 1965), pp. 1–30.
[14] Preface to *Philosophical Studies*, p. viii.

he never looked back. As is suggested by Bertrand Russell's moving comments about the relief and joy Moore brought to him by enabling him to trust again in the world's reality, Tom Regan's view that Moore is a "liberator," which we shall discuss at length and mostly oppose, seems in this instance to be right on the mark.[15]

To someone with Moore's views, the philosopher's task is not just to defend the claim that we are directly in touch with the things of the world; it is also to show what these things are. The great difficulty has been that philosophers suffer from a deep-seated impulse to obscure the things they observe. He thus considers that his ruthless exposure of the "naturalistic fallacy" by the OQA will give philosophers a chance to go back to just before the moment when they made the first false judgment of identity that set everything off on the wrong foot – and not make it. Previously when philosophers had made such a judgment, whatever it happened to be, they had never been able to completely unmake it. Their impulse had always been to construct a philosophical system to mitigate their error when only a renunciation of it would do.

The response to Moore's argument that William Frankena has made obvious is that any *argument* that sets out to *prove* that an identity judgment is false must beg the question.[16] This requires us then to go beyond Moore's express understanding of the OQA. Rather than see it as a failed attempt to prove what he came close to recognizing as being unprovable,[17] we should see it instead as something that helps us to get our bearings about what we honestly *find* about value – that it can be understood in, and accepted on, its own terms only. The rest of *Principia*, by offering a full-scale theory that makes rich sense of our honest findings, enables us to answer the question whether any scruples we might have about them can be so deep and well taken as to lead us to reject them. The answer is the same as that concerning any scruples we might have suggesting that we do not really have knowledge of the external world: "No." So any reading of *Principia* that, as the one proffered in *The Philosophical Review* does, severs the OQA from its metaphysical and epistemological underpinnings, will leave it without the resources to address skepticism and all its attendant feelings of bewilderment and loss.

Looking at *Principia* as entirely of a piece makes Moore interesting company for Wittgenstein. Moore can be seen to anticipate Wittgenstein's diagnosis that the philosophical intellect suffers a kind of bewitchment that creates a deep and abiding sense of alienation. Like Wittgenstein, Moore suggests a program of therapy whose aim is to restore to philosophers their sense of being at home in the world. But

[15] Bertrand Russell, "My Mental Development," in *The Philosophy of Bertrand Russell*, Paul Arthur Schilpp, ed. (La Salle, Illinois: Open Court, 1972), p. 12.
[16] "The Naturalistic Fallacy," p. 113.   [17] *Principia*, p. 143.

rather than requiring philosophers to do what Wittgenstein himself could never do – give up philosophy – Moore assumes that his therapy will allow them to continue to philosophize. It will do so by giving them the means to keep their nerve in the face of the doubts that are the source of their alienation: Moore holds that it is only an impulse philosophers give in to while doing philosophy that is alienating, not philosophy itself. But given his claim that all philosophers prior to Sidgwick had given in to this impulse, he should have been at least a little bit troubled by the possibility that philosophy itself is the source of alienation.[18] It ought to have occurred to him, as it did to Wittgenstein, to wonder whether a skeptical metaphilosophy must go all the way down with philosophy. Moore's belief that the philosophical impulse to obfuscate can be eliminated without trace merely by his exposure of it is *very* naive. It turns out then, and for similar reasons, that Moore's relation to Wittgenstein is similar to his relation to Plato. Wittgenstein's willingness to raise doubts about philosophy, when combined with his penetration and immense poetical gifts, gives his investigations a tragic grandeur that Moore, who left no room for tragedy in the world, cannot sustain.[19]

Wittgenstein is said to have remarked of Moore that he showed how far one could get in philosophy without a great intellect.[20] Even if he did not mean this remark to be a compliment, there is a way to read it as such: It takes a very great prosaic mind to withstand the philosophical temptation to try to make things more or less than they are. Likely, it was this remarkable cast of mind that also enabled Moore, of all those who knew Wittgenstein, to take his measure most accurately for philosophy, to indulge in neither hysterical denunciation nor sycophantic adulation when he began his great therapeutic exercises. It is a literary staple that a sidekick knows some things the hero does not. Does Moore, in his insistence that the world has a nature that is not to be shaped by what we say or think about it, not only express the view we cannot help but accept when we are not philosophizing, but also the wiser philosophical view? When the critique that philosophical attempts to explicate reality are the result of tricks played by language is itself subject to critique, is not Moore's naïve view that the world has an ultimate, explicable nature the one left holding the field? Irony, understood as the attempt to hide from and acknowledge failure simultaneously, only makes sense if we *know* there is a reality we must try to live up to.

One way of responding to such questions as these is to refuse their terms. Philosophy consists of a series of negotiations between dichotomies, with the ones it must negotiate at any particular time being

---

[18] Ibid., p. 17.
[19] Ibid., p. 219. We discuss Moore on tragedy in the book's last chapter.
[20] *Bloomsbury's Prophet,* p. 187.

bequeathed to it by history. As it has been for more than half a century now, the task of objectivist ethical theory is to find a way of chastening Moorean confidence with Wittgensteinian humility. As the authors of *The Philosophical Review* article explain, many philosophers consider it to be their task to show "morality [to be] a genuine and objective area of inquiry," that need not appeal to any grand notions of an "independent metaphysical order."[21] One might continue in this vein by saying that because they have learned from Wittgenstein how to be suspicious of them, philosophers now have a better chance of avoiding the stupefying commitments that traditionally have been made in the name of such an order. Being more careful of the dangers they themselves create, they will be more disciplined in their refusal to make use of notions they have officially discounted. Nevertheless, as long as they exercise extreme caution, they may – must – borrow from the tradition of which they are so wary. Although the scale of the resulting theories will be smaller than what generations of earlier philosophers have been used to seeing, they will, for that very reason, be more human and more plausibly sustained.

The refusal of duly chastened philosophers to make use of grandiose notions will lead many nostalgic philosophers to worry that what is lacking in these accounts is just what is most important. Therefore, a crucial part of these projects will consist of debunking, of applying the Wittgensteinian insight that the monsters philosophers have tried to keep at bay by creating adamantine metaphysical structures, are really just the shadows of those structures. Once started on the project of building such a structure, at no matter what stage they find themselves in it, philosophers have been unable to put to rest their fears that something is amiss with it, that it is not yet strong enough really to keep those monsters out. These fears spur further efforts at construction and repair, which create more shadows in a never-ending dialectic of futility.

It goes against received opinion to recognize that for the most part, Moore stands up well to criticisms of this kind. Although there are times when he suffers from a somewhat prolix and gnarled style, in his hands it does not make the truth seem baffling or obscure. His style is rarely suggestive of one who must first convince himself before he can convince others. His plain words bespeak his fundamental conviction that goodness is simply *there* – we find it. His great confidence does often serve him poorly as a critic, however, making him much too impatient of those who have failed to see as clearly as he. On too many occasions, he takes a hammer to views that call for a scalpel. Especially in his discussion of evolutionary ethical theories, his impatience leads him to smash away at points that would, when properly understood, serve his own views.

---

[21] "Toward *Fin de siècle* Ethics," pp. 130–1.

One place where we do find him straining is in his discussion of ethical egoism. This is not surprising, as it is over this issue that the encounter with moral skepticism becomes most troubling. The fear of being played for a sucker looms large both in everyday life and philosophy. Still, the indignant tone Moore takes in this discussion poorly serves what is supposed to be a purely logical demonstration – he seems to be trying to badger the egoist into silence. His constant repetition of the charge that the egoist is "irrational," invoked almost as if it were a mantra, suggests a certain amount of desperation; even if he is at ease with his argument, he rightly senses that others will not be. It might be that Moore's straining shows him to suffer a weakness that sends him to the wrong place in his attempt to understand and deal with egoism's attractions. Perhaps the flaw in our thinking that makes egoism enticing has to do with a flaw in our *character* that his moral psychology is either not rich enough or not worked out enough to come to grips with fully.

Occasionally, Moore uses odd figures. Consider, for instance, his claim that good is something we are unable to pick up and move about with even "the most delicate scientific instruments."[22] Such figures have a charm that heightens *Principia*'s quality of innocence; this very prosaic mind still leaves a great deal of room for wonder. As Keynes notes, his innocence adds a most touching quality to his discussion of love and friendship.[23] At first, his tone appears to be much too abstract to tell us anything interesting about the flesh and blood of real life. But eventually one comes to wonder whether that tone enables him to find an element of purity that is common to our most mundane personal transactions and our most intimate and passionate moments. And although he writes distantly and diffidently of these things, his insistence on the indispensability of the body in love makes him one naïf who does not blush.

His ability to express his views in terms that do not stray beyond the resources of his philosophy also serves to keep Moore rather immune from self-deception. He is one philosopher who does not fall into the traps he most warns others against. In this, he compares favorably to some of his debunkers. He would never, for instance, think that the metaphysical-moral commitments of objectivity can be rendered less troubling by the simple expediency of having the "objective, categorical demands . . . ultimately issue from deep within the moral agent" rather than from the "external" "metaphysical order."[24] Surely, the skeptic's catcalls upon being told of objective moral "demands" has little to do with the "place" of their origination. Moore would have called those so easily impressed by their own metaphors "naïve and artless."[25]

---

[22] Ibid., p. 124   [23] "My Early Beliefs," p. 250.
[24] "Toward *Fin de siècle* Ethics," p. 137
[25] The phrase comes from his critique of Mill, *Principia*, p. 66.

He would also have been skeptical about the claim that although the weight of objectivity cannot be borne by goodness, it can somehow be shifted onto the entire corporate body of ethical concepts. As was recognized by Aristotle, the philosopher in whose name this claim is so often made, all the other finely honed notions used in the making of ethical judgments are forever in service to one basic question: Is a thing good or is it bad? Difficult philosophical questions about the nature of good cannot be made to disappear by having good slip into the crowd of the concepts it leads. And if we remain focused on the master ethical concept, we will be less likely to think that truisms about how each of us is acculturated into some particular ethical scheme both render us credulous with regard to that scheme and incapable of understanding any other. Moore was never so naïve as to think that the solution to moral-epistemological worries lies in making self-satisfaction and a lack of imagination prerequisites of moral understanding – skeptics will consider themselves *vindicated* to be told that there are different logically impregnable ways of making morality up. Once again, Moore insists on the truth of something we cannot help but believe (but *not* that it is true because we cannot help but believe it): There is a world independent of any of the ethical schemes we happen to employ to which they must all be responsible.

But if Moore avoids falling into the conservative metaphysical-epistemological trap of thinking that whatever different people cannot think their way beyond is true ("for them"), many philosophers seem to assume that the weight of his thought makes him far too eager to embrace a more conventional kind of political-social conservatism. Their fear is that his metaphysics and epistemology lead him to radically underestimate the intrinsic worth of the fully "autonomous" moral agent. This in turn makes him far too acquiescent in whatever rules, arrangements, and mores a particular society happens to have. The line of thought that leads to this conclusion starts with the observation that in order to engage in serious moral reflection, one must be searching and fearless; one must be willing to explore the possibility that *anything* might be good. Even though Moore admits this possibility as far as logic goes, the suspicion remains that he loses his nerve and forecloses too quickly on fearless moral exploration.[26] The *psychological* logic of his view, wedded as it is to the metaphor of having one's reflections and decisions guided by the property good, finally leaves him overly beholden to the established orders that "guide" one in so many different ways. Lying in the background of this criticism is the paradoxical and quintessentially modern thought that the fundamentality of the value(s) of autonomy and freedom requires people to *choose* the values by which they are to be guided.

[26] Abraham Edel, "The Logical Structure of Moore's Ethical Theory," in *The Philosophy of G. E. Moore,* Paul Schilpp, ed. (Evanston and Chicago, 1942), pp. 170–6.

Tom Regan, who both admires Moore and sympathizes with accounts that seek to "liberate" moral agents from various forms of authority, categorically denies that there is anything in Moore's philosophy committing him to any such form of conservatism. In fact, he argues the opposite case: Moore's metaphysics and epistemology *protect* the freedom of the individual – there are places where Regan makes Moore sound like an existentialist *in extremis.*[27] This book rejects such an interpretation of Moore. Although we deal with Regan at length in the main body of the text, we shall take a moment here to look at one line of his thought in order to show just how far removed Moore is from some of this age's most characteristic preoccupations and confusions.

As Moore himself does, Regan attaches great importance to the indefinability of the property good. He starts with the familiar observation that if good were definable in either naturalistic or metaphysical terms, it would be a "closed question" what things are good. "The Science of Morals" would cease to exist, as experts from the defining science would take it over completely. But Regan goes beyond what Moore explicitly says when he emphasizes the importance of good's being indefinable even in *nonnatural* terms. Nonnaturalistic indefinability protects the moral judgment of the individual from encroachment by *moral* science. He writes:

At the deepest level it is the autonomy of individual judgment about what has intrinsic value . . . that Moore relentlessly seeks to defend. *Individuals* must judge for themselves what things . . . are worth having for their own sakes. No natural science can do this. No metaphysical system can do this. Not even the Science of Morals can do this. Every attempt to take this freedom (and this responsibility) away from the individual rests on the same kind of fallacy. . . . The *raison d'être* of Ethics is to prove that there are some things – and these the most important things in human life – that no science can prove.[28]

The first thing to say is that Moore would simply be bewildered upon being told that the fact that "individuals must judge for themselves" whether something is valuable is of *any* import. This is something that is true of *all* judgments, whether their predicates be definable or indefinable, ethical or nonethical, scientific or nonscientific. The mistake of attaching significance to the fact that individuals "must" make "their own" judgments is similar to the psychological egoist's mistake, exposed long ago by Butler, of attaching significance to the fact that individuals have "their own" desires. As a desire's being one's own does not foreclose on the possibility of something other than oneself being its object, so does a moral or other kind of judgment being one's own not foreclose on the possibility of its being based on what somebody other than oneself judges. One who "judges for himself" that it is better to defer to the judgments

---

[27] Especially in the chapters "The Autonomy of Ethics" and "The Liberator," pp. 183–250. MacIntyre offers roughly the same reading of Moore from the negative side.

[28] *Bloomsbury's Prophet,* p. 204.

of others lets those others "make his judgments for him." There is then
no fuel for Promethean fires in the fact Regan makes so much of. This is
a good thing. As Aristotle might have asked, if individuals were on their
own in some deeper way than this, how would the young ever learn from
the old? How would the foolish ameliorate their foolishness? How would
even the wisest of us get along?

Above all else, Regan seems to fear a theory that would have moral
questions settled by something akin to an algorithm. His worry is that this
would make acts of moral judgment lifeless and mechanical. But this fear
is not Moore's; he thinks that there is a set of moral truths that, had we
complete knowledge of it along with all relevant nonmoral information,
would provide an exact answer to every moral question. It is nothing
metaphysical that prevents our reaching these answers, but the fact that
the world is rich and our knowledge of it – including our knowledge of
our own creative capacities – limited. Regan's fear of scientific thinking
seems to be based on the crudest of caricatures, according to which it embraces the ethos of conformity to the point of tyranny. But even in normal scientific times, there is contention and creativity in the sciences
every bit as exciting as any to be found in philosophy or the arts. This is
so even though all scientific controversialists recognize themselves as being obligated to follow certain (unclosed) canons of thinking in the pursuit of truth. As science makes room for both truth and gadflies, so too
can ethics.

Even if we allow Regan to be exaggerating for effect when he claims that
the *raison d'être* of ethics is to prove that there are things about life no science can prove, he does think that the unprovableness of its judgments is
what saves ethics from being soul deadening. Because it cannot be proved
to one that her moral judgments are false, no army of soldiers, scientists,
or priests can make her think otherwise. Regan also suggests that the unprovableness of a moral judgment is connected to the indefinability of its
fundamental term. But Moore insists that whether their terms be indefinable or definable, a great many *nonmoral* judgments are also unprovable.[29] And even though they are unprovable, since the moral judgments
of the hidebound and the free spirited alike must stand before the bar of
truth, truth trumps authenticity. To *judge* (*not* "for oneself") what is good
or bad is in no way to *choose* what shall be good or bad. To think otherwise
is to remain under the influence of that most powerful and pernicious of
twentieth-century philosophical spells, verificationism.

If Regan is wrong, are other critics right who maintain that the weight
of Moore's philosophical apparatus forces conservatism on him? Moore
would indeed be nonplussed by the thought of a serious person finding
the murder of an elderly shopkeeper to be an admirable expression of

[29] *Principia*, pp. 143–4.

antiauthoritarianism.[30] Since he does think that responsible behavior must be guided by goodness, he conveys no sense at all that we are making moral law when we decide what is best. It is no surprise then that he finds freedom to lack intrinsic value. Still, even if he refuses to join in the rush to make the poorly understood values of freedom and autonomy the centerpieces of morality, his conservative political-philosophical views are in no way forced upon him by his metaphysics or his metaphors. Although he rejects it, his theory leaves open the possibility that freedom is a part of organic unities having great intrinsic value. He allows for and perhaps accepts the thought that freedom is very good as a means.[31] But finally, on the paramount conservative issue of stability versus change, with eyes wide open, Moore does conclude that complacency toward standing orders is less dangerous than complacency toward untested new orders. A century has just closed in which fatuous optimism about the effects of unmooring people from their characteristic patterns of thought and behavior has helped to free them to carry out programs unprecedentedly bloody for regimes unspeakably dreary. His recommendation at the beginning of that century that we be *very* careful about risking those admittedly imperfect moorings seems then not to be naïve, but prescient.

We shall begin to bring this introduction to a close by considering the earlier hint that although he does not realize it, the deepest impulse of Moore's philosophy is, as Wittgenstein's is, to end philosophy. Moore's great aim in ethics is to expose and expunge philosophy's revisionary impulse in order to defend the things we know to be irreplaceable in any sane way of life. This requires a transformation of philosophy so profound as to be impossible for most philosophers to envisage: Some things philosophers must simply accept. But promulgating such a position within philosophy appears to undermine it. Even as he purports to locate the things lying not so much beyond as before dispute, he invites dispute. To make an official philosophical pronouncement that certain things are not open to serious question is to raise the suspicion that really, they are.

Moore might try to defend his own philosophizing against this line of thought by saying that his metaphysical explications of the things we know provide the means of permanently silencing the skeptic. With their metaphysical lines permanently protected, ethicists will now be able to proceed to the work in casuistry that has been too long neglected. He could also note that it is no part of his view that all the parts of a philosophical theory must be uncontroversial because the things it serves are. However difficult it has been for philosophers to do it, as he tries to show in his own career, one *can* prevent uncertainty in the philosophical

[30] Norman Mailer, "The White Negro," in *Advertisements for Myself* (New York: G. P. Putnam and Sons, 1959), p. 347.
[31] *Principia*, p. 186.

sphere from leaking into the sphere of what is known prephilosophically. But Moore needs to be more alert to the possibility that one explores the philosophical sphere only if one thinks of the prephilosophical sphere as *needing* explication or "support." That possibility makes the known the merely knowable. One who really thinks of the known as needing no support, as "going without saying" – would say *nothing*.

Moore is certainly naïve if he thinks for even a moment that an impulse as deep as the skeptic's could ever be eradicated. Since it never will be eradicated, it could turn out, on the metaphilosophy he seems most committed to, that philosophy will continue to have a role to play in human life, albeit one much less exalted than what it has usually reserved for itself. According to this view, the only worthwhile form of philosophy is *reactionary;* the sole job of philosophy is to resist philosophy. Because ordinary thought's inarticulateness provides it with some protection against skepticism, it is not something to be bemoaned. Nevertheless, once it is taken in by skepticism, its inarticulateness leaves ordinary thought incapable of responding to skepticism with anything but a sputter. It is, therefore, the job of reactionary philosophy to offer resistance, usually piecemeal, to revisionary philosophy's illegitimate encroachments on ordinary thought. Even if reactionary philosophers do on occasion put forward large-scale positive theories, being in the form of preemptive strikes against various skeptical challenges, they remain defensive in character. One who comes to such a view of philosophy might find Moore's exclusion of philosophy from the catalog of things having intrinsic value to be most revealing and most moving. Philosophy is good only as a means to the dissolution of intellectual clots that the wrong kind of philosophy creates. This would suggest that Moore pursues philosophy not because he finds it to be intrinsically interesting, but because he recognizes an obligation to help others dissolve the clots they suffer from. His long philosophical career is then an impressively patient and quiet one of self-sacrifice.

One might find this entire line of thought to be troublingly antiintellectual. By its lights, the highest form of wisdom is not merely to accept that things are what they are; it is never even to *consider* that they could be anything else – it has the pig defeating Socrates on both counts. We can safely assume that Moore would have been disconsolate to have found his thought leading to such a conclusion. A way of fending it off that is suggested by other, related lines in his thought is to see philosophy and other intellectual activities as purely aesthetic in character, to see them, that is, as concerned solely with beauty and not at all with truth. This enables human beings to rise above the pig without suffering alienation and also allows philosophy and other refined modes of thought more freedom than views do that see them as engaged in the pursuit of truth. One might find that this makes the quarantining of philosophical thought from ordinary thought beneficial to both. One might also find that by not having been too hasty in accepting the values of freedom and self-creativity, Moore is able to uncover the realm in which these goods are to be found in their purest, most precious form – it is in *thought* that we are at our freest and most creative. Still, we are likely to conclude that the price of severing philosophy from truth is one Moore would have found too high. At the end of this book, we consider a way of maintaining a connection between philosophical and other kinds of systematic thought and truth. If successful, this would enable philosophers and others of the intellectually engaged to have, along with the boldness of free imaginative flight, less dangerous commitments to puzzlement and truth.

Perhaps it will not be amiss to close this introductory discussion by allowing Moore his own irony. Whatever its origins finally happen to be, a philosophical program of skepticism can only be sustained by the profoundest kind of credulity. It must be something extraordinary that allows one to maintain, in the face of the direct awareness that good is what it is and not another thing, such propositions as that good is set by the course of evolution, or that it is nothing but pleasure, or that it waits upon the will of God or man. But as Moore had occasion to observe in his own work in the history of ethics, no matter how sharp the skeptical edges of their intellects be, philosophers' theories are finally blunted by their own rock-headed good sense. The credulity that sustains skeptical philosophy never goes all the way down to the bottom of things. This might appear to provide us with only the smallest of comforts, as the depth philosophical credulity does reach is enough to make the human condition one of bewilderment and woe. But it does leave open the hope that we all have moments of peace when, with guards down, we find ourselves humbly accepting the reality of goodness and the world's many good things.

1

Simplicity, Indefinability, Nonnaturalness

Lay of the Land

The revolution G. E. Moore wishes to effect in *Principia Ethica* begins with his famous claim that the property good is simple, indefinable, and nonnatural. Upon their full recognition and acknowledgment that good has these properties, philosophers will no longer commit the "naturalistic fallacy" of identifying or confusing good with anything else.[1] This will restore to philosophers the plain truth they have mysteriously lost sight of, that good, the property in which all value is grounded, is *utterly* unique. The importance of this for ethics cannot be overestimated. Having wandered for twenty-five-hundred years in a fog of their own making, philosophers have now been given a chance to achieve not only a fully satisfactory understanding of good, but also a fully satisfactory understanding of the *things* that are good. The sense of dissatisfaction that has clung to ethics with the fog will disappear as intellect discovers what instinct has always known, that there are things enough to make life worth living.

Visionaries are not always patient. So it is no surprise that Moore's *Principia* account fails to do full justice to the nature of these properties and the role they play in the determination of good's nature. The sketch offered here, to be fleshed out in future chapters, seeks to correct this defect. Very broadly, Moore argues that good's logical and ontological independence from *all* other properties is grounded in its simplicity and indefinability, with indefinability being much the more important of the two. He appeals mostly to nonnaturalness to explain why philosophers have failed to grant good its independence. Moore's official views are that to be simple is to have no parts and that to define a thing is to list its parts and their arrangements. So what is simple is indefinable and conversely; in fact, based on this account, the two properties could be identical. Although that is probably not his view here, he does glide blithely from one of these properties to the other in his early discussion of them.[2] By a non-

---

[1] See G. E. Moore, Preface to *Principia Ethica, Revised Edition*, p. 17, where he makes the distinction between identifying and confusing two properties much more explicitly than in the pages of *Principia*. See also Frankena, "The Naturalistic Fallacy," pp. 108–10.

[2] Panayot Butchvarov, "That Simple, Indefinable, Non-Natural Property *Good*," *Review of Metaphysics*, Vol. XXXVI (Sept. 1982), p. 57 and *Skepticism in Ethics* (Bloomington, Indiana: Indiana University Press, 1989), p. 60. For Moore's sliding, see especially pp. 6–8.

natural property, Moore means one that is outside time. It is because a confusion of good with some temporal, natural property finally lies behind every attempt to define it that Moore calls them all instances of the *naturalistic* fallacy.[3]

Matters are far too complicated, however, for good's independence from other properties to fall into place so neatly. Many properties meeting Moore's official criteria of simplicity and indefinability lack the full ontological independence he considers good to have. But there is a second conception of indefinability he implicitly and at one point, rather explicitly, appeals to that enables a case to be made for good's being *uniquely* independent of other properties. When he appeals to this conception of indefinability, he either fails to notice or to acknowledge completely how different it is from his official one. This one weakens or perhaps even severs for all properties the connection between indefinability and simplicity his official view posits. It also, in the case of good, makes for a strong connection between indefinability and nonnaturalness. Moore develops these hints in detail in later work, where he focuses exclusively on nonnaturalness as the source of good's independence.[4]

From *Principia* on, Moore is adamant about distinguishing *real* definitions, which he later came to call analytic definitions, from *verbal* definitions, which tell how a certain word is used, or what things are called by a word.[5] One way to describe the difference between the two kinds of definition is to say that if his ontology of value allowed it, real definitions would be immeasurably more important than verbal definitions: They reveal to us reality itself rather than reality as filtered by a language. Many who have absorbed the doubts raised by a further century of philosophizing about language will look with suspicion or something stronger on the claim that it is possible to get beyond language to "reality itself." They are reminded that this most penetrating and scrupulous of thinkers addressed similar doubts concerning the relation of thought and language to reality and stood his ground against them for the remaining half century of his career.

It is only in the sense of a real, or analytic, definition that Moore holds good to be indefinable.[6] (Presumably, every word, including the word "good," has a verbal definition.) For a thing to be analytically indefinable is for it to be an ultimate constituent of reality.[7] The claim that good is in-

[3] *Principia*, p. 13.
[4] "The Conception of Intrinsic Value," in *Philosophical Studies*, pp. 253–275 and "Meaning of "natural"," in *The Philosophy of G. E. Moore*, Paul Arthur Schilpp, ed. (Evanston, Illinois: Northwestern University Press, 1942), pp. 581–92.
[5] "Analysis," in *The Philosophy of G. E. Moore*, p. 661 and "What is Analysis?," in *Lectures on Philosophy*, (New York: Humanities Press, 1966), p. 159.
[6] *Principia*, p. 6.
[7] Ibid., pp. 9–10. It is a nice question whether Moore would consider this statement to be analytic or synthetic.

definable thus takes us to the heart of Moore's ethical project and its most dramatic problem. Before he writes a single word, by his choice of Bishop Butler's maxim as the book's motto, he takes himself to be proclaiming that ethical wisdom lies in simply *accepting* good's ultimacy. But it has been just about impossible for philosophers to do this. What is it that so confuses philosophers that they are led to deny good's ultimacy, or even just to puzzle about it, when at a level more basic and important than the philosophical they never for a moment lose sight of it? And what should we conclude about the nature of ethical understanding if it *depends* on the denial of good's ultimacy? Is it then based entirely on illusion?

According to Moore's official conception of indefinability, the one mostly guiding his understanding of how good is to be distinguished from the properties determinative of other sciences, a property's ultimacy lies in its having no parts to be parsed. He suggests early in the text that it follows for any property meeting this condition that there are no other properties in the light of whose nature it can be explicated, but at other places he shows some awareness that it does not. Although he never states it outright, its not being explicable in terms of other properties eventually becomes not a consequence of its having no parts, but a further, *separate condition* of indefinability. Although this is not a matter he discusses, this condition enables there to be degrees of ultimacy, as things may be understood in terms of other things to greater or lesser extent. Had he brought this condition more to the forefront of his discussion, it would have given even greater resonance to his claim that good can be understood in *no* other terms.

The model guiding Moore's official account of definition is provided by that which he does on concepts of ordinary spatio-temporal objects. Being in too much of a hurry, he fails to deal sufficiently or perhaps at all with the fact that he is drawn to two different conceptions concerning the kinds of things of which these objects are composed, which their definitions or analyses must therefore mention. Officially, he starts where ordinary thought does in its conception of what the parts of such things are. In his own example, he considers the parts comprising a horse to be "four legs, a head, a liver, a heart, etc. . . ."[8] We might call these the *literal parts* of a thing. Moore does not take his example of analysis any further than this, but since these parts are themselves complex, he must assume that

---

[8] Ibid., p. 8. This is an appropriate time to remember that according to Moore, although concepts or properties may be objects of thought, their natures are completely independent of thought and language. In order to aid the reader, this book shall adopt the convention of employing single quotes when these nonlinguistic items are being represented and double quotes when words are being represented. This is to deviate from Moore, whose use of quotes varies from work to work. (In *Principia*, he tends to use single quotes indifferently.) Occasionally, to avoid clutter, when it is clear that a nonlinguistic concept or property is being referred to, words referring to them will appear without quotes.

it is possible to burrow beyond them to the simple and indefinable parts of which they are composed. Many would think that such burrowing will eventually bring us to the subatomic particles of physics, but this is not the direction in which the thought of this unscientific thinker goes.[9] When he offers an example of a simple, indefinable property to shed light on what he says about good, he famously – or is it infamously? – offers the property of being yellow, which he claims to be different from any property happening to correspond to it in physical space.[10] This example strongly suggests a conception, one in terms of sense data, for example, according to which simple and purportedly indefinable *qualities* like colors, smells, and textures are the kinds of things of which objects are composed.[11] Moore fails to consider the difficulties involved in reconciling these two different accounts of what it is to be a part of an object. In effect having two different ways of understanding the nature of definition and indefinability, he winds up with two different conceptions of what it is for a property to be logically and ontologically independent of other properties.

As we follow Moore's official account to the place where it falters, we shall explore certain issues in his metaphysics, epistemology, and philosophy of science in more detail than he himself does. Our aim is to get a sense of how on his view the logical relations between the different properties of a science provide the materials for a systematic understanding of the world. Although he fails to consider matters beyond the level of generality provided by his example of the concept or object 'horse', we can see what a definition of a more general object like 'animal' would be like. Because it is more abstract, we need to make use of a more abstract notion of parts in order to define it. Rather than listing such parts as legs and livers, the definition lists such "parts" as being self-locomotive and food-taking. Although they are obviously not the literal parts of any animal, for an animal to instantiate such properties it must have certain parts. While the definition of 'animal' leaves open what more specific parts are required for a thing to instantiate these properties, the definition of a *kind* of animal such as 'horse' does not. Having four legs, etc. is a horse's way of being self-locomotive. So whether we start with the more general definition in the zoological chain of being and look down, or with the less general definition and look up, it is a matter of the respective definitions that horses are animals. We shall return to this most important point shortly.

---

[9] Suitably, Moore's reference on p. 4 to the ether is shortly to be rendered anachronistic.

[10] *Principia*, p. 10.

[11] Further evidence that he was drawn to this conception at the time of *Principia* is provided by his saying later in "Meaning of "natural"," p. 582, that he *no longer* holds the view according to which brown and round are "parts" of a penny. But even though he says this here, he seems to have remained attracted to such views his entire career.

Since the definition of a more general, higher-order object contains fewer parts than the definition of a less general object, there is a sense in which the more general object is simpler. But since the instantiation of each of its parts requires the instantiation of lower-order parts, in a deeper sense, it is not. The highest-order object in a chain would remain definable even if it were to have just "one" – extremely complex – property. The mind's ability to treat a complex general property as (relatively) simple by ignoring (most of) the details involved in its instantiation is indispensable if we are to discover the real order that makes the world something other than a booming, buzzing confusion. But it will contribute to serious error if it encourages philosophers to reason by analogy that although good may *appear* to be simple, really, it too is complex.

The natural hierarchies of objects or properties that we have appealed to in order to flesh out Moore's official account of definition provide us with a way of understanding his claim that a definition states the parts that invariably compose a whole.[12] It might sound as if Moore holds that for any *particular* thing to be a horse, it must have four legs. But consider that these general objects are *ideals* that particulars fit more or less closely.[13] Any particular horse having fewer than four legs we recognize as lacking in something. Adding this extra Platonic flavor to Moore's account makes it possible for particulars to belong to kinds to greater or lesser degree, which seems right. Although we would not wish to say that a creature becomes less of a horse by losing one of its legs in an accident, we might conclude that an embryo or very deformed creature is not fully a horse.

Moore says very little about the relations between analytic and verbal definitions. It is a rare word that sets necessary and sufficient conditions for the objects it refers to. Also, it will often be indeterminate whether or not certain properties belong in the cluster of properties gathered up by the definition. Is it possible that there is also some looseness in *analytic* definitions? Immediately, it would seem to be most in the spirit of Moore to deny this possibility – words may be vague, but nature is exact. He seems to take it for granted that without exactness in nature, there is no possibility of truly systematic knowledge of it. This seems to leave one with two alternatives concerning the vast array of inexact verbal definitions we use to come to try to understand the world: Either dismiss the pretensions of the "sciences" trying to make use of them, or make what must appear to be utterly arbitrary decisions about what the exact analytic definitions are around which the inexact verbal definitions hover.

Although it is not just definitions of such sociological words as "game" that appear to be inexact, we need only to consider them to see why Moore

---

[12] *Principia,* p. 8.
[13] We shall have much to say about Moore on the nature of ideals in the book's last two chapters.

would dismiss the first of the above alternatives out of hand. His certainty that certain of these objects, namely (the appreciation of) art objects, are *good* leaves him certain that they *are*. So is he then forced to accept the dissatisfaction engendered by the conclusion that these things have exact natures that remain forever beyond our intellectual grasp? Finally, although he does not seem fully to realize that his view has this implication, Moore must allow that the natures of these objects are not completely determinate. A spirit of artistic innovation makes it impossible for one to specify once and for all the properties a thing must instantiate in order for it be a piece of music, or sculpture, or any other kind of art object. Although the following Platonic suggestion might be one that Moore could not accept (and one that most twentieth-century tastes would find insufficiently "hard-headed"), some might find that it is a dynamic quality of good itself that makes for the indeterminacy of good things. It is the good of human *creativity* that keeps the nature of art objects forever open. In a casuistic system more plentiful than Moore's, *life* is too rich for biology to be perfectly neat. With this thought in mind, one could very cheerfully accept the Aristotelian recommendation that we look for no more exactness in a science than is appropriate to it.

This sketch of Moore's theory is consistent with his discussion of the different meanings that are had by the question "What is good?" An answer to this question can specify particular existents, which are not of interest to the science of ethics, or concepts of varying degrees of generality that have the property of being good, or finally, it can say how "good is to be defined."[14] The same sorts of answers can be given to the question, "What is an animal?" One can point to a particular animal, with which, except as a representative, the science of zoology is not interested, or one can describe a species or broader class of animal, or lastly, one can give the most general definition of animality. Moore finds there to be a crucial difference between the two sciences, however, which he considers to stem from the fact that in zoology the master concept is definable, while in ethics it is indefinable. Because 'animal' is definable, all such propositions as "Dobbin is an animal," "Horses are animals," and "Mammals are animals" are *analytic*. Assuming for the sake of the example that friendship is good, the concomitant ethical propositions "Dora's (particular) act of friendship is good"; "Romantic friendship is good"; and "Friendship is good" are all *synthetic*. Although a thing's being good follows from its being an instance of friendship, one does not logically imply that it is good when one asserts it to be an instance of such. A different kind of necessary relation obtains between being a kind of friendship and being good than obtains between being a horse and being an animal.

---

[14] *Principia*, pp. 3–6.

The language of parts gives us a way of describing this difference in re-lation. The analytic necessity of propositions in the nonvalue sciences has to do with there being mapping relations among the parts of the objects of different generality that comprise the natural hierarchy. For instance, the part 'self-locomotive' found in 'animal' maps on to the parts 'hoof', 'leg', etc. found in *horse*. These parts in turn map on to the parts of particular horses by virtue of which *they* are self-locomotive. Each part, 'leg', 'self-locomotive', etc. is at home at some level in the hierarchy. This is the level that contains the object of which, in Moore's sense, it is most a part. But be-cause a part maps on to the parts of objects found at other levels, in an at-tenuated sense it is also a part of those objects. 'Good', however, lacks any parts for mapping. So the necessity that obtains between a thing's goodness and its good-making properties has to be maintained in some other way.

But if the notion of parts provides a means of understanding the way in which good's independence from these sorts of properties is main-tained by virtue of its indefinability, it cannot account for its independence from other sorts of simple properties found in the hierarchy of qualities, for instance, the properties 'yellow', 'color', and 'quality'. We can begin to account for the difference between good and these proper-ties by noting that even though they lack parts, the properties on differ-ent levels of these hierarchies must be partly understood in terms of one another. Despite what Moore says early in *Principia*, in order to know what yellow is, it is not enough to attend only to that about it that is "simply dif-ferent from anything else."[15] One must also attend to that which it has *in common* with many other properties, starting with its being a color. (It is difficult to envisage how one could attend to yellow *at all* who did not also at least subconsciously attend to its being a color.) Going in the other di-rection, one cannot know what color is without attending to the fact that there are different ways of being a color, although it is true that one need not attend directly to any one of these ways. This provides a sense in which yellow and color are *mutually* definable, with yellow being more depen-dent on color than color is on yellow.

Near the end of *Principia*, Moore appeals to a kind of definition quite similar to this. Even though his example concerns the nonnatural prop-erty 'beauty', nothing seems to preclude it from being applied, after tweaking, to natural properties as well. According to Moore, beauty is de-finable in terms of good. For a thing to be beautiful is for it to be some-thing it is intrinsically good to appreciate. He says that this definition:

has the double recommendation that it accounts both for the apparent connec-tion between goodness and beauty and for the no less apparent difference be-tween these two conceptions. It appears, at first sight, to be a strange coincidence, that there should be two *different* objective predicates of value, 'good' and 'beau-

[15] *Principia*, p. 10.

tiful,' which are nevertheless so related to one another that whatever is beautiful is also good. But, if our definition be correct, the strangeness disappears; since it leaves only one *unanalyzable* predicate of value, namely 'good,' while 'beautiful,' though not identical with, is to be defined by reference to this, being thus, at the same time, different from and necessarily connected with it.[16]

The reader gets no hint about whether to be startled by Moore's not noticing how different this kind of definition is from his official account, or by his noticing it but not finding it to be anything worth mentioning.[17] Its having parts or not is on this account irrelevant to beauty's definability. What make beauty definable are the relations of metaphysical and epistemological dependency in which it stands to good. We can neither know what it is to be beautiful nor identify something as beautiful except in its terms. The fact that the definitional dependency between beauty and good goes in only one direction enables us to locate more accurately the difference between good and the simple natural qualities. Good is the only one of these properties whose nature is not *at all* implicated in other properties. Because higher- and lower-order natural properties differ in their degree of mutual dependency, they differ in their degree of ultimacy, with none of them being *ultimate*. Good, though, is ultimate.

The order of ultimacy between natural properties we find here is the reverse of the one we find when we look to Moore's official account of indefinability. On that account, natural properties, being the ones of which natural objects are composed, are the ones giving natural objects their *substance*. Take the natural properties away and not even a bare substance remains.[18] Moore must allow either that the substantiality of a natural property is in inverse proportion to its generality or that all of a natural object's substance comes from its most specific properties. In either case, this provides a sense in which the less abstract lower-order natural properties are more ultimate, more a part of the world, than the higher-order ones. This gives us a means to highlight even further the difference between good and natural properties: Good's ultimacy in no way diminished by its insubstantiality and abstractness.

Despite his acceptance of an instance of a definition of one thing in terms of another as being philosophically important, Moore does not try to fit these kinds of definition in with or alongside parsing definitions in his official account. On the contrary, he insists in the first chapter that even the definitions of objects of which it would ordinarily be said that it is in their nature to be a part of other objects, are not *at all* in terms of the objects of which they are parts. Failing to consider that it will be in a sense

---

[16] Ibid., pp. 201–2.
[17] He had also, at p. 60, defined *approval* as the feeling that a thing is good without mentioning its deviation from his standard kind of definition. We shall see that these are not the only places where Moore casually adds to his official view.
[18] *Principia*, p. 41.

much different than the literal one that a thing's being a part of something is a part of its definition, he claims that such definitions lead to the self-contradictory notion of a part (such as an arm) containing the whole (the body) of which it is a part.[19] The context of his discussion makes it clear that he fears the monistic strain in the thought of the British Hegelians. If the requirement that definitions be in terms of other things is taken to the farthest reaches, we will not be able to understand *anything* until we understand *everything*. Appearance and reality will then collide; instead of there being many discrete things, there will be only one thing. Although this is not the only place where we find Moore's thought to be marred by a fear of views, which could, in certain hands, have such unpalatable ramifications, this might be the place where it is the most marred.

Having brought Moore's half-articulated thoughts on definition and ontological independence closer to the surface, we can now do the same for his thoughts on the unconscious strategies of dissimulation that are both served by and serve all the various attempts to define good. Moore is insistent that a denial of good's uniqueness and ultimacy is ultimately a denial of its being. Whether or not philosophers acknowledge it, the end of all definitions of good is the same – the elimination of good from the inventory of things found in the universe.[20] It is putting it mildly to say that our very deep awareness of good puts obstacles in the way of all such definitional projects. Philosophers thus try to soften that awareness by effecting good's elimination in a series of steps. It is as if they think that good's final disappearance will not be noticed if its nature is attenuated gradually enough.

Without offering a reason for his opinion, Moore suggests that attempts to identify good with a complex property have a greater initial plausibility than attempts to identify it with a simple property.[21] Perhaps he thinks that it is easier to have our awareness of good trail off into wisps as a result of our tracking something complex and often very general than it is to have it be completely swallowed up by something simple and oftentimes quite immediate. One might respond to this suggestion that the hard work of keeping a complex property in mind alongside of good should make it obvious that the complex is something different from good. But such a response loses sight of the insidiousness of the definitional project. The more we ponder a purported definition of a thing, the more does our confidence in our immediate and instinctive awareness of that thing wane. The awareness that has been immediate will no longer appear to be so. And even if it does still *appear* to us that our awareness

---

[19] Ibid., pp. 33–4.
[20] At the very beginning of *Some Main Problems of Philosophy* (London: George Allen & Unwin Ltd., 1953), Moore states that providing such an inventory is the main task of philosophy.
[21] *Principia*, p. 15.

of good is immediate, we will remind ourselves that appearances are often deceiving.

Another might think that on Moore's official account of definition, projects that seek to identify good with another simple property lack the plausibility to be taken seriously for even a moment. On that account, those who purport to have discovered such an identity could only be doing one or the other of two things. First, they could be offering a verbal definition, which in these cases would take the form of a synonym. But such a claim as that "good" and "pleasant" are synonyms is decisively defeated by appeal to standard usage. Further, the claim that the expressions are synonymous undermines the revisionary nature of these projects, since the only way to make sense of these projects is to suppose that they are motivated by the thought that the theory of value embodied in ordinary thought and language is profoundly in error.

The second possibility is that such philosophers are attempting to promulgate what for simple properties is the analogue of a real definition. But the project of promulgating a definitional analogue must also be revisionary (whereas the complexity of items subject to real definitions makes it possible for them to be directed toward discovery as well as revision). If the proponents of such an analogue are not merely to be uttering the banality that something is the same as itself, they must be saying that what we have mistakenly thought to be a distinct entity really is *not*, but is some other thing whose existence and nature is less controversial. Immediately, it appears that its element of revisionism undermines this project as well. The simplicity of such things as good and pleasure makes it easy for one to think of them simultaneously. Since recognizing their nonidentity is as easy as thinking of them, anyone who tries to identify them would appear to be subject to instant ridicule.

But this is where an appeal to Moore's unofficial kind of definition gives the proponents of such identity claims the wiggle room they need. First, they can try to get us to accept some degree of attenuation of good's nature by having us think of good *in terms of* the defining property rather than *as* that property. Remember also that most or all instances of these kinds of definition reveal relations of mutual dependency between properties. So we can also be encouraged to think of a defining property, say pleasure, in terms of good – we might, for instance, be told about differences in the *quality* of various pleasures. Or perhaps pleasure will have its nature attenuated by being identified with some other thing, something complex perhaps, say happiness (which might, as beauty and approval do, have to be explicated in terms of good). Inevitably, although not logically so, these stratagems result in pleasure, "which is easily recognised as a distinct entity,"[22] absorbing good completely. Good is sooner or later

---

[22] Ibid., p. 16.

explained away in terms of pleasure – it is said that good is *merely* pleasure. Thus do philosophers say in a roundabout way what they do not have the self-awareness or courage to say outright: Good is *not*. And thus do cleverness and intelligence become not aids to clear thinking, but impediments.

If Moore gets a great deal of mileage out of the claim that good is indefinable, he also creates serious difficulties for himself when he lets indefinability completely overshadow nonnaturalness in his early attempts to establish good's independence from other properties. Good's independence is at least as much an ontological as a logical matter and the ontological issues are at least as approachable by an investigation of nonnaturalness as by an investigation of indefinability.[23] Passages on pages 11 and 14–15, where Moore discusses some of the problems he takes to arise from the failure of philosophers to see that good is indefinable, nicely illustrate the problems his single-mindedness creates. Far more troubling than their unpleasant tone of hyperbolic denunciation is the despair over the history of philosophy that tone is born of. By likening previous disputes about the nature of good to one about whether a triangle is a circle or a straight line and by claiming that to view yellow as definable commits one to "hold[ing] that an orange [is] exactly the same thing as a stool, a piece of paper, a lemon," Moore turns philosophy into an exercise in pathology. He denies to philosophers the ability even to *notice*, let alone correct, the mistakes that arise in the course of their inquiries. He has them suffering from an irresistible compulsion to endlessly iterate their mistakes as their theories recede ever further from reality. His impatience with dialectical thinking, so odd in one who is himself a master dialectician, suggests that the proper procedure for understanding the world is not to investigate and analyze, but simply to *wait* for the insight that sets everything right. This is to abandon the way of the philosopher for the way of the mystic, or perhaps for the person who does not think very much. Philosophy's debt to the shattering insight is undeniably great. But as Moore himself exemplifies so well in most of his own career, unless there is argument and counterargument and patient, detailed explication, there is no tribunal for that insight and hence no philosophy.

These passages also show how perilously close Moore comes to maintaining that the failure of a philosophical work to be absolutely clear at its very outset about the logic of its inquiry causes it to deal completely in illusion. But if in spite of their many errors earlier philosophers have not managed to hold on to important insights about the very same thing as

---

[23] But see Thomas Baldwin, who writes on p. 30 of his "Ethical non-naturalism," in *Exercises in Analysis* (Cambridge: Cambridge University Press, 1985), that the distinction between natural and nonnatural properties is primarily *logical* rather than ontological.

he is describing, Moore's exposure of their errors becomes, if not unintelligible, pointless. Their work would be no more relevant to his work than a child's gibberish is. On the other hand, if even the most wrongheaded of philosophical theories remain in touch with reality, then whatever their flaws, there is a chance for them to provide support for his own theory. For one, they can vindicate his faith in the irrefragableness of our immediate awareness of good. For another, it has to be impressive if his theory can provide the means to diagnose the mistakes of earlier philosophers and retrieve and properly place their insights. In his not very scholarly but always interesting and provocative history of ethical theory, Moore attempts just this kind of diagnosis. At the heart of that history, we find, not indefinability, but nonnaturalness.

Moore begins his history by dividing ethical theorists into two camps, the naturalists proper – the empiricists – and the metaphysicians.[24] What divides these camps are the different ways they have of inadequately treating good's nonnaturalness. At one point, Moore suggests that the naturalistic fallacy is an instance of a more general problem, the mistreatment of *all* nonnatural properties.[25] The empiricists crudely deny that there are any such properties, while the metaphysicians, being subtler, do at least recognize the category of nonnaturals, even if they then try to go back on it.[26] The mistreatment of good always starts with the same mistake. The vast majority of propositions we entertain have existents as both subject and predicate: "Ethical truths are immediately felt not to conform to this type and the naturalistic fallacy arises from the attempt to make out that, in some roundabout way, they do conform to it." Philosophers do this by supposing that a nonnatural property "*necessarily* exists together with anything with which it does exist."[27] Moore's emphasis on "necessarily" is not meant to suggest that there is a mistake in supposing necessity to be involved in the being of nonnaturals. Two plus two is necessarily four and friendship is necessarily good. The mistake lies in supposing that the necessity has anything to do with *existence*. If our understanding of nonnatural properties gets tied in any way to existence, we will inevitably fall prey to understanding them in terms of natural properties, the ones that really exist. We will then come to think that what is true about nonnatural properties *depends* on what exists.

The only way the empiricists have of accounting for the necessity of propositions concerning nonnaturals is in terms of the things that have *actually* existed. Thus they cannot make room for counterfactual propositions – they are even forced to say that mathematical propositions would not be true without the existence of just these things that have existed![28] So saying that the metaphysicians do a slightly better job than the em-

[24] *Principia*, p. 124.   [25] Ibid., p. 125.   [26] Ibid., pp. 110–12.
[27] Ibid., p. 124.   [28] Ibid.

piricists of dealing with nonnatural properties is damning with very faint praise indeed. Refusing to accept nonnatural properties for what they are, properties that do not exist in time, metaphysicians attempt to explain away their special character by defining them in terms of a *super-sensible* reality.[29] Even if officially it is "more" real than the world of natural objects, when the smoke clears and the mirrors are removed, this reality is revealed to be a pale reflection of the natural one – its being sensible trumps its being "super." When it comes to a mathematical proposition, for instance, metaphysical philosophers "have no better account of its meaning to give than either, with Leibniz, that God's mind is in a certain state, or, with Kant, that your mind is in a certain state, or finally with Mr Bradley, that something is in a certain state."[30] In ethics, instead of simply saying, as a naturalist might, that to be good is to be pleasing to some person or another, the metaphysicians say that it is to be pleasing to *God,* or to a *rational will.* This greater subtlety gives them a subtler way of imperiling what is as plain as $2 + 2 = 4$. They halfway manage to convince themselves that they must wait upon such superfluities as whether God exists or whether history embodies a rational principle before they can conclude that love is better than hatred.

What we think, including what we *think* we think, affects how we feel. So the errors of those who think incorrectly about value are of the greatest moment. Consistent hedonists do what Mill could not quite get himself to do, recommend piggishness if that is what brings pleasure. Metaphysicians, thinking that the truly valuable things can only be found in a world which, even if it mirrors this one, somehow lies beyond it, either become fatalists about this world or suffer some form of religious or quasi-religious dissatisfaction that leaves them yearning to escape its too solid flesh.[31] Moore's final message is one naturalists already profess but do not understand. So he directs it instead to the metaphysicians, who he thinks, however misguided, to be superior: Although it is not the best world possible, *this* is the world that justifies existence.

The Argument for Indefinability

Let us turn now to the argument by which Moore purports to prove that good is indefinable, the OQA, along with the Private Language Argument the most famous and influential "argument" of the century. We begin by presenting at length the passage in which Moore makes his argument:

(1) The hypothesis that disagreement about the meaning of good is disagreement with regard to the correct analysis of a given whole, may be most plainly

[29] Ibid., pp. 111–12.   [30] Ibid., p. 125.
[31] Ibid., p. 205. We discuss Moore's attempt to deal with this kind of disappointment in the book's last two chapters.

seen to be incorrect by consideration of the fact that, whatever definition be offered, it may be always asked, with significance, of the complex so defined,
whether it is itself good. To take, for instance, one of the more plausible, because
one of the more complicated, of such proposed definitions, it may easily be
thought, at first sight, that to be good may mean to be what we desire to desire.
Thus if we apply this definition to a particular instance and say 'When we think
that A is good, we are thinking that A is one of the things which we desire to desire,' our proposition may seem quite plausible. But, if we carry the investigation
further, and ask ourselves, 'Is it good to desire to desire A?' it is apparent, on a little reflection, that this question is itself as intelligible, as the original question, 'Is
A good?' – that we are, in fact, now asking for exactly the same information about
the desire to desire A, for which we formerly asked with regard to A itself. But it
is also apparent that the meaning of this second question cannot be correctly analyzed into 'Is the desire to desire A one of the things which we desire to desire?':
we have not before our minds anything so complicated as the question 'Do we
desire to desire to desire to desire A?' Moreover any one can easily convince himself by inspection that the predicate of this proposition – 'good' – is positively different from the notion of 'desiring to desire' which enters into its subject: 'That
we should desire to desire A is good' is *not* merely equivalent to 'That A should
be good is good.' It may indeed be true that what we desire to desire is always also
good; perhaps, even the converse may be true: but it is very doubtful whether this
is the case, and the mere fact that we understand very well what is meant by doubt-
ing it, shews clearly that we have two different notions before our minds.

(2) And the same consideration is sufficient to dismiss the hypothesis that
'good' has no meaning whatsoever. It is very natural to make the mistake of supposing that what is universally true is of such a nature that its negation would be
self-contradictory: the importance which has been assigned to analytic propositions in the history of philosophy shews how easy such a mistake is. And thus it is
very easy to conclude that what seems to be a universal ethical proposition is in
fact an identical proposition; that, if, for example, whatever is called 'good' seems
to be pleasant, the proposition 'Pleasure is the good' does not assert a connection between two different notions, but involves only one, that of pleasure, which
is easily recognised as a distinct entity. But whoever will attentively consider with
himself what is actually before his mind when he asks the question 'Is pleasure
(or whatever it may be) after all good?' can easily satisfy himself that he is not
merely wondering whether pleasure is pleasant.[32]

It is breaking no new ground to point out that Moore's presentation of
the OQA is quite muddled. In fact, it is shocking how slapdash he is with
something he considers so important. The standard and most plausible
reading of the passage breaks it into three parts, the first being just the
first sentence, the second stopping at the sentence beginning with "Moreover," and the third going perhaps all the way to the end of the second
paragraph, which we have not quoted in full. It then joins the first and
third parts together to form the main argument and treats the second
part as containing either a subsidiary argument or a non sequitor.

This reading ignores Moore's own verbal cues, which suggest that he
considers the beginning of the third part to be not an argument, but

[32] *Principia*, pp. 15–16.

rather a phenomenological appeal in support of the argument immediately preceding it. But the concern with differences in the significance of questions that is expressed in the first and third parts gives them a great deal more in common than either has with the second part, concerned as it is with differences in the complexity of questions. Further, no perfectly general point can be plausibly assayed about differences in the complexity of second-order questions. Assume, for instance, that good is asserted to be identical with a simple like pleasure. Even if we are confident that the question whether A's goodness is good has a different meaning than the question whether A's being full of pleasure is good, (we may be too puzzled by the first of these questions to have any opinion about what it means), there is no difference in the complexity of these questions, just as there is no difference in the complexity of the parallel first-order questions concerning just A. Since, as we shall see, Moore expresses confusion elsewhere about the difference between arguments and phenomenological appeals, it does not speak against the standard view that it has him not completely understanding his own strategy. It is also to be noted that he never publicly opposed what quickly became the standard reading of the argument.[33]

The argument can be pithily stated. The answer to a question whether a property purported to be the defining one for 'good' actually *is* good is always "significant," or nontautologous. Since the answer to a question whether something asserted to be good is good is tautologous, good and the property purported to be its definition must be different. In the third section, Moore provides the argument with its explication. Two different things can be meant by the claim that a property is good: It can be meant 1) that the property is *identical* with good or 2) that the property has the *further* property of being good. This is to say that the ascription of goodness to something can be either analytic or synthetic. Those who try to define good take a significant, synthetic proposition and treat it as analytic. The lack of equivalence between a statement that is really analytic and one that is mistakenly treated as such is shown by the fact that while we cannot doubt the former, we can doubt the latter. Moore might have made this point more clearly by contrasting the significance of the following pair of statements: "A, which is good, is good" and "A, which is what we desire to desire, is good."

In the second paragraph, where, officially, he considers and rejects the alternative "that 'good' has no meaning whatsoever," that is, that there is no such thing as good, Moore continues the point and draws out the further pernicious consequences that stem from the attempt to define 'good'. When he does so, he ensnares those who try to define not just 'good', but

[33] Richard A. Fumerton, *Reason and Morality* (Ithaca and London: Cornell University Press, 1990), p. 70.

any concept or property, in that most famous of philosophical conundrums, the paradox of analysis. Moore's conditions of analytic adequacy require all analyses to be either trivial or false. An analysis states that an identity obtains between the object denoted by the analysandum and the object denoted by the analysans. If the identity does obtain then by the terms of Moore's argument, the analysis is *trivial*, stating no more than a tautology. But if the analysis is nontrivial, "significant," there is no identity between the two and the analysis must be *false*. In *Principia*, Moore evinces no awareness that the sword he wields against those who define 'good' is double-edged. He fails to consider that the argument can be applied against his own sketch of the analysis of the concept 'horse' as well as his analysis of 'ought': He does not think that zoologists are merely saying that a horse is a horse and considers the claim that 'ought' means productive of the best consequences to be of great philosophical importance (as it is). So the first criticism to be made of the OQA is that, at least in the form Moore presents it, it proves far too much, making it impossible for analysis to be an intellectually worthwhile activity. As Moore says of Mill's alleged commission of the naturalistic fallacy, this problem is so obvious, "it is quite wonderful how [he] failed to see it."[34]

The argument poses a second problem. On a very plausible interpretation of it, it just begs the question. Consider the claim "The question "Is what we desire to desire good?" is significant." How do we determine that that question is significant? If we do so just by inspecting the properties denoted by the respective expressions in the question, we reverse the epistemic order that is supposed to obtain between our determining a question to be significant and our recognizing two properties to be different. Perhaps then the "argument" is really an implicit phenomenological appeal. But in that case, unless there is something that the recognition of a question's significance does to make it easier to see that the properties are different, Moore would be advised just to have us look directly at the properties to see that they are different.

If it is possible to determine questions to be significant by some other means than the inspection of properties, we could have a non-question-begging argument. Interesting articles by Frank Snare and Stephen W. Ball offer Moore a way to do just that. They rationally reconstruct his argument in a way that makes our recognition of the significance of a question a linguistic-behavioral matter based on our ordinary understanding of English.[35] Because we are fluent speakers of English, the significance

---

[34] *Principia*, p. 67.

[35] Frank Snare, "The Open Question as Linguistic Test," *Ratio*, Vol. XVII (1975), pp. 123–9. Stephen W. Ball, "Reductionism in Ethics and Science: A Contemporary Look at G. E. Moore's Open Question Argument," *American Philosophical Quarterly*, Vol. 25 (July 1988), pp. 197–213. Snare is more explicit than Ball that his version of the argument is *not* the one Moore understood himself to be presenting.

of the relevant question is something we recognize immediately and *un-self-consciously*. According to Ball, the OQA catches us "in the act, so to speak, of actual linguistic behavior, *not* of meta-linguistic theorizing."[36] Snare, comparing his distinction to Ryle's famous one between knowing-how and knowing-that, speaks of a grammatical intuition that is "merely a matter of having a practical knowledge . . . not a propositional knowl-edge of the rules of grammar."[37] These distinctions are not unlike the one Moore makes in *Principia* between knowledge of verbal meaning and knowledge of analytic meaning. It is also like the distinction he makes in "A Defence of Common Sense" and elsewhere between *understanding an expression's meaning* and *knowing what an expression means*, between what we may call ordinary meaning and philosophical meaning.[38] In these re-constructions, Moore's argument is to the best explanation of the lin-guistic-behavioral data. It holds that our intuitive recognition of the sig-nificance of a question is grounded in a difference in properties, which as ordinary speakers we need not recognize in an explicit or self-conscious manner, but which as philosophers we must explicitly come to recognize if we are to make any philosophical progress.

Although this version of the argument does not *immediately* appear to be question begging, dangers do await it. For one, there are problems concerning the ability of ordinary speakers to recognize that a question about a sophisticated philosophical definition is significant. What, for in-stance, will a nonphilosopher say who is asked whether the question, "Is that which a person *qua* rational agent strives for good?" is significant. This question is difficult enough for *Moore* to answer. Given what he says in the OQA, the answer has to be yes. But as we shall see, his argument against ethical egoism, which suggests that a person who denied the iden-tity of these notions would be guilty of a contradiction, impels him in the other direction.[39] An expression that is part of this definition does not seem to *have* any ordinary meaning, leaving us with nothing to appeal to in order to determine whether the question is significant. If this is so, the reconstructed argument has a smaller scope than Moore's original and many of the most interesting definitions lie beyond its purview. If we try to get around this fact by applying the test in these cases to *philosophers'* "intuitive" understanding of terms, the obvious problem is that their un-derstanding will differ according to what more encompassing theory they already hold. So far then, with definitions such as this one, the recon-struction will only have succeeded in finding a more roundabout way for philosophers to beg the question against each other.

[36] Ball, "A Contemporary Look," p. 209.
[37] Snare, "Open Question," p. 126.
[38] "A Defence of Common Sense," in *Philosophical Papers* (London: George Allen & Unwin Ltd., 1959), p. 37 and "The Justification of Analysis," in *Lectures on Philosophy*, pp. 165–7.
[39] See Chapters 6 and 7 for a discussion of Moore's argument.

Assuming for the moment that ordinary speakers can always tell whether a question is significant, we also need to wonder about the scope of and our knowledge of the principle that is crucial to the argument. This is the principle that a question's significance is always due to a difference in the properties denoted by the different expressions in the question. It is hard to believe, as Snare recognizes, that this principle holds in all cases.[40] If it does not hold in all cases then we cannot be certain that good is an indefinable property, since it may provide one of the exceptional cases.[41] Remember also that we are not allowed to ground our knowledge of this principle in our ability just to inspect the respective properties denoted by pairs of expressions to see that they are different. Perhaps one will try to argue that the principle can originally be based on the inspection of pairs of properties as long as none of the expressions denoting them are "good." Having established the principle in this way, we can then extend it to pairs of expressions one of which is "good" without inspecting the properties *they* denote. By doing this, we do enable the principle to be based upon the inspection of properties. But since it is not based on the inspection of what "good" and its purported definitions denote, we do not beg the question. We would also need to argue that even though we do not inspect the properties in the cases where one of the expressions is "good", we have reason, based presumably on induction, for believing that the principle holds in these cases as well.

But if this is the origin of the principle, one of two things would follow. The first would be that we are able to do with "good" and the expression purported to be its definition what we did with the expressions upon which the principle was based: directly inspect the properties denoted by them to see that they are different. If Moore thinks that we can do this in this case, he would again be advised just to have us do it. The second would be that there is some difficulty presented by the property good that makes it not open to inspection as the properties are upon which the principle is based. There being this difference between good and the other properties would then make one very suspicious about the relevance of the test in cases involving good. The fact that good is not open to the same kind of inspection could plausibly be taken as evidence that the difference between it and the other properties makes the principle inapplicable here.

In order to avoid this general dilemma in all its guises, the linguistic principle being appealed to must be more theoretical and methodological in nature. The principle is not something we base upon the direct in-

---

[40] "Open Question," p. 129.
[41] Actually, *no* version of the OQA can establish the indefinability of good as something *certain*. Moore says we must apply the test to every definition in turn. He obviously thinks we will soon run out of plausible candidates and give up the game. Still, we can never be certain that we have canvassed every plausible definition. See Ball, p. 209.

spection of properties or something we somehow "prove," but something that provides a framework for the study of linguistic behavior and the explication of the semantics of ordinary discourse. This in effect is what Ball and Snare try to make of it. But in order to be confident about accepting such a sophisticated principle, we need at the least to know a great deal more about the philosophy of language and the philosophy of mind than Moore discusses here. This supports a point we shall make a number of times: that because of all it requires, the OQA is hardly something we have a right to accept *at the beginning* of philosophical investigation. Rather than a fully fleshed out, incontrovertible argument, Moore can only be offering an argument sketch or hypothesis about good that the rest of the book has the task of defending. Because he thinks of himself as offering a more powerful argument than is really available to him, a great many of *Principia*'s claims will have to be tempered – to the benefit of his overall argument.

Moore fails to resolve in his own mind the tension between *proving* a proposition with premises different from it and bringing forth points that help one to have a clear perception of the proposition's truth. There is a passage in his discussion of the metaphysical philosophers that nicely captures this tension: "In face of this direct perception that the two questions are distinct, no proof that they *must* be identical can have the slightest value. That the proposition 'This is good' is thus distinct from every other proposition was proved in Chapter 1."[42] He seems to be saying that he proved to us that good is indefinable simply by getting us to see that it is! The tension in Moore's procedure lies in part in the very conservative nature of his ethical project, which is much in the spirit of his later epistemological project of defending our commonsense knowledge of the external world. Argument or not, Moore is not showing us something completely new, but something we have long known but somehow lost sight of. Remember what he says about the connection between the naturalistic fallacy and good's nonnaturalness: We originally intuit that good is not an existent property, but then try to make out in the roundabout way of a definition that it is. Reflection on the significance of a question enables us to cut through the thickets we have created to get back to what we originally intuited and never completely forgot – that by virtue of its being nonnatural, good can be understood solely in its own terms.

So although Moore thinks of himself as offering an argument, what he actually does by having us reflect on the significance of a question is shake us out of a prejudice against accepting good's full-fledged nonnaturalness. On this view, he is like the boy who tells the philosophical emperor that he is wearing no clothes.[43] He not only needs courage to make his

---

[42] *Principia*, p. 126.
[43] Paul Levy in *G. E. Moore and the Cambridge Apostles* (New York: Holt, Rhinehart and Win-

bold claim, but a genius of uncommon plainness to resist the very deep philosophical impulse to obfuscate the simple truth of the matter. If we read him in this way, we can capture the tension between his offering an argument and his begging the question in the following way: There is a sense in which he is begging the question because he is asking us finally just to see that two properties are different. But what keeps him from *merely* begging the question is the fact that he provides a new technique to get us to recall something we used to, and at some level, still know. Engaging in intuitive linguistic reflection on a question's significance takes us out of the mode of poisonous self-consciousness that philosophy either puts us into or results from and returns us to the purity of our original awareness of good. Finally then, Moore's "argument" is not an argument, but a means for the attainment of an epiphany.

Even as they attempt to make a full-fledged argument out of Moore's discussion, Ball and Snare partly capture this fact in their insistence that the reflection we perform in its name be at the level of our everyday understanding of language. Any level deeper than that and the spontaneity is lost that is the conduit to the plain truth. The recognition of a question's significance sets the stage for the epiphany that finally comes without the obfuscating mediation of reflection. Presumably, the crucial difference between this later awareness of good's indefinability and the one we previously had is that *we will not let the later awareness slip away.* So Moore's project becomes one more in a very long line of attempts to return us to, and keep us in, a state of innocence. What is striking is that in this case, the innocence is epistemic rather than moral. (Although many philosophers, perhaps Christian ones most prominently, will connect our epistemic corruption to the corruption of our will.)[44]

Moore's procedure here is not unlike the one he employs in "The Refutation of Idealism," published in the same year as *Principia.* Although there is much sophisticated argumentation and discussion in that paper, what is finally most striking about it is the way in which it cuts the Gordian knot of a tormenting philosophical problem: "how we are to 'get outside the circle of our own ideas and sensations.'" The "solution" lies in seeing that there is no problem; just to *have* a sensation is to be outside the circle.[45] Moore's arguments and discussion are aimed at getting us to see just that. He writes, "I am suggesting that the Idealist maintains that

---

ston, 1979), p. 12, notes that A. J. Ayer uses this figure to describe Moore in *Part of My Life.* Stuart Hampshire also uses it in "Liberator, Up to a Point," a review of Tom Regan's *Bloomsbury's Prophet, New York Review of Books,* March 26, 1987, p. 39.

[44] Although we shall have a great deal to say on the subject of Moore and innocence in the book's last two chapters, we may note at this time that it is part of Moore's own innocence not to entertain deeply the possibility that our epistemic corruption is the result of some sort of willful moral corruption.

[45] "The Refutation of Idealism," p. 27.

object and subject are necessarily connected, mainly because he fails to see that they are distinct, that they are two at all." Also, "My main object has been to try to make the reader *see*" that consciousness and its object are unique.[46] Similarly, he "proves" to us here that good is unique by getting us to *see* that it is.

This way of looking at the OQA fits in with some important things Moore says about proofs in *Principia*. He points out that neither he nor anyone else can prove a thing to be good or bad.[47] This is not something that should concern us, however. Our inability to prove to a madman such obvious facts as that there is a chair rather than an elephant beside him does not make us one whit less confident that we will not be trampled. What bothers us about value claims is not the fact that they cannot be proved, but the fact that there is so little agreement about them.[48] But this failure to achieve widespread agreement is due to the difficulty of the subject, not to its having no proofs. (And on the subject of what the greatest goods are, there is widespread agreement of a very important kind.)[49] It would also seem that if we cannot prove that an object like the madman's elephant is illusory, then we also cannot prove that a property is indefinable. What could we say to either the hallucinating or the blind that would ensure that they see only and all of what is there? With the place of proofs and arguments thus taken down a notch, it need not trouble Moore that the OQA is not really an argument that proves its conclusion. Those who are properly epistemically equipped will still receive the benefit of his exercise.

But finally, we must conclude that as with all other attempts to regain lost innocence, this one fails. If we really were to return to our original pristine state of awareness, we could no longer have the reflective philosophical understanding that is the goal of Moore's book. In the state to which we returned, we would take things too much for granted, would lack the kind of wonderment that is needed to motivate a sustained philosophical inquiry. And if somehow we were to become curious again, we would again be prey to the beguilement of the intellect that made us fall the first time. Moore has a great deal of trouble countenancing the fact that for distinctly philosophical understanding, the danger of a special kind of confusion must always be imminent. There are risks in self-conscious reflection that always accompany its rewards. Given his claim that all philosophers until Sidgwick have been under the sway of the naturalistic fallacy, Moore should have realized that there is something very deep about the kind of confusion he attempts to expose and eradicate – it is not *mere* confusion to be easily overcome. There are no guarantees that we will not fall back into it again and again.

---

[46] Ibid., pp. 13, 45.   [47] *Principia*, p. 75.
[48] Ibid., pp. 75–6.   [49] Ibid., pp. 188–9. See Chapters 9 and 10.

Moore might respond that the desirable state we achieve under his tutelage is not quite the one we found ourselves in originally. In our new state, we will have been chastened by the recognition that we let such an invaluable insight slip away. Having been so chastened, we will not let it slip away again. If we ever do find the epiphany beginning to evanesce, we have a procedure of reflection to help us retrieve it. So we can have the intellectual benefits of self-conscious philosophical awareness, can account for the special poignancy and depth of philosophical understanding, while avoiding its pitfalls. To argue in this manner is to begin to recognize that the value of philosophical understanding is tied to the risks of falling into a special and pernicious kind of confusion that is created by philosophy's refusal to take for granted what seems obvious to the plain intellect. But if we are to treat with full seriousness this refusal to take things for granted, we must nurture the thought that there are *serious* alternatives to the correct philosophical view. As Moore shows in *Principia,* it is much too easy for one to be condescending and dismissive toward a theory if he "knows" before studying it that it is guilty of the naturalistic fallacy. However wrong they be even in their essentials, we must recognize not merely the possibility, but the *necessity* of there being well-conceived and compelling alternative philosophical theories. Without such alternatives, the refusal to take the plain awareness of value for granted becomes inexplicable obduracy; we cannot then take account of the achievements of a finely wrought and fully articulated philosophical understanding. Because of the great difficulty he has in crediting such reflections, we shall consider in the last chapter of this book whether Moore must finally be an opponent of philosophy, or a proponent of a reconfiguration of it that leaves it no longer concerned with truth. These possibilities would surely be of grave concern to him, as they would seem to leave him without a ladder to stand on.

But for now, let us bring these airy metaphilosophical musings back to the earth of Moore's text. In the penultimate sentence of his presentation of the OQA he writes, "Everybody is constantly aware of this notion, although he may never become aware at all that it is different from other notions of which he is also aware."[50] If this kind of confused awareness is possible, then another kind of awareness, whose importance he came later to recognize, must also be possible.[51] This kind, the direct opposite of the one he has been so concerned with, is one in which one is aware of *two* properties, but mistakenly thinks of them as being only one. The possibility of this state puts into question the assumptions of full-blown realism, is as explanatorily powerful in the other direction, as the kind of awareness he makes so much of. It is there to be appealed to in order to explain why both ordinary people and philosophers think that two ques-

[50] *Principia,* p. 17.   [51] *Some Main Problems of Philosophy,* p. 220.

tions are different when really they are the same, why they think that the words "good" and "pleasant" denote two properties rather than one.[52]

The unsurprising conclusion is that there simply are no definitive proofs for the deepest positions in ethics or any other branch of philosophy. All one can do is to put forward various points for our intelligent consideration, place theories in their widest possible contexts, and draw out their deepest implications. If all this sounds vague, it cannot be helped; the proof of the pudding is in the eating. Although one may suspect quite early on that a philosophical theory is going deeply wrong, one must have the patience to allow it to unfold in its entirety. Moore claims to have won a first-round knock-out when all that philosophy allows are slow, painfully won split decisions – although it is true that much of the work of winning these decisions is done by those who are brash enough to seek knock-outs.

[52] Frankena, "The Naturalistic Fallacy," pp. 112–14.

2

Good's Nonnaturalness

Background

The topic of this chapter is Moore's claim that good is *nonnatural*. Our aim is to achieve a deeper understanding of Moore's views on the nature of nonnaturalness and of the entire ontology within which Moore places his theory of value, a sense of the difficulties imposed upon his conception of intrinsic value by nonnaturalness, and finally, some clues as to how we might deal with these difficulties in a manner enriching to his theory.

To remind ourselves, according to *Principia*, the difference between natural and nonnatural properties has to do with their relation to time. Simply, natural properties exist in time while nonnatural properties do not. Since a natural object is completely exhausted by its natural properties, no nonnatural property can be a *part* of a natural object. The two kinds of property best satisfying the criteria of naturalness on this account are: 1) the most determinate properties of colors, textures, sounds, etc. exemplified by objects in the physical world and 2) such mental items as feelings of pleasure and pain. When it comes to the consideration of properties more general or abstract than these, Moore's bare-bones analysis of the distinction between natural and nonnatural properties must be greatly extended and refined. Moore does a little of this work implicitly in *Principia* and much more of it explicitly in later work, without nearly doing all of it. The refinements he makes and the ones we make in his name, especially as they are concerned with the nature of those very subtle "objects," states of affairs, show the delicacy of articulation he is able to bring to the defense of blunt pre-philosophical conceptions, in this case, the conception of the total objectivity and utter uniqueness of value. Given the delicacy required by a satisfying philosophical articulation of this conception, we must treat very lightly the *philosophically* blunt way of stating it he chooses for his later work – that only value properties are nonnatural.[1]

In order to shed light on Moore's views in *Principia*, we shall examine two papers he wrote prior to it, "The Nature of Judgment" and "Identity," written in 1899 and 1901, respectively.[2] The first of these papers is a wa-

---

[1] Moore, "Conception," p. 259 and "Meaning of "natural"," pp. 591–2.
[2] Moore, "The Nature of Judgment," *Mind* n.s., 8 (April 1899), pp. 176–93. "Identity," *Proceedings of the Aristotelian Society* n.s., 1 (London, 1900–1901), pp. 121–45. The essays are

tershed for him, marking his movement away from idealism to the realist theories he maintained for the rest of his career. In it, he argues that
the world is composed of *concepts*. Concepts are possible objects of
thought and a judgment is a synthesis of concepts. Concepts are not anything psychological, however, it being indifferent to their nature whether
or not anyone thinks them. In fact, our ideas are nothing different from,
but *are* the concepts themselves. We are thus *not* to understand the truth
of a judgment as being dependent on "the relations of our ideas to reality." He writes:

When, therefore, I say "This rose is red," I am not attributing part of the content
of my idea to the rose, nor yet attributing part of the content of my ideas rose and
red together to some third subject. What I am asserting is a specific connexion of
certain concepts forming the total concept "rose" with the concepts "this" and
"now" and "red"; and the judgment is true if such a connexion is existent. Similarly when I say "The chimera has three heads," the chimera is not an idea in my
mind, nor any part of such idea. What I mean to assert is nothing about my mental states, but a specific connexion of concepts. If the judgment is false, that is not
because my *ideas* do not correspond to reality, but because such a conjunction of
concepts is not to be found among existents.[3]

So before "The Refutation of Idealism," Moore has begun his bold
move of emptying the mind of "contents" whose relation to a mind-
independent reality must always be problematic. Anticipating the later
paper, his view is that in thought the mind just grasps the mind-
independent objects *themselves*. The paper also makes a noteworthy double distinction between existents and nonexistents. There is first the distinction between existent and nonexistent *objects*. As the nature of a concept is independent of its being thought, so is it independent of there
being any existents. It would thus be wrong to think of concepts, which
are universals, as being existents or parts of existents.[4] What distinguishes
the existent rose from the nonexistent chimera is the fact that the simpler concepts constituting the rose stand in relation to the concepts existence and time, while those constituting the chimera do not.[5] Although
he speaks of the concept "this," which might lead one to think that his
view requires substances or bare particulars, this is not the case. Anticipating the views of *Principia*, an existent object just consists of concepts
standing in relation to other concepts, including the concept existence.
To analyze an object is to "break it down" into its constituent concepts.

   Mirroring *Principia*'s distinction between natural and nonnatural properties, Moore also distinguishes between concepts that are capable of
standing in relation to the concept existence and ones that are not. Al-

reprinted in *G. E. Moore: The Early Essays*, Tom Regan, ed. (Philadelphia: Temple University Press, 1986), pp. 59–81, 121–47.
   [3] "The Nature of Judgment," p. 179.
   [4] Ibid., p. 181.   [5] Ibid., p. 179

though he is not much concerned with nonnaturals here, he does say some things that anticipate his *Principia* account of them. Since it is a condition of an object's becoming existent that it stand *in relation* to the concept existence, existence cannot be a part of the object. Moore speaks briefly of a *sui generis* relation that obtains between existents and the concept existence. It is "something immediately known like red or two."[6] In *Principia*, he makes room for another such *sui generis* relation, that which stands between individual goods and the property good.

The second paper, "Identity," is motivated by a change of mind on the problem of individuation. Near the end of "The Nature of Judgment," he argues that objects are individuated "by the different relations in which the common concepts stand to other concepts."[7] But in "Identity," he argues that if the "predicates," or properties, of different objects were identical, they could not be individuated by the relations in which they stand to the properties of other objects. Consider two red spots, one of which is surrounded by yellow and the other by blue. One who holds that the red in each spot is identical will say that its two different instances are individuated by the different relations in which they stand to the yellow and the blue. But this will not work, since on this view, "The one surrounded by yellow is also surrounded by blue: they are not two but one, and whatever is true of that which is surrounded by yellow is also true of that which is surrounded by blue."[8] One will thus be forced to say that the *same thing* both is and is not surrounded by blue; he considers this a *reductio* of the position. He thus concludes that the different property instances are numerically different but "conceptually identical," or exactly similar, *particulars*.[9] This nominalistic strain is tempered, however, by the claim that each particular stands in relation to one and only one universal, which he likens to a Platonic form, that determines the nature of the particular.[10] Two particulars, like the reds in his example, are conceptually identical if they stand in relation to the same universal. Their standing in relation to the same universal is involved in the very definition of the conceptual identity of particulars.

In this ontology, room is again made for the distinction between natural and nonnatural properties. Objects are not composed of universals but of simple particulars, each of which stands in relation to the one and only universal determining its nature. In fact, when we think of *one* thing as having two or more properties, we are usually mistaken. An assertion that a piece of cloth is both black and woolen, "is not to be understood as an assertion that one individual has two predicates, but that two individuals have a certain relation."[11] Perhaps this explains why Moore can speak in *Principia* of a natural property existing *by itself* in time. Each par-

---

[6] Ibid., p. 181.   [7] Ibid., p. 182.   [8] "Identity," p. 110.
[9] Ibid., p. 111.   [10] Ibid., p. 114.   [11] Ibid., p. 127.

ticular property is logically independent of all others, even if, as does a color, it also requires at least one other particular to be instantiated along with it.

One of the things distinguishing particulars from universals in this ontology is the fact that particulars exist while universals do not. Because all universals are nonexistent, a thing's being a universal cannot by itself account for its being nonnatural. We need then to make a distinction between universals that determine the nature of particulars and ones that do not. Absent such a distinction, we will not be able to explain why there are not existent simple particular *goods* as there are existent simple particular reds and sweets. In the paper, for a different reason, Moore makes a distinction between kinds of universals that can also be applied to this one. It is obvious that a complex has properties that none of the constituents of the complex have.[12] When we ascribe one of these properties to the entire complex, we are making a different assertion than that a relation or set of relations obtains among the different particulars comprising the complex. Therefore, these properties are not parts of the object in the way that simple particular properties are. They thus satisfy one of *Principia*'s criteria of nonnaturalness. We can also see that simple particulars have properties that do not determine their nature. If, to use one of Moore's own examples, a complex has the property of being so many, then each particular has the property of being one.[13] This property plays little or no role in the determination of an object's nature. While it is true of any particular that it would not be the thing it is were it not one, its being one does not determine *which* one it is. Moore calls such nondetermining properties *class-concepts*.[14]

If we apply this distinction to good, we get the following account: From the fact that good is not a property that determines the nature of anything, it follows that no good thing is conceptually identical with the property good. This points to a way in which one can commit the naturalistic fallacy within this ontology. (The fallacy's great versatility enables it to be committed within every ontology!) To commit the fallacy is to place good in the wrong category of universal, to think of it as one of the universals that does determine the nature of the simple particular things exemplifying it. Once it is placed within the wrong category, the tendency toward moral monism, the view that only one kind of thing is good, becomes irresistible. In this ontology, the simplicity of pleasure makes hedonism the version of monism most likely to be irresistible.

Another class-concept Moore mentions is the *determinable* red.[15] We might be tempted to think that there is some relation like conceptual identity holding between different determinate universal reds that is to be analyzed in terms of the relation in which each of them stands to the

[12] Ibid., p. 126.   [13] Ibid.   [14] Ibid., p. 117.   [15] Ibid., p. 124.

higher-order determinable red. But Moore has two reasons, which we have already encountered in *Principia,* for denying this. (Although the implicit appeal to a second kind of definition applies a chastening element to the first of those reasons in *Principia.*) The first is that he considers universals to be "mere points of difference."[16] The second is his fear that such a view leads to extravagant idealist commitments to "concrete" or "self-differentiating" universals and to things having "identity in difference."[17] To anticipate a concern on the horizon, on this model, all determinables are nonnatural. This makes the category of class-concepts less than a perfect home for good. He tells us later that he never thought of good as a determinable and places determinables explicitly into the class of natural properties.[18] But at this time, he has not yet turned his thoughts explicitly toward the ontology of value and thus has not yet thought about how to distinguish good from natural determinable properties.

It is probably in "Identity" that Moore's inclination to see analysis as being required always to go downward toward the most determinate natural properties of a thing is at its strongest. The unchastened view that universals are mere points of difference seems to prevent them from having any features open to analysis in terms of more general properties. Also pointing analysis down is the claim that there are not single objects having two different properties such as being black and being woolen, but rather two different objects standing in relation to each other. Both of these views hint that it is an arbitrary matter what unities the mind finds among, or better, imposes on, the world's simple objects. The first of these views does not seem to allow that there is anything more in common between an instance of red and an instance of green than there is between an instance of red and an instance of sweet. The view that what we ordinarily consider to be single objects really are not seems to prevent the object consisting of the particular blackness and particular wooliness of Moore's example from being any more of a unity than the "object" consisting of that same blackness and a particular cottony quality in a pink shirt.

Fortunately, in his work after "Identity," Moore never allows the downward conception of analysis to have complete ascendancy over the upward. In *Principia,* remember, the second sense of definition he appeals to is one that goes up to the more general. He also recognizes an obligation to make sense of the fact that it is not an arbitrary matter which properties are seen by the mind as forming unified wholes. His view suggests that there are *natural complexes,* complexes that really do have some kind of unity within their complexity. Such complexes as animality are, at the requisite levels of abstraction, the objects of the various sciences. To al-

---

[16] Ibid., p. 120.   [17] Ibid., p. 125.
[18] Moore, "Meaning of "natural"," p. 583.

low that it is not arbitrary which objects are seen as forming unified wholes, it is important that we let the objects at different levels of analysis stand on their own feet, that we not seek fully to *reduce* one level of object to another.[19] This is to suggest that objects instantiate more or less fully a number of different natures, that there are various degrees of looseness without arbitrariness in the identity of objects at different levels of analysis, and also in the relations obtaining among the particular qualities that combine with each other to form objects.

Not the least important consequence of allowing a spirit of ontological expansiveness to accompany the spirit of analytical rigor is the way in which it can be used to enrich Moore's moral epistemology. His overall theory is at its best when it allows the world to contain many more different kinds of natural *goods,* of which we start to become aware very early in life, than he officially recognizes. Perhaps, for instance, we grasp the complex object health and its goodness, while being quite ignorant of the exact properties constituting health. Such a view makes the rough and ready, but nevertheless very deep, agreements in the opinions of human beings about what things are good much more a matter of insight than of indoctrination.

Later Refinements and Problems

"The Conception of Intrinsic Value" was written in the teens and first published in 1922.[20] In this great paper, Moore extends and refines his *Principia* views on the distinction between natural and nonnatural properties. He then refines those views in response to criticism by C. D. Broad; Broad's criticism and Moore's response are both found in *The Philosophy of G. E. Moore,* published in 1942. The greater subtlety of Moore's later views does not prevent them from continuing in the vein of *Principia.* In fact, he uses their greater subtlety to sharpen the distinction between natural and nonnatural properties and asks the distinction to carry even more weight than it does in *Principia.* He winds up holding that *only* value properties are nonnatural and makes nonnaturalness *solely* responsible for value's being an intrinsic feature of the world.[21]

Before we examine the details of "Conception," let us clear up a terminological difficulty that Moore points to in his reply to Broad.[22] Moore claims that the value of a thing is a property whose instantiation *depends solely* on its intrinsic nature. Thus it is a property that is intrinsic to the thing. But because it differs from those properties constituting the thing's

[19] Butchvarov, *Skepticism in Ethics,* p. 60.
[20] Moore, Preface to *Philosophical Studies,* p. vii.
[21] Moore, "Conception," p. 259. Although Moore uses beauty as his example of an intrinsic value property in this paper, we shall speak of the property good.
[22] Moore, "Meaning of 'natural'," pp. 583–5.

nature, it is *not* an intrinsic property. He is thus forced to say that although value is a property and is intrinsic, it is not an intrinsic property! In his reply to Broad, in order to avoid confusion, he distinguishes between natural intrinsic properties and nonnatural intrinsic value properties. Although we shall follow him in this change as much as possible, we shall occasionally have to rely on his original, "awkward" terminology.

We begin with Moore's claim that value depends solely on the natural intrinsic properties of a thing. For this to be the case, two theses must be true:

> (1) that it is *impossible* for what is strictly *one and the same* thing to possess that kind of value at one time, or in one set of circumstances, and *not* to possess it at another; and equally *impossible* for it to possess it in one degree at one time, or in one set of circumstances, and to possess it in a different degree at another, or in a different set. . . . (2) . . . if a given thing possesses any kind of intrinsic value in a certain degree, then . . . anything *exactly like* it, must, under all circumstances, possess it in exactly the same degree. Or to put it in the corresponding negative form: It is *impossible* that of two exactly similar things one should possess it and the other not, or that one should possess it in one degree, and the other in a different one.[23]

To understand these theses correctly, we must have a sure grasp of their modal terms. Moore insists that the impossibility being invoked is not merely *causal*.[24] If it were, the theses would fail to preclude certain kinds of subjectivist analyses. It is causally possible, for instance, for two exactly similar things to elicit exactly similar responses in anyone who perceives them in exactly similar ways. This would allow for an analysis of value in terms of perceivers' attitudes. The requisite impossibility must be such as to guarantee that things having intrinsic value have the same amount of it *no matter what* any perceiver's attitude toward them happens to be.

But the proper rendering of the modality of these conditions alone does not insure the nonnaturalness of value. These conditions could obtain even if good were an intrinsic *natural* property, for example, the property of being a state of pleasure. In order to preclude naturalistic analyses in terms of pleasure or any other natural property, another thesis must be maintained: Although it is solely dependent on the intrinsic natural properties of an object for its instantiation, goodness is not one of those properties. Rather, a special relation of dependence obtains between the natural properties of an object and its goodness. According to Moore, this relation serves to make value properties utterly unique; he "cannot think of any other predicate which resembles them in respect of the fact, that although not *itself* intrinsic, it shares with intrinsic properties the characteristic of depending solely on the intrinsic nature of what possesses it."[25]

---

[23] Moore, "Conception," pp. 260–1.   [24] Ibid., pp. 267–8.   [25] Ibid., p. 273.

In order to see how the fact of intrinsic value's being different from but completely dependent on natural intrinsic properties precludes different sorts of naturalistic theories, consider two different examples of such theories: 1) "The assertion "A is good" means "A is pleasant" and 2) "The assertion "A is good" means A is a state of pleasure."[26] The first type of theory is precluded by the fact that while a thing's intrinsic value is solely dependent on its intrinsic natural properties, its pleasantness is not. The pleasantness of a thing is at least partly dependent on the attitudes of the people experiencing it. Some people find a thing pleasant – like it – and others do not. On the second type of theory, a state of pleasure is an intrinsic natural property of a different, more inclusive object than the object of which the pleasantness of 1) is an extrinsic property. To combat this type of theory, it must be maintained that its goodness is not an intrinsic natural property of that object. But since its being a state of pleasure is an intrinsic natural property of the more inclusive object, it is allowed that the goodness of that object is *dependent* on the state's being one of pleasure.

We can flesh out our understanding of the way in which the two crucial features of nonnaturalness keep one from conflating being good with being pleasant or being a state of pleasure by examining an argument of Broad's and Moore's response to it. Broad claims that the pleasantness of a taste is always "derivative" upon certain of its "non-hedonic" properties, such as its sweetness. As he puts it, there must always be an answer in pleasure-neutral terms to the question, "What makes the thing pleasant?" In like manner, he finds goodness to be derivative. The goodness of a certain experience, for instance, is dependent upon its being a sorrowfully tinged awareness of another person's distress. But the pleasantness is supposed to be natural and the goodness not. He writes:

Now Moore counts pleasantness as a *natural* characteristic. If he is right in doing so, it is impossible to identify the nonnatural characteristics of a thing with the derivative sub-class of those of its characteristics which depend solely on its intrinsic nature. For by that criterion pleasantness would be a nonnatural characteristic just as much as goodness.[27]

Moore responds that Broad's criticism rests on a failure to distinguish between two senses of the word "pleasant." Each of these senses applies to a different kind of thing. When we become clear about what kind of thing each applies to, we see that in both its senses, pleasantness is quite a different kind of property than goodness. According to the first sense, pleasantness is an *extrinsic* property. Therefore, "the fact that it is "natural" can have no tendency to show that there are any natural derivative *intrinsic* properties."[28] As an example, Moore considers numerically dif-

26 Ibid.
27 C. D. Broad, "Moore's Ethical Doctrines," in *The Philosophy of G. E. Moore,* p. 61.
28 "Meaning of "natural"," p. 588.

ferent but qualitatively identical tastings of caviar. To some people such tastings are pleasant, while to others they are not. Since, *pace* Berkeley, the bare taste is the same whether one finds it to be pleasant or unpleasant, neither its pleasantness nor its unpleasantness is an intrinsic property of the tasting of caviar. Thus as Moore says, the pleasantness is derivative and extrinsic and on a different plane than good, which is derivative and intrinsic.

When we wish to account for the contribution to goodness that the pleasantness of things makes, we must turn to the larger sorts of wholes to which the second sense of "pleasant" applies. Continuing with Moore's example, "pleasant" applies in this instance "not only [to] an experience of tasting caviare but also an experience of feeling pleased with the taste." Of this larger object, the property of being pleasant is *not* derivative. As Moore points out:

> A state of things which can be properly described by stating that it is a state of things in which some person is *both* tasting the taste of caviare *and* being pleased with the taste, cannot be exactly like a state of things . . . in which some person is tasting the taste of caviare but *not feeling pleased with the taste*.[29]

Since the second sense of "pleasant" names a natural, nonderivative property of a more inclusive whole, its pleasantness is one of its *good-making* properties. (To remind the reader again, we shall say more later about such larger wholes, "states of things" in Moore's terminology, "states of affairs" in others'.)

Moore admits in "Conception" to being unable to say what exactly it is that distinguishes natural from nonnatural properties. All he can do is give a "vague expression" of the difference. He says that natural properties "describe" an object while nonnatural properties do not:

> If you could enumerate *all* the [natural] intrinsic properties a given thing possessed, you would have given a *complete* description of it, and would not need to mention any [nonnatural] predicates of value it possessed; whereas no description of a given thing could be *complete* which omitted any [natural] intrinsic property.[30]

In his reply to Broad, Moore notes that this account is not quite accurate as it stands.[31] Although they are natural intrinsic properties, an object's determinable properties need not be mentioned in a complete description of it. Since these properties follow from the object's determinate properties, mentioning them in addition to the determinate properties describes the object no further. So the natural intrinsic properties consist of the most determinate properties that describe the object *and* the determinable properties entailed by them. This characterization makes it impossible for good to be a determinable and in this discussion

---

[29] Ibid., p. 589.   [30] "Conception," p. 274.
[31] "Meaning of "natural"," pp. 586–7.

Moore claims never to have thought of good as a determinable. By explicitly disallowing this possibility, he makes it obvious that he requires a special and unique relation of necessity to obtain between a thing's natural properties and its goodness.

Clearly, Moore has brought great concentration, care, and subtlety to the subject of nonnaturalness in both "Conception" and his reply to Broad. As his discussion of the example of the enjoyment of caviar shows, he is considering "parts" and "objects" whose analyses must be quite a bit more nuanced than those that apply to brute physical objects. One might even think that we should completely abandon talk of parts and objects in coming to grips with his views. In support of this recommendation is the fact that Moore says in his reply to Broad that he no longer thinks of its brownness and roundness as parts of a penny.[32] So if *we* are to continue to make use of the notion of parts, we must do so with great care.

Despite the greater subtlety of his later account and his unhappiness with his earlier way of making the distinction, Moore still deeply retains the spirit of *Principia*. The distinction between the tasting of caviar and the enjoyment of the tasting of it is similar to the distinction he makes in *Principia*, as part of his argument against the view that pleasure is the sole good, between pleasure and the consciousness of pleasure.[33] The greater flexibility of his later work lets us give a more exact characterization of the distinction than could be given in *Principia*. Enjoyment is a distinct element of an experience, being something that can be *identified* by itself, even though, because it must always be the enjoyment *of* something, it cannot exist by itself. It counts as natural because it has duration and belongs to wholes that can exist by themselves.

Even with the new characterization, the distinction between natural and nonnatural properties is at its starkest and easiest to grasp at the level of the most determinate properties. But once we start to consider subtler sorts of properties, it is not so obvious that there is as sharp a distinction between natural and nonnatural properties as Moore thinks. To start, is good really so unlike determinable properties that it must be placed in a category utterly separate from them?[34] Questions posed in terms of descriptive and nondescriptive predicates seem no less trenchant. To cite something he realizes but does not make enough of, there are many different ways of describing.[35] Are there not then degrees of descriptiveness? If the most important and interesting task of philosophy is "To give a general description of the *whole* of the Universe,"[36] is there not a sense

---

[32] Ibid., p. 582.   [33] *Principia*, pp. 87–91.
[34] Butchvarov, "That Simple, Indefinable, Non-natural Property *Good*," pp. 58–62, *Skepticism in Ethics*, pp. 62–3.
[35] "Meaning of "natural"," pp. 591–2.
[36] Moore, *Some Main Problems of Philosophy*, p. 1.

in which we are describing *the universe* when we say that there is intrinsic value in it?[37] Such a sense would provide Moore with the clearest way of distinguishing between his view and the views of such opponents as emotivists and prescriptivists, who also maintain that to say of something that it is good is not to describe it. These and other philosophers like them might feel less hostility toward allowing good into their ontology if they see that a richer typology of properties is available once they take their eyes off the paradigm natural properties. Even if we continue with Moore to consider value to be utterly unique, there is great heuristic value in remembering his *Principia* distinction according to which many properties are nonnatural. Showing good's likenesses to some of these other properties helps make a belief in it seem less "superstitious."[38]

It is not just from the global perspective that the ascription of goodness can be seen to be descriptive. Consider an example from art. Suppose that one person A sees that a piece of sculpture is beautiful and therefore good while another person B does not. Since the two can agree on the most cold-blooded inventory of the thing's parts and arrangements, there is the Moorean sense of description according to which the dispute about its goodness is not descriptive. But there are other ways of describing and *seeing*, ways familiar to gestalt psychologists, for instance, upon which they do not agree. This kind of seeing is not a matter of espying different parts, but a matter of seeing the same parts in a different way (seeing that the duck is also a rabbit). When A tries to get B to see that the sculpture is a good piece of work, she attempts to get her to "see the thing in a new light" and not merely to get her to "change her attitude" toward it. If A succeeds, B sees the grace or the power of the piece she had not seen before. The sculpture makes sense or raises questions for B when before it had not. In learning to see the piece in this way, B is learning how it achieves (its) good.

In most cases, the perception of goodness is dialectical and expansive. We cannot get an exhaustive understanding of a thing's goodness – nor even of the thing – by focusing on it alone, but only by comparing it to other things and placing it within the classes of things into which it fits most comfortably.[39] This makes the investigation and description of things from which their goodness is seen to follow wide-ranging and theoretical. We do not realize just how wide-ranging and deeply enmeshed within theory these things are because we begin to learn the theories so early in our lives and so deeply that we take them for granted. (Our training in aesthetic theory begins even before crayons and bedtime stories.)

---

[37] Ibid., pp. 26–7.   [38] "*Conception*," pp. 258–9.
[39] Butchvarov, *Skepticism in Ethics*, pp. 69–70. In "The Limits of Ontological Analysis," in *The Ontological Turn*, E. D. Klemke and Moltke Gram, eds. (Iowa City: University of Iowa Press, 1974), pp. 3–37, Butchvarov claims that all understanding is comparative, going beyond the bare description of things and requiring classification.

It only *seems* to us now, in some cases, that we just "see" the goodness of things as we see the yellowness of them. Moore's own account in *Principia* of the ascription of beauty to a thing is at a very great remove from the widely accepted caricature of his view on the perception of value according to which we need only to perform the quickest inventory of a thing's most determinate natural properties before rendering a judgment on whether goodness emanates from it.[40] But perhaps because he never again engages in the same detail of aesthetic discussion, he does not consider in his later career how far his views on the ascription of goodness or beauty can get from the starkly drawn distinction between descriptive and non-descriptive predicates that his official conception of analysis appeals to.

In *Principia* remember, Moore defines the beautiful as "that of which the admiring contemplation is good in itself." He then elaborates on this definition:

> To assert that a thing is beautiful is to assert that the cognition of it is an essential element in one of the intrinsically valuable wholes we have been discussing; so that the question, whether it is *truly* beautiful or not, depends upon the *objective* question whether the whole in question is or is not truly good, and does not depend upon the question whether it would or would not excite particular feelings in particular persons.[41]

By the lights of this definition, when we ascribe beauty to a thing, we do more than say that it has a certain property that follows from the properties mentioned in the bare description of it. The ascription of beauty ranges beyond the individual thing to which we are ascribing the beauty and places it explicitly into one or more classes of thing. It is thus intrinsically classificatory and comparative. Even though we need not think explicitly of these classes of objects when we ascribe beauty to something, we have some vague sense of them in mind; the membership of the thing in such classes is part of what we mean. Although it may be in spite of initial appearances, we do have part of our eye on those classes and not just on the thing to which we are ascribing beauty.

Notice also how subtle and complex Moore's view on the ascription of beauty in such cases is. He claims that "to say that a thing is beautiful is to say, not indeed that it is *itself* good, but that it is a necessary element in something which is: to prove that a thing is truly beautiful is to prove that a whole, to which it bears a particular relation as a part, is truly good."[42] But in order to decide whether the larger whole consisting of the *cognition* of the object is good, we do not directly examine *it*, but instead the aesthetic object that is a *part* of it and other specific and general aesthetic objects to which the aesthetic object is related. In fact, we can only *create* the intrinsically valuable whole, the appreciation of the aesthetic object,

---

[40] We shall take issue with this caricature again in Chapter 4.
[41] *Principia*, p. 201.   [42] Ibid., p. 202.

by studying one of its parts, the aesthetic object. If we are still studying the part, the larger whole is obviously not yet completed for examination. There appears to be a most interesting similarity between this procedure of creative discovery, wherein we create an intrinsically valuable larger object by looking for value in a smaller object, and the procedure Socrates recommends for living the best kind of life.

Moore also speaks of "proving" that a whole to which the part bears a particular relation is good. But since he has already told us that we cannot *really* prove that a thing is good, he must be considering a proof in some weaker sense of the term. To prove that a thing is good in this sense is to show that it is a member of the class of acts of aesthetic appreciation, whose goodness has been established in the preceding pages of *Principia*. Showing something controversial to be an act of aesthetic appreciation can get quite complicated. The long and the short of it is that we show that a controversial object is sufficiently like things uncontroversially belonging to that class as also to warrant inclusion in it. This introduces a conservative element to the methodology of such proofs. But that conservative element is offset by the fact that a successful proof expands the class of objects we recognize as being worthy of appreciation. Proving something to be aesthetically valuable will in certain cases be long and revisionary rather than short and conservative.

For instance, to rehearse what has been going on in American households and in popular and learned journals for over two decades, one shows to noninitiates that listening to rap is sufficiently similar to other kinds of aesthetic experience as also to warrant classification as an aesthetic experience. One way to do that is to show that rap is sufficiently similar to one or more of the members of the class of African-American musical objects, rhythm-and-blues, or reggae, say, as also to be included in it. One may also compare rap to other forms of music and other declamatory and poetic forms. But keeping our eye just on the defense of rap as being similar to other forms of African-American music, one who is challenged about *them* can defend their merits by pointing out their likenesses to other kinds of music. (One may also feel that their musicality is so obvious as to need no argument.) One can then defend the forms that provided the second comparison class by comparing them to others. This process can go on for quite some time before something is simply accepted as musical.

While the defense has so far been conservative, there is also a revisionary element in the proof of the aesthetic worthiness of rap. In order to show that rap is a distinct art form, that it has *its own kind of beauty*,[43] at some point one must highlight the features that make it unique. Because rap does have its own unique beauty, before we had ever listened to it, we

---

[43] Ibid.

had not known that something could be beautiful *in that way*. If we have been successfully prepared to hear rap's beauty, our study of the more specific will have enriched our understanding of the more general. The inclusion as music of something so close to the spoken word and so heavily rhythmic deepens our appreciation of the source of music in the conversation and movement of everyday life. Our receptivity to beauty grows along with our admiration for human inventiveness as we are exposed to this new kind of beauty.

To repeat, when we appreciate something aesthetically, we do not just study and learn about *it*. We look at its relations to many other things and their relations to many other things and learn about them all. By following Moore himself, we have strayed *very* far from the paradigm he is supposed to blindly accept according to which we need only note the most determinate properties of a thing before deciding whether the nonnatural property of beauty or goodness follows from it. There is no reason to think that there is not a similar complex dynamic involved in the study of Moore's other great good, friendship, or any other goods we may happen to find.

Final Refinements

Our final discussion concerns the possibility of maintaining of certain other kinds of "objects," most importantly of those known as *states of affairs,* that their intrinsic value depends solely on their intrinsic nature. Maintaining this view will require us to stretch even wider the conception of objecthood that Moore propounds in "The Conception of Intrinsic Value" and his reply to Broad. One of the most interesting features of Moore's work in this area (as in others) is its ability to join a spirit of expansiveness – more probably than he recognizes – to a spirit of analytical austerity. Although we must remain respectful of certain of its limitations, which at the levels of abstraction being considered are not exactly weaknesses, it does appear that a reasonable Moorean explication can be given, for any object that can plausibly be considered to have intrinsic value, of the distinction between the property it exemplifies of being intrinsically valuable and the properties it has as a part of its intrinsic nature that make it intrinsically valuable.

Let us begin by considering the nature of things much like art objects: tools and artifacts – knives, can openers, cars, and so on. Borrowing an example from Philippa Foot, we can envision that a thing found in another culture, with spatio-temporal properties identical to the properties had by a thing our culture uses for cutting, is there a decorative object, not a knife.[44] If this is so, then any intrinsic value that such things as

---

[44] Philippa Foot, "Goodness and Choice," *Virtues and Vices* (Berkeley: University of California Press, 1978), p. 134.

knives have *qua* tool, or any intrinsic value they contribute to as parts of
larger wholes, cannot be due solely to their simple determinate spatio-
temporal properties and the determinable properties entailed by them.
Any such value is heavily, perhaps solely, dependent upon their having a
function and their performing it well. There is nothing whose function
is determined by its spatio-temporal characteristics alone.

One response to this problem is that these things have only *instrumental* value. Since the instrumental value of a thing may vary depending on
whether it is used for cutting or for decorating, its intrinsic natural properties need not go beyond the spatio-temporal ones. It will be difficult for
Moore to accept this conclusion, however. Such objects are beautiful according to the *Principia* definition that what is beautiful is that of which
the admiring contemplation is intrinsically good. In most instances, these
things can only be rightly admired by one who knows what they are *for.*
Even if one rejects Moore's argument that the mere existence of beautiful objects has intrinsic value, it remains that these objects, being worthy
of admiration, are capable of being intrinsic parts of larger wholes having
intrinsic value.[45] We must then have a more nuanced account of their natures, an account that makes their use a "part" of them. To help develop
this conception, we again remind ourselves to be respectful of the fact that
the different higher-level natures a thing instantiates are not completely
reducible to its lower ones. Although it is true that at one level of analysis
a thing just is its brute spatio-temporal properties, *qua* artifact, it is more
than that. In the full description of a thing as an artifact, one must appeal
to aforementioned facts about the culture in which it was made and the
relevant intentions of its maker(s). Once having brought these features
of a thing into play, we can say of our knife and their decorative object
that even though their determinate physical spatio-temporal are identical, they do not belong to the same kind and hence are not identical.

When put so strongly, this reply sounds odd. If two things are composed of the very same determinate properties, the same *stuff,* how can
they not be the same? One replies by repeating that there is more to belonging to a certain kind than having the right stuff. The objector is forgetting that analysis must proceed at different levels, must assume different perspectives. From the right perspective, it is no longer odd to say
that for a thing to be a certain kind of artifact, certain social facts must
obtain. When we say that these properties are a part of what it is to be a
knife, we must remember that we are now using a very abstract and attenuated sense of the term "part."[46] To make this thought more plausi-

---

[45] For Moore's "Beautiful World Argument," see *Principia,* pp. 83–5.
[46] A remark of Butchvarov's in "The Limits of Ontological Analysis," pp. 26–7, is apposite:
"The analytical understanding regards the features and circumstances in terms of which
it seeks to understand the nature of the object as possibly only *analogous* to parts of the
object, not necessarily as literally parts of the objects."

ble, consider the reaction of archaeologists to a cultural object they discover of whose function they are ignorant. They cannot classify the object, say what it *is*, until they know its function. Does its function not then seem to be a "part" of its nature?

To bring facts about functions into the analysis of these objects, it will be helpful to make a distinction similar to one we make with acts of enjoyment and with beliefs. Even though we cannot describe the nature of a particular act of believing without saying what it is about, we recognize that what it is about does not affect its nature *qua* belief. In some manner such as this does a thing's being a knife depend upon social facts without those facts literally being part of the physical thing that is the knife. It is conceded that Moore might not have been happy to see his account go so far in this direction. Remember the contempt he expresses for the claim that its being a part of the body is part of the analysis of being an arm.[47] Still, his view seems not only to allow, but to require this kind of expansion if we are to continue to maintain that the intrinsic value of a thing is solely dependent on its intrinsic natural properties.

Perhaps it is more obvious with functional objects than with others that we will have to move some distance away from one of Moore's guiding conceptions on the nature of good's dependency on the natural properties of objects. For something to be a functional object, it is enough that its makers have had some very general intentions about what it was supposed to do. Any more precise intentions concerning the object are thus irrelevant to its nature *qua* functional object. Insofar as an object's value is dependent on how well it performs that general function, it is possible for its value not to depend on its most specific spatio-temporal properties. Mark McGwire's baseball bat may be equally lethal whether it is colored black or white, or even whether it weighs thirty-two or thirty-three ounces. Unsurprisingly, given the similarity of functional objects to art objects, this point also seems to hold for art objects. Part of the beauty of a painting, for instance, can lie in a contrast that could have been brought about by any number of different specific colors. So despite what Moore says in *Principia,* the most specific properties of an art object need not be "*essential* to its beauty."[48] A little more thought suggests this point to hold across the board for value. The goodness of a certain act of friendship depends on its being an act of *encouragement,* not on its being a pat on the back or the saying of a particular word. Anyone who worries that value does not then touch all the way down to the bottom of things is reminded here that the relation between lower and higher levels of objects is not fully reductive and also of Moore's unofficial conception of definition that ties ultimacy in natural properties to general properties rather than specific.

---

[47] *Principia,* pp. 31–3.   [48] Ibid., p. 202.

A consideration of artifacts brings us now to those most important and abstract kinds of objects, states of affairs.[49] Immediately upon moving to states of affairs, we can say that the state of affairs that consists of a thing's existing while having been made in a certain culture by people with certain intentions is different from the state of affairs that consists of a physically identical thing's existing while having been made in a different culture by people with different intentions. This suggests a principle that only seems paradoxical at first glance: States of affairs containing different physically identical objects may have different natures and hence different amounts of intrinsic value.

Perhaps the thought that *all* value attaches to states of affairs is found in *Principia* and other of Moore's works without much being made of it. At one point in *Principia*, Moore says, against the metaphysical philosophers who find value only in what is eternal, "But when we assert that a thing is good, what we mean is that its existence or reality is good."[50] The method of isolation for determining the amount of an object's intrinsic value also suggests that what it is for an object to have intrinsic value is that the state of affairs consisting of the object's existing all by itself has intrinsic value. Later, in *Ethics*, Moore offers as the analysis of the claim that A is intrinsically better than B, "'it would be better that A exist quite alone than that B exist quite alone.'"[51]

The claim that all value resides in states of affairs might leave one uncomfortable for a number of reasons. One might object on phenomenological grounds that we find value in *the thing itself* and not just in its existence. When we wonder whether a thing is intrinsically good, we consider *it* and not its existence. Recalling for a moment the ontology of "The Nature of Judgment," the nature of a concept is prior to and independent of the concept existence – the chimera is the same thing whether it exists or not. "The Refutation of Idealism" also seems to require that the mind engage directly with nonexistent things. One well-known response to views such as these is that to think that there is a significant difference between thinking of an object and thinking of an object's *existence* is to fall prey to an act of philosophical sleight of hand. Kant's famous dictum that existence is not a predicate (that it does not *describe*) is an attempt to head off the dangers that come from indulging in such lines of thought. Still, insofar as we are concerned specifically with Moore, we are likely to have to allow a great deal of room for Meinongian views, as he holds that it is in the *nature* of an art object to be unreal.[52]

It should be mentioned here that it might be the case that certain kinds of facts are relevant to the determination of the value of some states of affairs, but irrelevant to the determination of the value of others seem-

---

[49] See Baldwin, *G. E. Moore*, p. 73.   [50] *Principia*, p. 120.
[51] *Ethics*, p. 39.   [52] See Chapter 10.

ingly rather like them. Consider, for instance, how a knowledge of the state of an artist during the time he created a work might sometimes be relevant to the value of our appreciation of his work. The fact that the artist composed a great symphony despite suffering a loss of hearing might make his achievement worthier of appreciation than it would otherwise be. The state of affairs consisting of our appreciation of the work while knowing of the creator's struggles with his disability might then have greater value than the state consisting of our appreciation of the same work while knowing that it had not been created by someone so afflicted. Conflicting with this thought is our inclination to say that just so long as there are the relevant general intentions on the part of the composer, the value of the work and its existence and our appreciation of it are independent of other facts about him. Grown-ups must accept that trying hard does not guarantee a thing's goodness (although some value might, *pace* Moore, attach to the trying).[53] One might also object that the view puts us on a dangerous slippery slope. Is a limitation of talent or even laziness and other kinds of moral or temperamental deficiencies an affliction the overcoming of which gives greater value to certain works or actions and our appreciation of them?

Before responding that the answer to this question is obviously *no*, consider the grandeur that Malcolm Lowry's struggles with alcoholism give to *Under the Volcano* or the depth that is added to Miles Davis's trumpet playing by his having to come to terms with a less than breathtaking technique. Similar questions pose well-known theoretical and practical problems in the more distinctly moral sphere. Remember Kant's worries about the moral worth of actions done by people who are temperamentally inclined to do the right thing. There is certainly something moving about people struggling with and rising above their limitations. Still, it is easy to point to other cases where we are inclined to say just the opposite of what we are inclined to say in these cases. In art, we find something thrilling about work, like that of the young Elvis Presley, that is the expression of easy, fecund genius. Morally, we consider a naturally good nature to be very good – and again, *pace* Moore, not just as a means. Likely, the suggestion we make in the book's last few pages that there are not just pure art objects that we appreciate but continua of *art-historical* objects, would, along with a similar point about objects of more distinctly moral evaluation, be quite useful in an extended discussion of these matters. Some of the different claims that seem true but inconsistent if about the same things, are actually about different things. This, of course, still leaves open the question how much each of these different kinds of things contributes to the value instantiated by the world taken as a whole.

Something we need to consider in dealing with these and related issues

[53] Ibid., p. 176.

is how to make the truth or falsity of certain beliefs intrinsic properties of acts of aesthetic appreciation. Consider the act of appreciating a portrait painting. A part of that act of appreciation could be one's belief that the painter accurately captured the subject's character, her role in society, and so on. The value of the act thus waxes and wanes with the truth and falsity of those beliefs.[54] But their truth or falsity do not seem to be intrinsic properties of these beliefs. The belief that the subject of a certain painting married into a family of prosperous merchants, for instance, is the same *belief* whether it is true or false. Returning to the language of "Conception," calling a belief true does not seem to describe it (which again seems to jeopardize Moore's claim that the ascription of goodness is uniquely nondescriptive). If its truth is not an intrinsic property of the belief, then it does not seem that it can be an intrinsic property of the state of affairs of which the belief is a constituent. Since the value of the state of affairs is partly dependent on this property, it would appear to follow that the value of the state of affairs is not solely dependent on its intrinsic properties.

One deals with this problem by making a point similar to the one Moore made when responding to Broad about the pleasantness of things. There are two different kinds of states of affairs to which the truth of a belief is importantly related. The first of these, analogous to the first kind of pleasant object Moore discusses, consists of *just* the contemplation of the work. The truth (or falsity) of the belief is extrinsic to this whole just as the pleasantness is extrinsic to the first whole Moore describes to Broad. The second, larger state of affairs, analogous to the whole consisting of the tasting of caviar plus the enjoyment of it, consists of the appreciation of the work plus the truth of the relevant belief. The truth of the belief is intrinsic to this whole. Just as a state of affairs in which the tasting of caviar is being enjoyed differs from one in which the tasting of caviar is not being enjoyed, so does a state of affairs that has among its constituents a true belief that Y differ from one exactly like it but for its containing a false belief that Y.

One might find there to be something worrisomely artificial about such objects. Is it possible really to focus on *just* that state of affairs or must we implicitly be thinking about it as a part of something larger? One might worry that because the facts that make the belief true lie outside the act of appreciation, we cannot envisage that act existing by itself. If this is so, it seems to undermine the method of isolation as a test for intrinsic value and also to suggest that there is something ontologically incomplete about such acts of appreciation. To understand the thought lying behind this worry, consider an "object" consisting of a circle and its relation to the field within which it lies – *minus* the field. This is a kind of

[54] *Principia*, p. 195.

quasi-entity standing between the smaller whole consisting of the circle by itself and the larger whole consisting of the circle-within-the-field. One fears that in like manner, the act of appreciation-plus-truth is a quasi-entity standing between the act of appreciation taken without its truth and the larger whole that contains the facts that make the beliefs true. Must we really be thinking about one or the other of these things?

We can begin to dispel this worry by refining the isolation test for intrinsic value. When we wish to know whether a state of affairs consisting of an act of appreciation is valuable in and of itself, we do indeed think of it in and of itself. But we can do this while *putting aside* our knowledge that in fact, its existence is dependent on other things. This should arouse no more suspicion than our ability to focus our attention solely upon (and find value in) a single event, call it E, even as we recognize that because it was the effect of something, it could not have existed alone. The genetic dependence of E on its cause does not affect the fact that by itself, it is both conceptually and ontologically independent of it. It might seem that the analogy between E and an act of appreciation does not hold. The cause of E is only externally related to it while the relation of the fact to the belief it makes true is more intimate than that. To counter this worry, remember our brief discussion of the nature of belief. Even though we can only characterize an instance of belief by saying what it is about, the belief does not "contain" what it is about. Although we recognize that there must be something that makes a belief true, we need not be thinking of it when we think *that* it is true. Just as the larger causal nexus of which E is a part does not leak into its nature, so does the larger whole the belief is about not leak into the belief's nature. We can thus recognize the truth of a belief to contribute to the value of a whole without having to make that *of which* the belief is true a part of it.

The ontologically self-contained character of an act of appreciation holds despite what we might call its epistemic incompleteness. Even though the truth of the belief is a constituent of the larger, valuable act of appreciation, the one doing the appreciating cannot tell, just by performing the act, whether the belief in question is true or not. One cannot completely catalog the items comprising the whole from within, but has to look outside the complex to see whether it has truth or falsity. This makes the epistemic situation quite unlike the one found in the state of affairs consisting of one's enjoyment of the tasting of caviar. In that case, one does know, just by having the experience, that it is enjoyable – although one does not know thereby that it is worthy of being enjoyed. To the extent that the value of an act of appreciation depends on the truth of the beliefs contained in it, there is always a danger that we shall suffer deep and abiding illusion when we attempt to gauge its value. But that we are subject to illusion should be nothing surprising to a philosopher.

Let us turn to another issue concerning the relation of intrinsic value to states of affairs. If an object A (or its existence) is good, is there also a state of affairs consisting of the *goodness of A's being good* (or bad)? And if there are such states of affairs consisting of the goodness of a thing's goodness, are there higher-order states of affairs consisting of the goodness of the lower-order states of affairs' goodness? Though the regresses created by these states of affairs would perhaps not be vicious, it is putting it mildly to say that they would raise considerable difficulties. One response to these questions is that it is simply a category mistake to ascribe goodness or badness to the goodness or badness of something. If someone were to ask whether it is good that friendship is good, one might well find herself at a loss about what to say, just as she would be if she were asked whether the sweetness of something is sweet. What would it mean either to affirm or deny such a thing?

But perhaps there is a sense, and a most important one at that, according to which it can be either good or bad that certain things are good or bad. Many, for instance, appear to have found reason to regret that friendship is one of life's great goods. It is something sad, something "too bad," that human finitude imparts a troubling exclusivity to friendship, makes it to some degree selfish. One thus concludes that because the existence of this great good requires the existence of something bad, a world of *perfect* goodness is impossible. Or the thought may go in the other direction. In the last two chapters of this book, we shall consider what is perhaps the predominant view of Western casuistry – *that it is good that the world contains evil*. Many have held this view because of a belief that the manifestation of evil enables human beings to have a deeper and more valuable kind of awareness than any they would otherwise have been able to have.

Perhaps one can respond to the claim that it is bad that friendship is good by saying that what is really being regretted is nothing about friendship, but rather something about the limits of ourselves or the world that stifles its fullest flowering – the love of *all*. Or one might say that what is confusedly being noted is the fact that the pursuit of the intrinsic good of friendship can be extrinsically bad because of ways in which it leads to the ill treatment of those who are not friends. To the claim that it is good that the world contains evil, one might respond, as Moore does, that though the act of recognizing something to be good or bad can itself be intrinsically good, a thing need not exist for us to recognize this fact about it.[55] But finally, suppose it to be granted that a state of affairs having goodness or badness as a constituent can itself be good or bad. In the spirit of Moore, it would still seem that its goodness or badness follows from its constituents with a different kind of necessity than do the other properties that are intrinsic to it. The difference, for instance, between such a

[55] Ibid., p. 219.

state of affairs' being second-order (or higher) and its being good is sufficiently similar to the difference between an object's being colored and its being good to preserve the difference in necessity.

We close by reiterating a suggestion we made at the end of the first section of this chapter. When it comes to uncovering the value of things, the horse does not always go before the cart. We do not always first grasp a natural object and then discover its value. Sometimes, our sense of what things are *objects* is informed by our sense of what things are *valuable*. Using one of the preceding examples, it may be that we recognize the state of affairs of a belief's being true to be a self-contained object because of our implicit awareness that that is something where good is to be found. We think naturally and easily of the state of affairs containing the truth of the belief just because we have a strong, if originally inchoate, sense of the goodness of truth. To repeat, this is to raise the possibility, which we shall consider further in Chapter 5, of there being a great many different kinds of natural goods of which we have a deep instinctive awareness.

3

The Paradox of Ethics and Its Resolution

The Paradox of Ethics

The Open Question Argument (OQA) juxtaposes for us in the most dramatic way imaginable the revolutionary and conservative features of Moore's thought. Moore is a revolutionary in presenting an argument that lays bare the pretensions of a twenty-five-hundred-year-old discipline and at the same time, paves the way for great progress in it. The argument by which he achieves this breakthrough does not require that we wend our way carefully through labyrinthine passageways of premises, *scholia*, and subconclusions. On the contrary, it supposes no more acumen than can be mustered by a six-year-old child. At the same time, the ease of his argument highlights Moore's fundamental conservatism. His simple way of cutting through all manner of philosophical obfuscation restores to philosophers the things they knew when they were six.

For Moore's revolutionary argument to have this kind of conservative import, it must be the case that very early in our lives, before we are very self-conscious, we develop a very deep connection to good, which, because it is not developed in much reflection, cannot be completely lost to it. His argument reminds us of things we know in practice but have been unable to retain in theory. In order to explain this chasm between our sound ordinary understanding of good and our unsound philosophical understanding of it, Moore's view would seem to require that there be two rather distinct modes of awareness of good. Unfortunately, he does not offer anything nearly approaching a fully worked out view on the nature of our awareness of good. In his book on Moore, Robert Sylvester seeks to rectify this omission.

Sylvester finds that Moore leaves open two possibilities about how the mind comes to cognize the truth of propositions about the goodness of things. He calls these two different modes of cognition the a priori mode and the a posteriori mode. The a posteriori mode works upon concrete existents. Sylvester's example concerns one's cognition of the goodness of kindness: "There may be an actual occasion when a moral agent acts with kindness to another and where an observer sees the act and judges, correctly, that the act exemplifies value."[1] These rather immediate and

---

[1] Robert Peter Sylvester, *The Moral Philosophy of G. E. Moore*, pp. 72–3. Sylvester's view is that Moore "seems to be closer" to a posteriori propositions than a priori ones.

instinctive judgments would seem to be the ones out of which our prere-
flective awareness of good is comprised. After encountering a number of
such occasions early in our lives, the goodness of kindness becomes one
of the myriad of things we know of which we take no particular note. The
a priori mode of cognition comes afterward and is more reflective. It is
engaged in the entertaining and making of judgments in the abstract on
the goodness or badness of things. The consideration and ordering of
such propositions is part of the work Moore calls casuistry, work we all undertake to varying degrees. It is when we are in this mode of reflection
that we become aware of the necessity that obtains between various concepts and their goodness.

   Using this distinction on the OQA (which Sylvester does not do), we
can then say that our original insight that two questions are different
comes from the a posteriori mode of awareness. This insight, captured in
our linguistic intuitions according to Snare and Ball, acts as a guide for
our reflective a priori understanding, enabling us to see that any identity
proposed for good does not obtain. Moore's more general aim is to effect a synthesis between the two modes of the cognition of good, to enable the reflective intellect to provide the philosophical underpinnings
for what we know immediately and instinctively.[2] He wishes to take the
instinctive insights that come to us in a piecemeal fashion and make them
part of an articulate casuistical system. This is achieved by the discovery
of the principles that reveal the unity behind disparate moral phenomena. Because he has uncovered the naturalistic fallacy, the unity Moore
discovers, unlike the ones his predecessors have sought to impose, will
not be a straight jacket.

   It is because of our early un-self-conscious acquaintance with good
through particular instantiations of it that Moore is so optimistic about
the possibility of his argument showing the way to great theoretical
progress. Progress only requires that we go back to something we have
never completely left behind. To recall, immediately after presenting the
OQA, he expresses his optimism in these words:

Every one does in fact understand the question 'Is this good?' When he thinks of
it, his state of mind is different from what it would be, were he asked 'Is this pleasant, or desired, or approved?' It has a distinct meaning for him, even though he
may not recognise in what respect it is distinct. . . . Everybody is constantly aware
of this notion, although he may never become aware at all that it is different from
other notions of which he is also aware. But, for correct ethical reasoning, it is extremely important that he should become aware of this fact; and, as soon as the
nature of the problem is clearly understood, there should be little difficulty in advancing so far in analysis.[3]

---

[2] In *The Ethics of G. E. Moore: A New Interpretation,* John Hill endorses the second clause of
the sentence as an accurate description of Moore's project without speaking to the first.
[3] *Principia,* pp. 16–17.

This passage provides a way of posing a very difficult problem for Moore: How is he to reconcile his optimistic belief that ethical progress will follow once the relatively easy task of distinguishing good from everything else is performed with his pessimistic observation that that task has been botched for over two millennia? There are places in *Principia* where it is extraordinary how Moore manages not to be bothered by or even to seem to notice how much tension between pessimism and optimism his thought embodies. The satire in which he likens a dispute about different definitions of good to an argument about whether a triangle is a straight line or a circle precedes by only six pages the optimistic summation of the OQA we have just noted. The difficulties involved in retaining hope that people this befuddled will have "little difficulty advancing so far in analysis" is something he does not consider. In Section 36, the first of the chapter "Hedonism," he calls the failure to distinguish between *approval*, the feeling that something is good, and *enjoyment*, which does not contain any thought of good, a "vulgar" mistake and implies that with a little care it can be avoided. He says this in a sentence immediately following one in which he says that it is very difficult to distinguish between the two! Some of the tension of these passages is no doubt due to the superior tone he assumes in order to separate himself from his misbegotten forbears. But the problem remains even after we remove the venom from his remarks.

The fact that it has led so many astray from what they knew originally suggests that ethics can actually be dangerous to society. There is first the danger that the naturalistic fallacy will lead to the denial of a plurality of goods: "If we start with the conviction that a definition of good can be found, we start with the conviction that good *can mean* nothing else than some one property of things; and our only business then will be to discover what that property is."[4] The thought of the great impoverishment the world has suffered because of the many artists and art lovers who have surrendered to hedonism makes Moore's example of the happy drunkard breaking crockery while passing on *King Lear* very unhappy.[5] The troublesome relation between reflection and common sense can also lead to a problem quite the opposite of close mindedness. In an 1895 paper entitled "The Socratic Theory of Virtue," Moore contrasts the "faith" of the "honest workman" which, based on "long experience . . . is likely to be right in the main" to the dangers of free thinking: "By opening all moral conduct free to speculation . . . it may lead narrow men to wrong conclusions, and conclusions often changed."[6] As an example of this kind of danger, we may consider the great harm that vulgarized versions of existentialism have done to modern life by placing "authenticity"

---

[4] Ibid., p. 20.   [5] *Ethics*, p. 147.
[6] Levy, *G. E. Moore and the Cambridge Apostles*, p. 157.

above simple decency. "The White Negro," by Norman Mailer, a writer whose great talent has often dissipated in fad, perhaps provides the most striking American example of this kind of thing.[7]

Moore also suggests that ethics is dangerous to society at the end of his 1899 lectures *The Elements of Ethics*. In fact, he there expresses a conservatism so extreme as to confine ethics to the ash heap. He ends his lectures with this admonition:

> The pity is that some of the best minds are the most likely to be influenced by theories – to think a thing is right, because they can give reasons for it. It is something important to recognise that the best reasons can be given for *anything* whatever, if only we are clever enough: sophistry is easy, wisdom is impossible, the best that we can do is to trust to
> COMMON SENSE.

Since these lectures were presented to "honest workmen," it is an irresistible temptation to point out that if he had followed his own advice and canceled them, he would have avoided the misunderstandings and ill will they appear to have generated.[8]

No doubt, Moore thinks that any danger from these various quarters will lessen now that he has given us the key to progress. But if he fails to open philosophers' eyes, ethics will continue to be dangerous. Dangers remain even after philosophers come to the right conclusion about good's indefinability. Remember that Sidgwick was still so confused as to embrace hedonism and to fail to reject ethical egoism. There remains a problem even if it is granted, as it must be if our instincts are to be capable of leading us out of philosophical darkness, that the instincts of decent people are not likely to be overly corrupted by reflection. That being so, the proper kind of reflection can do no more than return to us in a *slightly* stronger fashion the insights that were lost by improper reflection. So the risks of reflective engagement with good still seem to outweigh the benefits.

These remarks suggest a defense of philosophy that is paradoxically based on the dangers of philosophy. It is inevitable that the mistakes of philosophers will escape the study, which is after all only a few steps from the pub and editorial office. Once it loses its immunity to the dangerous conclusions of reflection, instinct is incapable of returning to health by itself. There is thus a grave need for a distinctly philosophical antidote to reflection of the kind Moore provides in the chapter "Ethics in Relation to Conduct." This will consist of reflections that give to those whose instincts have been threatened the *intellectual* encouragement they need to trust in them again. These reflections will restore to them their confi-

[7] Mailer, "The White Negro," pp. 337–58. In Mailer's defense, his own very fine *The Executioner's Song* provides the materials for as pitiless a dissection of the fatuities of "The White Negro" as any critic could wish for.
[8] *Elements*, pp. xix, 41.

dence in the value of the small goods they still grasp immediately but no longer sufficiently believe in. They will contain reminders not to think themselves out of pursuing such small goods for the sake of elusive and perhaps even illusory larger ones. Alas, the ease with which so many philosophers and intellectuals of the last century found "the best reasons" to abandon these small goods and the insane constructions with which they replaced them suggests the paucity of the resources that philosophy makes available for combating philosophy.

Sooner or later (likely sooner), philosophers are going to seek to enlarge the scope of the defense of their discipline by arguing that the systematic, articulate knowledge of value is an intrinsic good much greater than that which can be provided by the commonsense awareness of it. Either it belongs to a third great class of goods, knowledge, mysteriously dismissed by Moore in his last chapter "The Ideal," or it belongs to his first class of goods, the contemplation of beauty, or aesthetic appreciation.[9] (A set of complexly related truths, being something it is good to contemplate, can be counted as an aesthetic object.) This defense of ethics enlarges the scope of intrinsically valuable activity and thereby deepens the contribution Moore's work can make to casuistry. Since it is always possible that the greatest overall good requires that some intrinsic goods not be pursued, it will be an important part of the defense of allowing ethical theorizing that some people have a philosophical impulse they cannot suppress and that allowing others to try to suppress it would cause more harm than good. (The argument would be similar to the one Moore makes that for as long as people have the desire to live, murder is wrong even if human life is bad.)[10] This suggests that Moore's ideal of the relation of philosophy to society at large is rather the opposite of Plato's. Philosophers are to be allowed to pursue their thoughts, but must keep mostly to themselves. Concerned as they are with general knowledge, philosophers are not to give any advice on particular matters.[11] Given the dangers of ethical theorizing, it might even be wise to *encourage* the disdain that thinkers and doers have for each other.

Let us now turn to the more distinctly intellectual problem the practical problem stems from. Moore must explain why some – highly intelligent – people are unable to recall something they never completely forget. Since the different awarenesses they are unable to reconcile all have the same object, it appears that Moore's explanation will have to exploit differences in the modes of those awarenesses. His choice of words occasionally suggests ways of doing this. Remember that in Section 36, while discussing hedonism, he describes approval as the *feeling* that something is good. Also, in Section 79, in a discussion of the metaphysical philosophers he says, "It does seem to be true that we hardly ever think a thing

---

[9] *Principia*, pp. 199–200.   [10] Ibid., p. 156. See Chapter 8.   [11] Ibid., p. 3.

good, and never very decidedly, without at the same time having a special attitude of feeling or will towards it." These passages suggest a line of thought according to which the original a posteriori apprehension of good has an emotional or conative element. Although this apprehension is tied to feeling or action, it contains the seed of its own transcendence in a purely intellectual apprehension. Going further than Moore could have, one might argue that the only way of achieving this purely intellectual apprehension is to become so puzzled or confused about one's original apprehension of good as to no longer take it for granted – and to stay puzzled about it for a very long time. This would be to make skepticism and self-misunderstanding *prerequisites* of philosophical understanding.

Suggesting an account for Moore that hinges on such remarks as these is very speculative. As he does so many times, he says enough to tantalize, but no more. Because he uses suggestive words offhandedly and does not explore their implications very far, we do not know whether to give them much weight. If this is maddening, it is also very moving: He manages to suggest solutions to problems he does not fully see. In this, *Principia* differs radically from his later work, so famous for the thoroughness, sometimes lapsing into tediousness, with which he explores every nook and cranny of his thought. It is as if Moore embodied in his own career *Principia*'s duality between spontaneous, confident awareness – which his achievement in *Principia* is to express philosophically – and studied, worrisome awareness. The speed with which he changed his manner of working after *Principia* suggests how sharp the break can be between the two kinds of awareness, and the fact that he came to consider the plodding *Ethics* better than *Principia* suggests just how much can be lost when the studied awareness of value so completely takes over from the spontaneous.[12]

The line of thought we have suggested would help to support a theme in Moore's critique of the metaphysical philosophers and to a lesser extent, the hedonists. This is that they fail to distinguish clearly the object of consciousness from the act by which it is cognized. That we must make this distinction is of course one of the great themes of Moore's work at this time, both here and in "The Refutation of Idealism;" it is the prescription grounding the heroic realism for which he is so famous. The fact that our original awareness of good is closely tied to action helps explain why philosophers fail to distinguish good from the awareness of it. When the metaphysical philosophers find in our original cognition of good an element that inclines one to action, it becomes too easy for them to treat the entire act of cognition as an indissoluble unity and the fundamental object of ethical theory. Finding ethics to be an inquiry "properly confined to 'practice' or 'conduct'"[13] they fail to analyze all the way

---

[12] Moore, "An Autobiography," in *The Philosophy of G. E. Moore*, p. 27.
[13] Ibid., p. 2.

down to the simple, indefinable component that would take them out of the practical sphere to the contemplative one of ethics proper. Meanwhile, the hedonists lose sight of good in the wake of the pleasant feeling its cognition engenders. Since pleasure so often arises upon the perception of good, hedonists wind up conflating good with pleasure. They then find pleasure to be the only justifiable end of action, the only thing intrinsically worthy of approval. They concern themselves with what approval has in common with enjoyment, pleasantness, while losing sight of its distinguishing feature, the thought that something is *good*.

The development of these suggestions, besides providing another way of tying together the mistakes of two of the great philosophical schools, also gives Moore his best chance of providing a reasonably charitable explanation of why the mistakes of the philosophical tradition are both ubiquitous and simple. Philosophers systematize the confusions that arise from their taking their early practical awareness of good as fundamental and then just never get beyond them. The incorrect philosophical theories they embrace too early in their studies prevent them from looking at the particulars of their own life with a clear gaze. Still, even if we can begin to make some sense of philosophers' initial puzzlement, there remains the trouble of explaining why they have *remained* puzzled for so long. At some point, the unreflective awareness they never completely lose that good is different from everything else should have intruded upon their systematically misleading philosophies and gotten them to recognize that they have erred. Until the dawn of the twentieth century, this never happened. Yet *now* philosophers are going to be struck like Keats upon reading Chapman. So Moore's problem remains even after we suppose him to have sharpened in this manner the distinction between the practical and the theoretical awareness of good.

The place where Moore comes the closest to resolving the difficulties we have been exploring is Section 87, in the chapter "Ethics in Relation to Conduct." While acknowledging that error has been rampant in the tradition, Moore expresses his great confidence that philosophers will soon agree with him on the self-evident principles of ethics. He tells us in the first sentence of that section that the reason philosophers will come to agree with him on these propositions, despite the fact that they cannot be proved, is that he has now proven "that good is good and nothing else whatever." Later he writes:

Certain it is, that in all those cases where we found a difference of opinion, we found also that the question had *not* been clearly understood. Though, therefore, we cannot prove that we are right, yet we have reason to believe that everybody, unless he is mistaken as to what he thinks, will think the same as we. It is as with a sum in mathematics. If we find a gross and palpable error in the calculations, we are not surprised or troubled that the person who made this mistake has reached a different result from ours. We think he will admit that his result is wrong, if his mistake is pointed out to him. For instance if a man has to add up 5

+ 7 + 9, we should not wonder that he made the result to be 34, if he started by making 5 + 7 = 25. And so in Ethics, if we find, as we did, that 'desirable' is confused with 'desired,' or that 'end' is confused with 'means,' we need not be disconcerted that those who have committed these mistakes do not agree with us. The only difference is that in Ethics, owing to the intricacy of its subject-matter, it is far more difficult to persuade anyone either that he has made a mistake or that that mistake affects his result.

The passage lends itself to two different interpretations, depending on whether or not the misunderstandings and mistakes referred to in its first two sentences are taken to suggest that previous philosophers have been misled by a distinctly different kind of awareness of good than the ordinary. The first reading does not find such a suggestion. Moore is simply expressing his optimism about the future of ethics now that he has cleared it of its fundamental mistake. The reason for his confidence is expressed in the first sentence. Unlike previous philosophers, he is not confused about what questions he is trying to answer. (But *how* could philosophers have been so long confused about their question?) This reading would be more apparent if in the second sentence Moore had dropped the phrase "unless he is mistaken *as to* what he thinks" or had written instead "unless he is mistaken *in* what he thinks." Since it is obvious that if he is right then everyone who disagrees with him is wrong, we can simplify the second sentence to: "Although we cannot *prove* we are right, we are confident that philosophers will come to agree with us upon our having cleared matters up."

The second reading finds a suggestion of a sharp distinction between the practical and the theoretical awareness of good. Previous philosophers have actually at the unreflective level accepted the conclusions about the nature of good that Moore is the first to formulate explicitly. But upon engaging in theory, they misread their own thoughts and failed to see that they held them. This interpretation is supported by the comparison Moore makes to arithmetical error. An educated person who simply miscalculates really does agree that the correct sum in his example is 21. So Moore is suggesting that we have unreflective, "sub-conscious" thoughts that we misidentify when we try to characterize and systematize them.[14] By making two changes in the first sentence, emphasizing "what" and adding "explicitly" before "think," we can make this reading clearer: "Though, therefore, we cannot prove that we are right, yet we have reason to believe that everybody, unless he is mistaken as to *what* he thinks, will *explicitly* think the same as we." A freer translation is: "Though, therefore, we cannot prove we are right, everybody who does not misread his thoughts will *explicitly* agree with us." This interpretation has Moore self-consciously playing the role of Socratic midwife.

---

[14] Moore's theory of desire, p. 68 ff., also seems to require a great deal of unconscious mental activity.

The rhetoric of the rest of the passage reveals a great deal of tension about the prospects for the future of ethics on either reading. At one level, the comparison of philosophical to arithmetical error introduces a note of optimism. Because of Moore's breakthrough, the errors that have been committed are now as "palpable" as the arithmetical error. Thus Moore's thought that one who has been wrong "will admit that his result is wrong, if his mistake is pointed out to him." But after a moment's thought, one wonders just how much reason there is for optimism. Moore's comparison expresses *contempt* for previous philosophers. They have failed at something ridiculously easy and have never bothered to re-think their results. If the simplicity of their errors is of this order, some-one with sense should have exposed them long ago. Now that they have finally been exposed, why should we think that their exposure will be ac-cepted by them? The only plausible conclusion is that philosophers are hopeless and Moore should despair of showing them *anything*.

But just when one comes to this view of the matter, Moore suggests that he was only making a logical point with the comparison, thus allowing philosophers to be subtler in their mistakes. The subject is intricate and it is not easy to see where ones goes astray. Of course, this also leaves lit-tle room for optimism. Why should we expect that all of a sudden Moore's argument will lead philosophers out of the darkness? Cassandra was not listened to and epiphanies are not guaranteed. (Again, as a matter of his-torical fact, Moore's work did, by his own lights, lead ethics into even greater darkness than it had previously been in.) So pessimism is the more appropriate response to either conclusion, that philosophy is easy and previous philosophers have been idiots or that philosophers have had a modicum of sense but the subject has remained beyond them.

There is another way in which Moore's comparison to arithmetic is problematic. The price of committing the naturalistic fallacy in mathe-matical theory is not nearly as high as it is in ethical theory. The intrica-cies of philosophical-mathematical problems and the many different false opinions philosophers have about the nature of mathematical enti-ties have no effect on their explicit awareness of a great many mathe-matical truths. Absent an explanation why philosophical error has prac-tical ramifications in ethics it lacks in mathematics, Moore's comparison does little to help him resolve his dilemma.

Resolution of the Paradox

"The Conception of Intrinsic Value" is much more in the spirit of the view that the everyday awareness of good is not so simple and straightforward as *Principia* makes it out to be. Nowhere in that paper does Moore sug-gest that we have an immediate awareness of good that contains every-thing we will ever be able to or need to know about it, that preempts any

philosophical qualms we might come to have regarding it. He accepts his
views to be controversial and offers no quick proof of them. In fact, he
does not attempt to prove them at all. To bring this spirit of tentativeness
to *Principia*, we must interpret the OQA in a way that weakens it, perhaps
along the lines of Ball and Snare, or perhaps even abandon it. The great
interest other philosophers have taken in the OQA might suggest that it
is the linchpin of his work. But the absence of any mention of the argument in *The Elements of Ethics*, much of which Moore carried over verbatim to *Principia*, shows it to be rather an afterthought.[15] A fully satisfying
understanding of good is not something that comes to one in the shaft
of light provided by a single argument, but is something that dawns on
one during the course of an exhaustive investigation of it.[16] We must then
find some way of allowing in Moore's name that earlier philosophers who
spent years of their lives on the subject of value were not guilty of failing
to note a simple point they already thoroughly knew as children.

One might object, quite fairly, that respect must be paid to the
metaphilosophical problem upon which Moore has, even if a bit heavily,
put his finger. Most of us *do* have an understanding of good that for the
most part works reasonably well in ordinary life, but that refuses to yield
easily to philosophical reflection. About our suggestion one has every
right to ask, *Why* does a satisfactory philosophical understanding of value
come slowly and with difficulty when we make judgments about the goodness or badness of things every day of our lives? Similar problems arise,
of course, with regard to the philosophical and scientific understanding
of properties other than good. But the way in which its simplicity, indefinability, and nonnaturalness combine to make good unique perhaps
makes this problem more troubling in its case than in others. For instance, immediately it does not seem open to one to say that we originally
have a many-leveled gestalt awareness of good, which we then refine more
or less successfully, as we do in the case of animality and perhaps causal-
ity. Because properties such as these are not so ontologically distinct from
the things instantiating them as good is supposed to be, it is not surprising that we have both a deep and a confused awareness of them.

But perhaps there are other ways of looking at good that allow philosophical confusion not always to be mere obtuseness, that allow the philosophical understanding of good to be a significant advance on the ordinary understanding of it. Although in developing these ways of looking
at good we will take advantage of its simplicity and indefinability, we are
not always going to be concerned with sharply distinguishing between
these two properties. It is part of these ways of looking at good that it is

---

[15] This to disagree with Thomas Baldwin. See note 10 to the Introduction.
[16] G. C. Field, "The Place of Definition in Ethics," *Proceedings of the Aristotelian Society*, Vol.
XXXII (London: 1931–2), p. 84.

not useful or even possible at every stage of inquiry to make a sharp distinction between them. In fact, we do not have a ready-made understanding of these properties to be applied straight off to properties of the order of subtlety of good; rather we must be ready to refine our understanding of them in the light of the difficult cases that good and other properties present. Since we do to some extent use our understanding of these properties to help us get clear about good, the very important conclusion follows that at the outset of philosophical inquiry, we lack the intellectual equipment needed to have an understanding of good on the order of sophistication and clarity that Moore thinks is possible.

This should be no surprise. If our immediate understanding of good were sophisticated and clear, ethics *would* be easy. Moore creates unnecessary problems for himself by tying himself to the thought that if we are to make distinctly philosophical progress, we must clearly see the indefinability of good at the very beginning of our inquiry. He seems to feel that there is something about philosophical investigation that makes us unable to clarify our fuzzy intuitions, or the notions we use to clarify them, as we go along. He seems almost Kantian on the matter, writing as if it were an a priori psychological truth that philosophical reason will reify rather than correct the errors in what it proposes. But the most he can be taken to have uncovered, the most he could have *wished* to have uncovered, is a contingent fact about how *most* philosophers have failed. His own criticism of Aristotle indicates that philosophers who commit the naturalistic fallacy need not set their mistakes in stone. He criticizes Aristotle for being unsystematic, which weakness he connects to the fallacy.[17] Aristotle's lack of system, even if it poses other problems, should have indicated to him that it is possible to philosophize in a provisional manner.

Moore's particular fear is that if we are not perfectly clear about good's indefinability at the very outset of inquiry, we will forever be seeking to deny our unreflective insight that value is unique and intrinsic. But however right we are to have this unreflective feeling about the distinct nature of good, it is mixed up, as anyone knows who has taught an introductory course in ethics, with other inconsistent opinions about it. The thought that good is utterly distinct from all else can only be clearly successfully articulated when it comes in sophisticated philosophical dress. Moore would have been better advised to have offered, in the spirit of "Conception," a hypothesis about the features good must have if (*some of*) our unreflective thoughts about it are to be refined and justified.[18] Work of great dialectical skill, on the order of the work he performs in that paper, is necessary to spell out the conditions that justify them.

---

[17] *Principia*, p. 176.

[18] It is the heart of Hill's thesis in *The Ethics of Moore* that this is what Moore actually does. But this way of reading Moore ignores the OQA. It is, we are arguing, what Moore should have done, not what he actually does.

Let us begin by trying to undo the damage wrought by Moore's unfortunate comparison of good to yellow.[19] This comparison does much to make it seem as if the grasping of the simple, indefinable property good is an all-or-nothing matter. As with yellow, one either sees good or is blind to it.[20] If one is blind, there is nothing more to be said. If one sees it, there is also little to be said: "If I am asked 'What is good?' my answer is that good is good and that is the end of the matter. Or if I am asked 'How is good to be defined?' my answer is that it cannot be defined, and that is all I have to say about it." Since these words appear on *Principia*'s sixth page, Moore must really think that there is *much* more to say about it, which highlights our problem. There is little to say about yellow and *pace* Moore, no sophisticated systematic "science" of yellow.[21] Even if it is simple and indefinable, good is elusive, subtle, and rich in a way that such determinate natural properties as yellow are not.

The reader may protest again that this is fine to say, but *how* can it be so? To say it is only to name the mystery. To meet this worry, we shall have to develop subtler conceptions of the properties of simplicity and indefinability as they are instantiated by good. We can begin to do this by pointing out a way in which the comparison of good to yellow also steers us wrong on the issue of good's simplicity. Moore says that to be simple is to have no parts – *no* parts. The comparison to yellow puts this fact in the wrong light. There is a very important sense employed by Moore according to which yellow actually has *one* part. This is the sense that is highlighted by the claim that the most determinate natural properties are the parts of which a complex natural object is composed. If these properties had no parts, then the complex objects composed of them would also have no parts. But that would make these complex objects *simple*. There must then be some very important sense in which at least the most determinate natural properties of a thing have one part rather than none.

Let us recall the ontology of "Identity" to get clearer on the difference between the simplicity of the determinate natural properties and the simplicity of good. Even if the different fully determinate *universals* referred to by the word "yellow" have no parts rather than one, these universals, unlike the universal good, determine the nature of particulars that do have one part. Because of this fact, there is a sense in which any understanding we have of the universal yellow or the particulars instantiating it must be complete. Following "Identity," since the particular yellow only differs numerically from the universal yellow, we think of the universal *through* the particular. If one thinks of or perceives a simple particular yellow, one

[19] Butchvarov, *Skepticism in Ethics*, p. 61; G. C. Field, "The Place of Definition in Ethics," p. 91, *Moral Theory* (New York: E. P. Dutton and Sons, 1921), p. 57.

[20] See Moore, *The Elements of Ethics*, p. 17, where he speaks explicitly of our not being blind to good. See also Frankena, "The Naturalistic Fallacy," p. 112.

[21] *Principia*, p. 14.

also thinks of the universal. If one has a simple particular shade of yellow or its universal in mind *at all,* one has *all* of it in mind. But because good does not stand in any such relation to simple particulars, one cannot think of it through a particular in the same manner. There is nothing one can grasp all of in order to grasp "all" of good.

This difference also makes unhelpful Moore's point that we cannot explain but only *ostend* to one who has never perceived it, what yellow is. Even if we need some mastery of the "language game" of color in order to ostend yellow, once this mastery is achieved, ostending it is easy. But this is clearly not the case with good. We can point easily enough to things that are good, but not so easily, if at all, to good itself. In a very important sense, we show that we do not have a completely satisfactory understanding of good if we even try to ostend it, even if only to ourselves in the "mind's eye." Making the same point in a different way perhaps, the spatial notions borrowed from properties such as yellow throw us off in our attempt to explicate the nature of good.[22] Because of the different relation(s) in which good stands to individual goods, we cannot "hold" good in mind in the same way we "hold" yellow in mind. This difficulty about good distinguishes it not only from such natural properties like yellow, but also from other such nonnatural (or, if only value is nonnatural, nonexistent) items such as numbers. Of all the things there are, good is among those least like an object to be singled out. So when we talk of fixing the property good before our minds, of its being a simple object of thought, we must be extremely careful not to be taken in by any of these terms' misleading connotations. If we are ruthless in purging these connotations from our understanding of good, we will be less inclined to think of it as something of which our awareness is all or nothing. We will grant that depending on what other things we know, there are many different degrees of attention we can fix on it.

If indefinability plays a crucial role in describing what is at issue in the claim that good is unique and independent of other properties, it is not obvious what role it plays in the early stages of a philosophical inquiry in justifying or defending this claim. Consider the following propositions: 1) Good is what the rational will strives for; 2) Good is what we desire to desire; 3) Friendship is good; and 4) Good depends solely upon natural properties for its exemplification. Moore says explicitly that the first, third, and fourth of these are true and the second he might consider to have a role to play in moral psychological theory. With the possible exception of the second then, all of these are propositions we must know in order to have a philosophically interesting conception of good. Having

---

[22] It might also be that a great deal of facile criticism of Moore's theory as requiring a "free-floating" property would be avoided if unsuitable spatial metaphors were avoided more assiduously by critics.

moved so far from the idea of the parts in the definition of an object being related to physical parts, can we not consider these to be "parts" of a
very complex definition of good?[23]

Presumably, Moore would insist that even if these propositions tell us
things that are completely true of good, they still do not *describe* its nature.[24] It is *because* of what good is that these things are true. So even if
they help us to discover what good is, they do so by helping us to pick out
good (in whatever attenuated sense it is possible to do that) rather than
by defining it. In this, these statements are comparable to the statement
that orange is the color most like yellow and red. In order to grasp the
truth of that statement, we must already be acquainted with or become
acquainted with *orange* as well as yellow and red. Besides the four we have
already mentioned, there are indefinitely many other more or less interesting things we can say about good that can be helpful in picking it out.
We do not wish to give any of them or *all of them together* pride of place as
the definition of good, but wish rather to say that singly and in combination, they point us to that property of which they are all true.

But let us reconsider the preceding proposition about orange. Suppose
we are able to recognize the color orange but have never noticed that it
is more like yellow and red than it is like other colors. Are we not then
learning something about the intrinsic nature of orange – and yellow
and red – when we notice this?[25] (And when we assert this proposition,
is there not a sense in which we are describing orange?) Learning this
proposition is certainly unlike learning the contingent proposition,
which does not teach us anything about the color, that a certain piece of
paper is orange. All or most of the propositions involving good are at least
a little bit like the first of these propositions, not the second. Even the
humble particular fact that appreciating a certain well-made artifact is
good, pointing as it does to the doctrine of organic unities, reveals something about good's rich a priori character to us.

The difference, already noted, between our awareness of a specific
color and our awareness of good, that it is much easier to isolate and hold

[23] Field, who on pp. 55–6 of *Moral Theory* wonders why on Moore's account "rational end"
is not a complex definition of good, sums up his discussion thus: "Mr Moore really finds
it difficult himself to think consistently of goodness as a simple, indefinable quality, and
is being constantly compelled, without realizing it, by the force of facts to introduce some
other elements into his idea of it."
[24] *Principia*, p. 36.
[25] We should probably amend our earlier statement that there is little to say about and no
science of yellow. If there are, for example, objective facts about what colors "match" or
"go well" with other colors, there might be a quite complex aesthetic science of color.
Much of painting and the other visual arts would then presumably be an exploration of
this subject. Ultimately, this science would be subsumed under the science of beauty and
thus also subsumed under ethics, the science of good. But to connect this thought to the
point we were making earlier, the more interesting point of comparison would not be
between good and *yellow*, but between good and *color*.

the color before our minds, makes the distinction between definitional and other necessary truths clearer in the case of a color than it is in the case of good. In spite of the difficulties we have just considered in fully making good on this claim, it *is* tempting to hold, as Moore does, that by holding it before our minds we can just *see* that orange is an indefinable and "distinct entity,"[26] even as we grant that there are more necessary truths to learn about it. Since we cannot hold good in mind in the same way, we *cannot* just see this about it. Moore implicitly recognizes this when he offers the OQA *as an argument*. If it is an argument with premises that take us beyond our ability to inspect properties, it appeals, as we have discussed, to controversial views in metaphysics, philosophy of mind, and semantics. Until we know more about the mode of reference for such sophisticated terms, we do not know exactly what they mean or what properties they refer to (assuming them to refer at all). This returns us again to the dialectical point that before we decide *what* we have before our mind when we think about good, we need to refine the philosophical notions we bring to bear on it. Speaking with Wilfred Sellars for a moment, this makes Moore's claims about the nature of good "promissory notes" to be cashed upon further philosophical rumination. Speaking with Wittgenstein, we must get away from the "picture" of there being an acute inner faculty that enables us to see good once and forever. We do not think about good simply by "inspecting" it.

One speaking for Moore might say that even if we do not at first hold good before our minds with perfect clarity, we must still be able to distinguish truths about good itself from truths about the necessary relations with other things into which it enters. Lacking this ability, we shall be sucked into the morass of monism. Thus we must have some sense that the truths about good are not a matter of definition. But Moore must allow, even if he does not realize it fully, that in the prephilosophical mode of awareness, we do not know exactly what the terms are of the propositions we are considering. We can cognize the truth of a proposition that, for instance, friendship is good without knowing what exactly good *or* friendship is. If this were not possible, there really would be no point to analysis, as the questions suitable to it would already have their answer. Moore must allow for the possibility that over time, we become more adept at sifting good out from the cluster of goods we come to know it by. Our knowledge of good and *the* good must grow together. This last point is of crucial importance to moral epistemology. We do not just happen to spot good and then note that it is exemplified by friendship or the other things that are good. Rather, we are directed to good, however haphazardly, by good things.

Nor is the epistemic dependency all on the side of good. If we do not recognize such things as happiness and health to be good, we do not cor-

---

[26] *Principia,* p. 16. Moore says this of pleasure.

rectly identify *them* either. This epistemic interdependence between good and the things that are good holds even if we finally decide that they are metaphysically independent of each other. Knowledge of this metaphysical independence is hard won, not the first step in philosophical understanding. We might say that since good "lurks" within these clusters, we are not able to and need not be able to identify good precisely in order to have some knowledge of the systematic relations that obtain between it and the various good things. This enables our epistemic situation with regard to good to be similar to what it is with regard to the definable properties determinative of other sciences. Just as we have a fairly wideranging but rough-and-ready knowledge of different sorts of animals and animality in general before we attempt precise analyses of them, so can we know many truths about good without knowing whether it has an analysis or is unanalyzable.[27]

For the purposes of ordinary life, it is unimportant whether good is complex or simple, with the complexity being found in the relations that obtain between it and the various goods. Our vast if shallow knowledge of good enables us to render most of our decisions concerning it with some degree of adequacy – we do not often need to test the limits of our everyday understanding of good. We can even get along moderately well with a somewhat egoistic conception of good, one allowing us to be mostly concerned with the effects of our actions upon ourselves and our loved ones. We can also get by with an unsophisticated, even primitive, casuistry. Even when it comes to the daunting task of raising a child, we can for much of the time act as if hedonism were true, as it is very important for any number of reasons to make a child's life pleasant. Although we also recognize the need to foster other goods such as knowledge and moral probity, we can give them all their due, more or less, without a great deal of conflict. For one, we realize that such things as knowledge and moral probity are indispensable to a truly pleasant life. Of course, there are the times that so engage novelists and playwrights when conflicts arise and our store of moral knowledge becomes depleted quite quickly. If we faced these crises more regularly, we would be less likely to think of our ordinary awareness of good as satisfactory.

At a more advanced stage of inquiry, there may be an important philosophical point that can only be carried by good's simplicity and indefinability. Recall again that Moore holds that the demands of the objectivity of value leave no room for special pleading – even though we all engage in some of it. Plain people have something on the philosophers who become skeptical of this and flirt with ethical egoism. But once the skeptical questions about egoism have been raised, it is not possible to go back

---

[27] In "A Defence of Common Sense," pp. 57–9, Moore makes a similar claim, that we know there to be physical objects without knowing their analysis.

to the innocent but ignorant stage of understanding that preceded it. As Moore does in his refutation of egoism, one must answer the skeptic in a distinctly philosophical manner that calls upon the simplicity and inde-finability of good. On Moore's view, the fact that good is a universal, in-divisible and *one*, grounds the point that it cannot be *had* by anyone. The fact that this point can only be made at an advanced stage of reflection may explain why Sidgwick mistakenly felt that both egoism and altruism were philosophically respectable positions. We must, as Sidgwick does not, consider metaphysical matters far beyond the purview of common sense in order to resolve the false conundrum with which he ends *The Methods of Ethics*.[28]

This general conception of ethical inquiry seems to require a more ho-listic Moore than the one we are used to seeing. This is a Moore who in-sists that we get a sense of the forest before we study the individual trees. Of course, after we have become familiar with the whole, reflection on var-ious individual issues will further sharpen our large-scale understanding. We must not, however, impose on this more holistic Moore Kuhnian im-plications he could not possibly have countenanced. If we wish to stay within the spirit of Moore, we must reject the suggestion of Alasdair Mac-Intyre that from certain vantages, different large-scale ethical theories are incommensurable.[29] Moore is nothing if not a realist about good. As a re-alist in the philosophy of science takes up the tasks of showing how the entities of science exist independently of human beings and their theo-ries, and how even incorrect theories can be about entities that really do exist, an ethical realist takes them up with good. Two theories positing rad-ically divergent goods are nevertheless both about *good*. And even if we happen to accept some ethical claims on the grounds of overall coher-ence, it does not follow that we accept a coherence theory of moral truth.

---

[28] Henry Sidgwick, *The Methods of Ethics* (Chicago: University of Chicago Press, 1962), pp. 496–509. For a further discussion of Moore on Sidgwick, see Chapter 7.
[29] MacIntyre, *After Virtue*, pp. 6–8. For further discussion of MacIntyre, see Chapters 4 and 5.

4

The Status of Ethics: Dimming the Future and Brightening the Past

Dimming the Future

This chapter continues the work of Chapter 3 by considering what a more realistic assessment of both the past and future of ethics will look like once we reject Moore's explanation that the difficulties of the field have been due to the endless making and remaking of a simple mistake. For the most part, Moore's account posits an ethical future whose brightness is matched only by the darkness of its past. But the denial of his claim that a simple mistake, in a plethora of forms, has made for a violent rupture in the consciousness of value enables the contrast between the past and future of ethics to be made much less stark. First, Moore's dawn of the century optimism receives a cold but welcome dose of reality. Since the publication of *Principia*, ethics has not benefited from an epochal breakthrough. Its difficulties and complexities continue to make such a breakthrough highly unlikely. At the same time, the reasons for tempering his optimism about the future are reasons for allaying his pessimism about the past. The numberless errors of previous generations of philosophers are what we should expect from the application of fallible, if impressive, intellect to a difficult domain. The future is not so bright nor the past so dark as this still young philosopher thinks.

Before we begin examining the complex of attitudes Moore brings to the past and future of ethics, we wish to make a metaphilosophical point about the value of progress in this and other philosophical fields. There is another standard of merit to accompany the progressivist standard, sitting so uneasily with his view that we all have a perfectly adequate prephilosophical awareness of good, that Moore borrows from the natural sciences. This emerges from a consideration of the point made in the first chapter that any well-wrought philosophical theory requires worthy alternatives. Since the various alternatives must be in fundamental disagreement about fundamental matters, it cannot be that their worthiness depends solely on their truth. In fact, when we are presented with a truly compelling philosophical conception, the question of its truth to a certain extent becomes niggling.[1] (Although there is something deeply moving about theories of great depth being deeply wrong.) Much of the in-

---

[1] Butchvarov, *Skepticism in Ethics*, p. 101.

terest of a work in ethics lies in the dramatic quality of the sense of life it conveys, of the vision it presents of the human intercourse with good, *whatever* good happens to be. As with great literature, certain achievements, including *Principia,* stand on their own feet. There is simply no "progressing" beyond them. Because there is this more aesthetic dimension of merit in ethical and other fields of philosophy, there will never be a time when each philosopher simply stands on the shoulders of her predecessors.

Although it is likely not the result of conscious deliberation, Moore's work is the aesthetic expression of the thought that something more important than progress is involved in the attainment of life's most important truths – namely, *return. Principia* beautifully brings to life the great dialectic of resistance and reconciliation concerning the simple truths about good and evil we all do somehow know. In Chapter 10 of this book, we shall say a great deal more about the incompletely realized non-progressivist elements of Moore's conception of ethics. The most extreme way available to him of preserving the integrity of prephilosophical thought against philosophical confusion is to make philosophy something *purely* aesthetic – something concerned with truth and reality *not at all.* The discussion in this chapter, however, is appropriate to a strategy less extreme than that. It is important to offer such a discussion because whether or not he has the right to, Moore consciously adheres to a conception of ethics that makes it capable of discovering the truth about reality.

Let us begin by considering Moore's attitudes toward the history of casuistry, the branch of ethics concerned with the questions, "What things are good in themselves?" and "What things are a means to good?" His attack on earlier casuistical work is rather confused and not entirely fair. At one point in his final chapter, "The Ideal," he proclaims that earlier attempts by unnamed authors to "construct an Ideal . . . omit many things of very great positive value. . . . Great positive goods . . . are so numerous, that any whole, which shall contain them all, must be of vast complexity . . . it is sufficient to condemn those Ideals, which are formed by omission, without any visible gain in consequence of such omission." He concludes that "no ideals yet proposed are satisfactory."[2] This claim is curious. Since his own view is that there are only two great intrinsic goods, friendship and aesthetic appreciation, he seems to have left himself subject to his own criticism. To the immediate charge of inconsistency, Moore's defender will point out that he allows, and in the case of aesthetic appreciation, insists that there are not only many different particular ways of instantiating those goods, but many different genres and subgenres of them. But once this response is used in his defense, it is fair to use it in the defense of others. So he is here arguing against "men of straw."

<hr>

[2] *Principia,* pp. 185 6.

Moore, who speaks so boldly at the beginning of *Principia* of both the disrepute of earlier efforts in casuistry and the great progress to follow upon his work, in later passages occasionally reveals ambivalence about its future, and even some ambivalence about its past. He says early that the defects of casuistry are due to a lack of knowledge, an inability on the part of casuists to "distinguish . . . those elements upon which . . . value depends" and insinuates that by the end of *Principia,* his work of clarification will have gone a long way toward clearing these matters up.[3] But he lowers expectations for the future of casuistry in his summary at the end of the book's final chapter. He speaks there of the field's great difficulties as requiring "patient enquiry" and says that he is more concerned with revealing the proper method for dealing with the issues than he is with establishing his own "platitudinous" conclusions.[4] Clearly, then, despite some strong claims, he is not completely confident about the nature of the impact of his work on casuistry.

He makes no bones about the difficulties faced by the second branch of casuistry, the one that takes up questions concerning the causes or necessary conditions of the intrinsic goods. There are obvious reasons why judgments in this field will remain provisional and controversial:

It is certain that in different circumstances the same action may produce effects which are utterly different in all respects upon which the value of the effects depends. Hence we can never be entitled to more than a *generalisation* – to a proposition of the form 'This result *generally* follows this kind of action'; and even this generalisation will only be true, if the circumstances under which the action occurs are generally the same. This is in fact the case, to a great extent, within any one particular age and state of society. But, when we take other ages into account, in many most important cases the normal circumstances of a given kind of action will be so different, that the generalisation which is true for one will not be true for another. With regard then to ethical judgements which assert that a certain kind of action is good as a means to a certain kind of effect, none will be *universally* true; and many, though *generally* true at one period, will be generally false at others.[5]

We might think that the situation is different in the first branch of casuistry, concerned as it is with the discovery and ordering of the intrinsic goods. It is plausible to hold that the study of friendship, being quite general in nature, need not be much concerned with the particularities of different eras and cultures and situations. The proposition that friendship is good is not merely an empirical generalization. Because we cannot envisage life as not being enriched by friendship, our confidence in the goodness of friendship withstands the thought that we could never gather up all the different kinds of friendship for a summary judgment. Still, it seems that Moore is overly confident about how much agreement to expect with propositions ranging beyond his two platitudes. There will

***

[3] Ibid., p. 5.   [4] Ibid., pp. 222–3.   [5] Ibid., p. 22.

certainly be disagreement over the details of any analysis one offers of friendship or aesthetic appreciation. One might even wish to contend the claim that friendship is good by noting, as Moore does, that certain deep and abiding human relationships are rooted in *evil*.[6] Although some will reply that these kinds of evil relationships cannot be friendships, perhaps because they lack some necessary ingredient such as love or mutual respect, others will charge that this is to be guilty of *legislating* that only worthwhile human relationships are to count as instances of friendship. One could strengthen worries along these lines by noting ways in which Moore includes their goodness in the description of both of his goods. Among their constituents are an "appropriate" emotion, one that in the circumstances is *good*, and the cognition of a "truly beautiful" quality, one it is *good* to admire. In effect, Moore secures agreement with his casuistical propositions by making them tautologies. A lack of controversy is thus a sign that further work needs to be done – what makes an emotion appropriate or a quality beautiful? It will not be the result of any work done in this field that it leads us to change our mind and hold that these things are not great goods after all. But we will never reach full agreement on the details of the subject; a richer understanding is always a more contentious one.

We also increase the possibility of casuistical controversy by going back to and expounding on a point Moore recognizes, that there are *many* different intrinsic goods. Moore mostly ignores these other goods because he considers a chasm to lie between them and the two greatest goods. But it seems more likely that the world's goods belong on something more resembling a continuum. By ignoring all the many other goods, which include the virtues and such things as health and (the consciousness of) pleasure, Moore loses out on much of what makes life worth living. Further, as we have already suggested and shall argue for more explicitly in Chapter 5, the acknowledgment of a more continuous arrangement of the world's goods enables us to present a more coherent picture of the way in which our awareness of good and *the* good develops.

Given the appeal common sense has for Moore, he might easily have come to consider the virtues to have intrinsic value. We often find ourselves with very strong opinions about the goodness of a particular courageous act or the admirableness of a particular kindly person. Given the unknowability of the future, we cannot account for these opinions by saying that they are concerned with what is merely good as a means. We can also make use of the doctrine of organic unities to alleviate concern about the inner qualities of criminals and thugs: Their courage is good even if it is part of a larger whole that is bad. The doctrine of organic unities and the larger sense of 'object' we have explored in Chapter 2 gives us the re-

---

[6] Ibid., p. 210.

sources to argue that Moore is wrong in thinking that virtuous action, that is, action done habitually without any *explicit* thought of good, is not intrinsically valuable.[7] The whole consisting of a person doing some good, of which, because of the training she has undergone and thinking she has previously performed, she need not be explicitly aware, is a complicated organic unity different from and having more value than the whole consisting of a person just happening to do some good. It might be that Moore is too concerned to separate himself from previous philosophers who in his eyes had overvalued the virtues. He wants to avoid the trap Kant has often been thought to have fallen into, of forgetting that there is more to life than being a dutiful grind. Moore rightly opposes those (who are they?) who think the virtues are the only things of value, but overdoes the criticism.[8]

Just the admission of more items into the catalog of goods makes more complicated the relation of Moore's work to past and future casuistical efforts. His history becomes less condemnatory as the errors of previous casuists become subtler and more reasonable than he credits. In a world filled with such a great number of goods, there are so many points to examine and considerations to bring forward that it cannot be surprising that there have been many false steps on the road to ethical knowledge. For instance, there can be a great deal of disagreement over different attempts to classify and rank the virtues *just because*, as Moore points out, there are so many of them that they cannot all be exemplified by one person[9] or even by one culture. This fact about the variety of the virtues, when extended to all the intrinsic goods, points to the possibility that change, even when things are going well, might be desirable, as it increases the number of different goods the world instantiates. (This version of the principle of plenitude, along with views about what fairness requires, and, it must be said, more than a little *resentiment,* seems to infuse much of the so-called multicultural movement.) Of course, these changes must not come *too* fast. The deepest plumbing of value requires that individuals and cultures settle in for the long haul. The world needs hedgehogs more than it needs foxes.

Moore says that ethics is like chemistry and physics in its concern for generality and not at all like history and geography, which he considers to be concerned solely with particulars.[10] But there remains an inexhaustible set of peculiar "objects" of special interest to historians, anthropologists, and sociologists – ethoses; societal and individual ideals; norms and forms of life – that must also be of concern to ethicists. Their interest lies not only in the crucial role they play in the formation and perpetuation of value, which makes them relevant to the second branch of casuistry, but also in the fact that they may themselves be things of

[7] *Principia,* pp. 175–6.   [8] Ibid., p. 173.   [9] Ibid., p. 166.   [10] Ibid., p. 4.

intrinsic value, either good or bad.[11] Given human inventiveness in the
face of changing circumstances, we can never be confident that all possible ideals and forms of life have been exhausted – in fact, we can be
quite confident that, as is the case with art forms, these things are inexhaustible. History and other disciplines show us that there are many more
kinds of valuable things than have been dreamt of in our philosophy.[12]

Because of the kinds of things they are and the various ways in which
they get tied to particular historical circumstances, it is untenable to think
that there can ever be fully settled analyses of these sorts of cultural objects. There will certainly never be the consensus about them that there
is about so many of the objects of the natural sciences. Because they are
ideals, an awareness born of the fact that their complete instantiation is
impossible must be brought to bear upon them. Even those who attempt
most heroically to practice in accord with ideals recognize that breathing
room must be provided for the messy realities of life. Further, especially
as one is concerned with ideals tied very closely to a particular time and
place, it is going to be an open question whether certain things are really
parts of the ideal or just accidents of history – do the horrors of Bolshe-
vism redound poorly on socialism or just on the Bolsheviks? One must
also look at roads not taken by history in order to study the unrealized
potentialities that might be a part of an ideal. Obviously, no particular negotiation of any such set of conceptual issues, to say nothing of any general set of recommendations for dealing with them, will ever come close
to attaining unanimous assent. Another related source of disagreement
is that certain other possible goods, such as tolerance and freedom, have
a kind of *logical* incompleteness to them. The old saw about toleration requiring that limits be placed on the toleration of intolerance shows that
because of its nature, no perfectly complete conceptual analysis of toleration can be assayed.

Even if at a particular time there were to be a great deal of consensus
on any of these sorts of social objects, it remains that social innovations
and the rise of new ideals imparts a retrodictive character to the study of
them. New forms cast shadows on the old, requiring us endlessly to revise
our judgments about them. To cite a contemporary concern, traditional
notions of honor and courage embodied by certain military and quasi-
military institutions have come under feminist fire for the prejudices, limitations, and unfairnesses they are supposed to harbor. But some of those

---

[11] Although difficulties in construing such large cultural objects as instances of friendship
or aesthetic appreciation might lead Moore to deny that they have any great positive value.

[12] Butchvarov's remarks on p. 113 of *Skepticism in Ethics* about our ignorance of "the good
of a society *qua* a society" are appropriate to this discussion. We are in part exploring the
possibility that there are types of societies that differ from one another in philosophically
important ways and hence the possibility that there are *different goods* for different types
of societies.

who have looked at different institutions and realms of life where such
ideals have become less prominent than they used to be have concluded
that these ideals are richer and more important than the critics have credited. An argument occasionally heard against the critics is that they have
ignored the depths of the particular human imperfections these ideals
are trying to rein in. If these ideals more effectively accommodate the ·
world's imperfections than other ideals whose level of a priori perfection
is too high for most people to live by, they are likely to win at least a temporary vindication. In general then, a warning similar to one issued by
Sidgwick in his discussion of utopian thought is most appropriate: There
are many ways for those who construct and quarrel over ideals to com-
promise with imperfect reality.[13] For as long as both theoretically minded
and practically minded people keep promoting and exploring new ideals
and old, there is no hope of these kinds of controversy ever being settled.
This, of course, is not something to bemoan.

    Let us briefly consider another controversy of many centuries standing.
In philosophical and political commentary written at all levels of abstraction and difficulty, we find a debate between two camps we can call the romantics and the pragmatists, or the liberal optimists and the conservative
pessimists. The romantics find that as an expression of a grand ideal,
something, the French Revolution say, has great value and is worthy of
both the great sacrifices that brought it into being and the great sacrifices
it brought into being. One of the things giving value to this ideal is the
way in which it points to the world's betterment. This gives the ideal value
as a means, but also something more. It imbues the actions constituting
the ideal's expression with a meaning and hence with a positive value they
would not otherwise have. The suffering created by the admittedly flawed
bringing to life of the ideal is not *mere* suffering, but is a part of a vast organic whole instantiating a great deal of goodness. Meanwhile, the pragmatists find the ideal to be very pernicious. In fact, they find that the more
captivating it is in its purity as an ideal, the worse it becomes. Members of
the revolutionary *avant garde* appeal to ideals in order to clothe their
meanness and will to power in moralistic garb. And even if the revolutionary persecutors are "well-meaning," irony makes it crueler to be mur-
dered by a Jacobin than by a more common thug. Obviously, there are
dangers in each of these attitudes of which any sensitive person must beware. At how much murder and mayhem have liberals winked because of
their captivation by the socialist ideal. And for how long did conservatives
tolerate such evils as slavery and Jim Crow because of the failure of their
imagination and their lack of nerve in contemplating new ideals.

    In the delineation of the strengths and weaknesses of ethoses, ideals,
and all other such forms of object, the obligation to respect incomplete-

---

[13] Sidgwick, *Methods*, pp. 21–2.

ness and life's messy realities, and to provide the resonant, living detail that comes only from paying close attention to particulars, makes history, which is concerned with both particular and general matters, a more useful model for ethics than physics and chemistry. Because there is no easy way of comparing different individual and societal conceptions of the good, we must tread lightly with any conception of the subject according to which we might one day discover a neatly ordered table of the ethical elements. As in the study of history and literature, we must tolerate a great deal of ambiguity. Ethics must remain fluid; sensitivity and an eye for nuance and paradox must always accompany analytical rigor.

When we consider whether all of these road blocks to consensus should lead us to despair about the state of ethics past or future, we can remember a point Moore makes concerning instances of disagreement about whether or not a thing is beautiful. Moore claims that in most cases where large numbers of people find a thing to be beautiful, they are likely to be right:

> differences of opinion seem to be far more often due to excessive attention, on the part of different persons, to different qualities in the same object, than to the positive error of supposing a quality that is ugly to be really beautiful. When an object, which some think beautiful, is denied to be so by others, the truth is *usually* that it lacks some beautiful quality or is deformed by some ugly one, which engage the exclusive attention of the critics.[14]

If we apply a similar thought to ethical controversy – it certainly applies to disputes between liberals and conservatives – we do not conclude that previous theorists and writers have been completely wrongheaded, but that they have said some things that are true but in need of further elaboration, and have mixed them up with other things that are false. This enables Moore to say what we all know: Although the field of casuistry is fraught with difficulty, much light has already been shed on it. Further, any light that has gone out over the years can be rekindled by sympathetic historical investigation. It takes but a moment's consideration to conclude that it will ever be thus. In considering what is possible for ethical theory at all its different levels, Moore might have taken heed of the admonition of the "highly unsystematic and confused" Aristotle that one should look for no more exactness in a science than it allows.[15] The reason why there cannot be great exactness and agreement in ethics is actually a cause for intellectual and perhaps even practical optimism. The world is such a rich and interesting place that it pays endless examination and reexamination. Ethicists, like historians, anthropologists, and other students of humanity, will never run out of interesting things to say, nor people of interesting ways to live.

---

[14] *Principia*, pp. 200–201.   [15] Ibid., p. 176.

All of this suggests an approach more welcoming to controversy and disagreement than the one Moore seems officially to countenance. It is not obvious that the field proceeds best when all ethicists think of themselves as involved in one great common labor. Even if from a god's eye perspective there is a perfectly ordered ranking of the world's goods, the facts about the largeness of the field and the limits of human understanding might require a pluralistic methodology that remains unconcerned with how things appear to that eye. Rather than have philosophers embrace a cooperativist and progessivist conception most at home in the physical sciences, rather than have them work on tidying up one great system, ethics is better off with many competing systems and views: "Let a thousand flowers bloom." This advice holds for the obvious Millian reasons. Any one system, however grand and sophisticated, is likely to leave out a great deal of the truth. The truth is better served when people put their views up against opposing ones. It also holds because it makes it more likely that when grand syntheses such as the one in *Principia* are assayed, there is much for them to synthesize. An approach friendly to controversy is also welcome for the fact that a great deal of beauty is lost when writers sacrifice their individual visions to normal ethical science. The cooperativist vision can easily become much too conservative, totalitarian even.

Brightening the Past

As the fluidity of ethical investigation works to temper Moore's optimism about the great progress to be made following the shedding of philosophical blinders, it also ameliorates his pessimism concerning the history of the subject. If the field's richness keeps us from attaining exact knowledge and large-scale agreement, it also makes the mistakes of previous philosophers other than irretrievable. Earlier philosophers have had many worthwhile things to say even when their work was riddled with error. As is shown by the example of Sidgwick, even so deep an error as hedonism need not vitiate the rest of a philosopher's work. (Sidgwick also shows that a philosopher's avoidance of the naturalistic fallacy does not foreclose on the possibility of his committing other serious errors.)

Moore allows himself this kind of generosity but is too overwhelmed by the discovery of the naturalistic fallacy to take advantage of it. Consider the following remark about the methodology and history of ethics he makes near the beginning of the chapter "Hedonism." In this passage, he explains and defends the methodological principles he uses in doing the history of ethical philosophy and exegesis on particular works:

It is, indeed, only when we have detected this [naturalistic] fallacy, when we have become clearly aware of the unique object which is meant by 'good,' that we are able to give to Hedonism the precise definition used above, 'Nothing is good but pleasure': and it may, therefore, be objected that, in attacking this doctrine under the name of Hedonism, I am attacking a doctrine which has never really been held. But it is very common to hold a doctrine, without being clearly aware what it is you hold; and though, when Hedonists argue in favor of what they call Hedonism, I admit that, in order to suppose their arguments valid, they must have before their minds something *other* than the doctrine I have defined, yet, in order to draw the conclusions that they draw, it is necessary that they should *also* have before their minds this doctrine. In fact, my justification for supposing that I shall have refuted *historical* Hedonism, if I refute the proposition 'Nothing is good but pleasure,' is, that although Hedonists have rarely stated their principle in this form and though its truth, in this form, will certainly not follow from their arguments, yet their ethical *method* will follow logically from nothing else.[16]

Moore embraces what might be called the method of *negative* synthesis. He distills out of the work of previous philosophers the mistaken core that he considers to vitiate the entirety of their work. But the admission that they also held doctrines other than the false ones he examines provides him with the chance to use a different, positive methodology. Instead of concerning himself only with the way in which the naturalistic fallacy infects their work, he could have tried to tease out the other insights, consistent with his own, that their work embodies in spite of the fallacy. If he had taken this tack, he might have been able to provide a deeper understanding, by more closely investigating the places where different working philosophers actually go off the track, of the pitfalls philosophers face in trying to get a properly reflective understanding of good. But his obsession with a mistake he considers to be primitive keeps him from reading other philosophers with the requisite sympathy, as an examination of his discussions of any number of them shows.

For a quick example, consider his remarks on A. E. Taylor. Moore quotes and derogates the following passage: "The primary ethical fact is, we have said, that something is approved or disapproved: that is, in other words, the ideal representation of certain events in the way of sensation, perception, or idea, is attended with a feeling of pleasure or of pain."[17] Even in this very brief passage, which suggests a version of the ideal observer theory, we can find things for Moore to treat sympathetically. Taylor talks about the ideal representation of an event, which perhaps indicates that he is trying to guarantee complete impartiality in the consideration of it and the entirety of its effects. While he may not fully realize it, Taylor is attempting to eliminate special pleading in order to find out whether something is *good*. It may also be that in speaking of approval as the primary ethical datum and in his incorrect definition of it, Taylor is confusedly trying to honor a point made by Moore, that a cognition of good containing the "appropriate" positive emotional response is of much greater value than a cognition of it lacking in emotion.[18] Taylor

[16] Ibid., p. 61.   [17] Ibid., p. 60.   [18] Ibid., pp. 189–90.

might also be groping for the point that our instinctive reactions have a high enough degree of reliability about what is good to guide the more contemplative intellect. So while not completely clear as to what he is doing and no doubt making grave errors, Taylor does have points of contact, at important places, with what Moore considers to be the truth.

Moving to another example, but for his hurry to impute the naturalistic fallacy to T. H. Green, Moore might have considered more seriously the distinction between the view that "'good' is merely another name for 'desire satisfying'" and the view that good is what satisfies the desire of a *moral* agent.[19] Even Mill, hapless by Moore's lights, can be seen to have been groping for insights consistent with Moore's views. Despite the fact that he chooses a profound mistake as his theoretical centerpiece, Mill does take seriously the deep psychological fact Moore takes too much for granted, that good deeply engages our desires. When Mill says that the only "proof" that something is desirable is that it is desired, he was appealing, through the fog created by his many errors, to our immediate inclination to desire those things we find good. It may also be that without fully realizing what he was doing, Mill, like Taylor, was recognizing the point that immediate inclination is often a more reliable guide to what is good than a purely contemplative grasp of it.

Such sympathetic readings would be more consistent with the Moore who allows that there has been some progress over the years in ethics, the one who says, just before he excoriates them, that in their half-hearted recognition of nonnatural properties, metaphysical philosophers have advanced beyond the naturalists.[20] If he had fully engaged himself in such readings, he would have made his history something more than a catalog of folly. By shrinking the chasm between his insights and others' failings, he would have made himself more the repairer of a tradition than its destroyer. To have pointed to the insights shining through the confusion would have made Moore's overall argument more compelling, as it would have supported his claim that no matter how confused they get, philosophers never completely lose sight of good. With the distance between himself and others lessened, it would have been easier for him to show how others who assumed many different initial perspectives were nevertheless groping for the insights he more completely reveals.

Had he taken this road, he might also have played a smaller role in theoretical developments he must have considered to be nihilistic. It is an often-noted irony that much of Moore's revolutionary impact was quite other than what he envisioned or hoped for. Besides the contribution his work has made to objectivist ethical theory, it has also given great sustenance to emotivists, prescriptivists, and other noncognitivists. Its contribution to these vastly different ethical theories provides the basis for a

---

[19] Ibid., p. 139.   [20] Ibid., p. 111.

more radical critique of Moore than any we have yet considered. The historicist moral philosopher Alasdair MacIntyre argues that historical circumstances enter so deeply into moral concepts that it is not merely the case, as Moore has it, that generalizations about the effects of certain kinds of actions and virtues hold at one time but not another. Nor is it merely as we have it, that the play of history makes it exceedingly difficult for one to analyze completely the nature of certain goods. Rather, Moore and all those who think of "'moral philosophy' as an independent and isolable area of enquiry"[21] are, because of their radically ahistorical and individualistic approach to the subject, not even capable of *understanding* the things these generalizations are supposed to be about. The very meanings of the moral concepts, like the meanings of all concepts, are tied to the ethoses and traditions that spawned them. This makes the ethical concepts from different eras and traditions incommensurable.[22] It also makes "The notion that the moral philosopher can study *the* concepts of morality merely by reflecting, Oxford armchair style, on what he or she or those around him or her say and do . . . barren."[23] (MacIntyre clearly includes Moore among those to be condemned even though his armchair was in Cambridge.)

MacIntyre's criticism of Moore works in two stages. First, he offers a critique of his procedure of rendering moral judgments as one that stifles inquiry and real debate and finally, that undercuts the possibility of moral judgments being rational. The emotivists and other noncognitivists, correctly thinking that Moore's account of how we "find" good inhering in things is not compelling as an account of *cognition,* but incorrectly thinking that it contains the germ of the correct account of moral "inquiry," offer their own explicitly noncognitivist views in its stead. The second line of criticism follows upon the first. The reason Moore and his noncognitivist followers are forced to rely on such a dead-end conception of moral investigation is that they are part of a movement that has cut morality off from the traditions and history that give it its lifeblood.

As has been argued for in the account of Moore on aesthetic appreciation, noncognitivists, critics like MacIntyre, and many others who do not often keep the same company embrace the same caricature, as simplistic as any that has ever been foisted on a great thinker, of Moore's views on the procedures of moral investigation. This Moore embraces an extraordinarily crude version of Robert Sylvester's a priori method of cognition of ethical propositions. He holds that all one needs to do is take a quick moment to "look at" or "inspect" concepts. One then gets to decide without further ado whether or not the simple property good attaches to them. Upon doing that, one gets to make moral pronouncements *ex cathedra.* In MacIntyre's words,

---

[21] MacIntyre, *After Virtue,* p. ix.   [22] Ibid., pp. 6–8.   [23] Ibid., p. ix.

Propositions declaring this or that to be good are what Moore calls 'intuitions'; they are incapable of proof or disproof and indeed no evidence or reasoning whatever can be adduced in their favor or disfavor. Although Moore disclaims any use of the word 'intuition' which might suggest the name of a faculty of intuition comparable to our power of vision, he none the less does compare good as a property with yellow as a property in such a way as to make verdicts that a given state of affairs is or is not good comparable to the simplest judgments of normal visual perception.[24]

On this view, Moore's theory, with its "highly impoverished view of how 'good' may be used," is not merely barren, but irresponsible and pernicious. Precious aesthetes ask silly hypothetical questions rather than engage in the serious work of limning the virtues. MacIntyre quotes Keynes on the kind of empty-headed talk the Bloomsberries engaged in:

'If A was in love with B and believed that B reciprocated his feelings, whereas in fact B did not, but was in love with C, the state of affairs was certainly not as good as it would have been if A had been right, but was it worse or better than it would become if A discovered his mistake?' Or again: 'If A was in love with B under a misapprehension as to B's qualities, was this better or worse than A's not being in love at all?'[25]

Since there are no rational procedures for settling such "disagreements" as these, the discussions concerning them degenerate into posturing and browbeating. (With what zest would Nietzsche have railed!) MacIntyre writes:

How were such questions to be answered? By following Moore's prescriptions in precise fashion. Do you or do you not discern the presence or absence of the non-natural property of good in greater or lesser degree? And what if the two observers disagree? Then, so the answer went, according to Keynes, either the two were focusing on different subject matters, without recognizing this, or one had perceptions superior to the other. But, of course, as Keynes tells us, what was really happening was something quite other: 'In practice, victory was with those who could speak with the greatest appearance of clear, undoubting conviction and could best use the accents of infallibility.'[26]

On MacIntyre's reading, Moore's theory immediately precedes the *reductio* into emotivism of the Enlightenment project of "moral individualism."[27] Upon the exposure of its cognitive bankruptcy, emotivism is seen to be not Moore's bastard, but his rightful heir.

We can agree that *Principia* suffers some impoverishment from Moore's failure always to add the detail that would give flesh to his thought. But this weakness need not be endemic to his work. More likely, it is due to the fact that he lacked a rich moral imagination – which may have been due to his innocence.[28] In any case, he saw himself as writing a prole-

---

[24] Ibid., p. 15.   [25] Ibid., pp. 16–17.
[26] Ibid., p. 17.   [27] Ibid., pp. 14–19.
[28] Levy, *Moore and the Cambridge Apostles*, pp. 11, 135–6, 293. Stuart Hampshire argues that Moore's innocence was a theoretical weakness in "Liberator," p. 39.

gomenon. If we bring to Moore the imaginative expansiveness he lacked, even the questions about love and illusion Keynes and MacIntyre have such fun with seem less misbegotten.[29] They begin, in fact, to sound like the stuff of great comedy and tragedy. Upon doing this for Moore, we are much less likely to think with the noncognitivists that his belief in a cognitive component in the answer to these questions is just an exercise in delusion or as MacIntyre, borrowing from Nietzsche has it, an exercise in the will to power.[30]

We can also grant to critics like MacIntyre that if not as a matter of logic then of temperament, Moore does not always seem to leave room for dialectical interplay between one's original intuitions and the (one hopes) coherent principles one develops as a result of reflection.[31] Moore makes few if any explicit comments about how to achieve "reflective equilibrium," how to settle the disputes sure to occur between our views on particular matters and our most thoughtful principles. This is odd, as this is an issue that exercised his great teacher Sidgwick. Again, perhaps he was overconfident about how neatly things would fall into place once he had cleared the field of ethics of its rubble. But Moore does actually provide some guidance on these sorts of issues, as Sylvester shows.[32] Certainly, his actual procedure is not nearly so vapid as the one upon which MacIntyre pours his scorn. When, for instance, he seeks to convince that Sidgwick is wrong about pleasure being the only good, he does not ask us just to "inspect" pleasure and "see" that the proposition "Pleasure is the sole good" is false. Rather, he makes a distinction in the philosophy of mind between pleasure and the consciousness of pleasure and offers a counterexample concerning the goodness of noncognized beautiful objects. In other words, he *argues* that Sidgwick's view does not cohere with our most considered moral and philosophical judgments. He provides us with a larger framework for the intuition about beautiful objects that helps to explain why Sidgwick is wrong and also why he makes this mistake. Perhaps Moore's Beautiful World Argument sounds prissy and unconvincing to the modern reader *as Moore presents it*. But if we consider that flesh and blood people actually do worry about preserving parts of the environment they or very few other people will ever enjoy, it acquires no little poignancy.[33] Certainly, Moore does enough here and elsewhere to show the careful reader that he has paid heed to

---

[29] If Moore had been more expansive, it is likely that he would not have been able to muster the bull-dogged focus that he brings to issues in his later work. What Moore points out about the virtues on p. 166 of *Principia* is true of philosophy as well. The diversity and complexity of the subject requires a diversity of talents and a division of labor.
[30] *After Virtue*, p. 22.
[31] Baldwin would be another such critic. See *G. E. Moore*, pp. 68–9.
[32] Sylvester, *The Moral Philosophy of G. E. Moore*, pp. 38–9, 60–9.
[33] Butchvarov, *Skepticism in Ethics*, p. 88.

his own warning that "We must not . . . look on Intuition, as if it were an alternative to reasoning."[34]

We can then uncover a Moore who allows for a great deal of give-and-take between opposing positions. Arguments that proceed in a piece-meal fashion are of lesser moment than those that tie many different points together. If we are concerned with an individual point of contention, we need to know how various proposals to deal with it fit into the entire moral landscape. It is not inspection but connection that is primary. We may surrender a deeply felt intuition if it does not fit into our always developing conception of the whole of the terrain. We are not locked forever into our initial prejudices.[35] Nevertheless, it must be emphasized that people can and do take stands on individual issues of greater or lesser moment and scope. One person "sees" as a general matter and in particular cases that individual liberty, being a great intrinsic good, takes precedence over security concerns while another "sees" that the benefit of the doubt must be on the side of security. At some point, moral discussion can and often does break down.[36] These claims are surely not shocking. The thought that there was once and can be again a golden age when ethical theory provided a framework for generating comforting solutions to difficult questions is as fatuously nostalgic as any that nestled in the bosom of Rousseau. Nor does the recognition that there never was nor ever will be such a time bring *strong* objectivist ethics into disrepute. It is not a requirement of ethical objectivism that it make either ethics or life easy.

---

[34] *Principia*, p. 144.

[35] This is to disagree again with Hill, who argues in *The Ethics of Moore* that on Moore's view, there can be no changes made in our commonsense moral beliefs as the result of ethical reflection. See pp. 33–4, 37–40, 74–5, 110, 120, 123–5.

[36] This to register disagreement with another of Hill's claims in *The Ethics of Moore*, pp. 123–5, that Moore is committed to holding that there can be no moral disagreements among people who agree on all the nonmoral facts. In making this claim, Hill forgets Moore's warning on p. x of the preface to *Principia* "that in every way in which it is possible to cognise a true proposition, it is also possible to cognise a false one." Interestingly, Hill anticipates some of MacIntyre's arguments in these pages, the last of his book.

5

The Origin of the Awareness of Good and the Theory of Common Sense

The Origin of Our Awareness of Good

In the first part of this chapter, we examine Moore's views on the origin and development of our awareness of good and the way in which that awareness is connected to action by the will. We will see how Moore is able to allow that the commonsense awareness of good we bring to philosophical reflection is more provisional than one who only listens to him at his most stentorian would think possible. Though common sense leaves us with very strong beliefs about good and the goodness of certain things, since they are not grounded in sustained reflection, they are jumbled together and in fact, are likely to be inconsistent. These facts give ethics its job and the parameters within which to work. Although the beliefs left to ethics by common sense undergo a great deal of change as they are scrutinized, defended or discarded, and systematized, the general picture in ethics is one of refinement, not revolt: Too much change and we will have switched the subject. In the chapter's second part, we flesh out this conception by suggesting avenues of argument Moore incorrectly disallows himself that show how a commonsense awareness of such natural goods as health provide a guide to ethical reflection. In doing all of this for Moore, we make him less revolutionary and more appealing.

The remarks most pertinent to the subject of our awareness of good and its connection to the will are found in Sections 77–85 in the chapter "Metaphysical Ethics." Moore is more concerned in these pages to argue against certain views than to put forward his own. Perhaps it is for this reason that his remarks are brief and provisional. But whatever the reasons, it follows that gaps and uncharacteristic hesitancies appear in the statement of his views. Also, what he says there is not always consistent with what he says elsewhere. So parts of our interpretation and some answers to important questions will have to be speculative.

The target of Moore's attack is Kant's "Copernican revolution." At the heart of that revolution is the supposition that the primary task of philosophy is to examine "Cognition, Volition and Feeling . . . three fundamentally distinct attitudes of the mind towards reality," rather than reality itself.[1] Kant and his idealist successors make the fatal mistake of

---

[1] *Principia*, pp. 129–30.

"supposing that to ascribe certain predicates to a thing is the same thing as to say that the thing is the object of a certain kind of psychical state."[2] In epistemology, they make the "very natural, though . . . utterly false supposition that for a thing to *be* true is the same thing as for it to be perceived or thought of in a certain way."[3] In ethics, the relevant psychic states are considered to be ones of will or feeling. In his discussion of hedonism, Moore had already dismissed the view that good is to be analyzed in terms of the feeling of pleasure. So here he focuses on what he calls "the commonest assumption of Metaphysical Ethics at the present day," that good must be analyzed in terms of will. If such a view were correct then an investigation of the "fundamentally real Will" would yield ethical conclusions. But because it is not correct, no such investigation is of "the smallest relevance to the proof of any ethical conclusion."[4]

The fundamental mistake of these views stems from their assumption that "preference" or will, "seems roughly to stand in the same relation to thinking things good, in which the fact of perception stands to thinking that they are true or exist. . . ."[5] Given this assumption, it is natural to suppose that a thing's being good is "identical with its being preferred in a certain way."[6] But the most that could be shown is that our preferring or willing something in a certain way is a *criterion* of its goodness – and is very unlikely even to be that.[7] As the mistake about cognition renders worthless "the whole mass of modern literature, to which the revolution has given rise, and which is called Epistemology;" so does the analogous mistake in ethical works keep them "from making the smallest contribution to the solution of ethical problems."[8]

The Open Question Argument fells this entire movement with one quick stroke: "That the assertion 'This is good' is *not* identical with the assertion 'This is willed,' either by a supersensible will or otherwise, nor with any other proposition has been proved; nor can I add anything to that proof."[9] But fortunately, Moore does not rely solely on the OQA. He anticipates and meets two responses to his denial of the identity between being good and being willed:

(1) It may be maintained that, nevertheless, they really are identical, and facts may be pointed out which seem to prove that identity. Or else (2) it may be said that an *absolute* identity is not maintained: that it is only meant to assert that there is some special connection between will and goodness, such as makes an enquiry into the real nature of the former an essential step in the proof of ethical conclusions.[10]

Moore meets the first objection in Section 79 by showing what the possible connections between the will and goodness are. Although none of these connections allow for an identity between the two, some of them

---

[2] Ibid., p. 129.   [3] Ibid., p. 133.   [4] Ibid. p. 129.
[5] Ibid., p. 133.   [6] Ibid.   [7] Ibid., pp. 133, 137.
[8] Ibid., pp. 133, 139.   [9] Ibid., p. 129.   [10] Ibid., p. 129

"may easily be confused with the assertion of identity; . . . therefore the confusion is likely to have been made." Against the second objection, he argues, mostly in Sections 83–84, that no connection but that of absolute identity has the slightest relevance for any ethical conclusion.

Let us now turn to Section 79, the one containing his suggestions about the origin of our awareness of good. Immediately, the section presents an interpretive dilemma. On the most literal reading of it, its two paragraphs contradict each other. We shall first present Moore's discussion, revealing the contradiction. We shall then suggest some adjustments to his discussion that remove it. These adjustments, based on an assumption that he misspeaks slightly, are rather mild and in the spirit of his summary of this section, found in Section 82. But it must again be noted that there is no way of making all of his scattered remarks on the will's relation to the perception of good consistent. This is most likely due to the fact that they are indeed scattered about. Because his main concern always lies elsewhere, he does not see fit to work out a detailed view in any one place.

Moore begins by considering the claim that willing (or a certain kind of feeling) is the source of "philosophical knowledge" of good. Maintaining the analogy with Theory of Knowledge, one who holds this may mean the following:

> just as, by reflection on our perceptual and sensory experience, we become aware of the distinction between truth and falsehood, so it is by reflection on our experiences of feeling and willing that we become aware of ethical distinctions. We should not know what was meant by thinking one thing better than another unless the attitude of our will or feeling towards one thing was different from its attitude towards another.

According to Moore, this just gives the "psychological fact that it is only *because* we will or feel things in a certain way, that we ever come to think them good; just as it is only because we have certain perceptual experiences, that we ever come to think things true." This he says is just a "*causal* connection – that willing is a necessary condition for the cognition of goodness." Because there is a causal connection between willing and thinking good, it would seem that there cannot even be a *partial* identity between them. If the first is a distinct thing necessary to bring the second thing into being, the two things must have natures independent of each other.

But if this is what Moore means by calling the connection causal, he is inconsistent with what he says in the next paragraph. He begins there by considering those who say:

> further that willing and feeling are not only the origin of the cognitions of goodness; but that to will a thing, or to have a certain feeling towards a thing, is the *same thing* as to think it good. And it may be admitted that even this is *generally* true in a sense. It does seem to be true that we hardly ever think a thing good, and never very decidedly, without at the same time having a special attitude of

feeling or will towards it; though it is certainly not the case that this is true universally. And the converse may possibly be true universally: it may be the case
that a perception of goodness is included in the complex facts which we mean
by willing and by having certain kinds of feeling. Let us admit then, that to think
a thing good and to will it are *the same thing* in this sense, that wherever the latter occurs, the former also occurs as a *part* of it; and even that they are *generally
the same thing* in the converse sense, that when the former occurs it is generally
a part of the latter.

Even though he begins this paragraph by examining the claim that
there is *more* to willing than its being the cause of the cognition of goodness, it follows from the rest of the paragraph that willing cannot be the
cause of this. Ignoring the qualification which he repeats but nowhere
discusses, he says here that it is possible that thinking something good is
a *part* of willing it. If there is just one complex, it would seem that the two
parts of it cannot be distinguished from each other as cause and effect.
Or, if there is a causal relation between them, it has been reversed. Rather
than willing being a necessary condition for the cognition of goodness,
as he first had it, he now has it that thinking something good is a necessary condition for willing and certain kinds of feeling.

The way out of the exegetical dilemma is to realize that without being
fully explicit about it, Moore is speaking in the two different paragraphs
of two different stages of moral awareness. In the first stage of awareness,
which is his topic in the first paragraph, we will without any (explicit)
thought of good; willing is the cause of our ever coming to think certain
things good. As we mature, reflection on our acts of willing creates in us
a general awareness of good; we then reach the second stage in our volitional life, discussed in the second paragraph. In this stage, a thought of
good does become a "part" of willing. A general connection is set up between the will and a thought of good such that a thought that a thing is
good precedes and leads to our willing it. So by the lights of this discussion, some version of what we may call the Socratic theory of the will, according to which we will what we think to be good, can be false originally,
but becomes generally true upon the attainment of a certain level of maturity and awareness. (Once again, Moore nowhere explains the nature
of the exceptions. This is one very important reason why we can only speculate about what his fully developed theory would look like.)

This interpretation of the history of the connection of the will to the
cognition of good is consistent with Moore's summary of his position,
found in Section 82. There are two important points he wishes to emphasize there. The first, which we now see to hold for the first stage, is
"that it is only because certain things were originally willed, that we ever
came to have ethical convictions at all." The second, which is about the
second stage, is this: "It may be further maintained, with some plausibility, that to think a thing good and to will it in a certain way are now as a

matter of fact identical." Still, Moore insists that no matter how close that connection between the thought of good and the will becomes in the second stage, "the two things are not, in the strict sense, identical." This is because there remains a distinctly noncognitive, volitional element in willing. We are now in a position to explain the fundamental error of the metaphysical philosophers who define good in terms of the will. Not going back far enough in time to the point before which the will was fully mature, they fail to distill from it that distinct element, the thought of *good,* that is not only logically separate but at one time actually *was* separate from volition.

Any interpretation of Moore on the issue of the connection between the thought of good and the will must be made with great humility, however. There are formidable difficulties to be found within these few sections alone. Let us consider sentences from Sections 79 and 82, respectively. In Section 79, he writes, "It does seem to be true that we hardly ever think a thing good, and never very decidedly, without at the same time having a special attitude of will or feeling towards it; though it is certainly not the case that this is true universally." The first thing to note is that Moore repeats his denial that the connection between thinking good and willing is universal even in the second stage, but is silent again about what prevents or breaks it. Nor does he say what it is "decidedly" to think that a thing is good. Does this just mean that one is very confident that a thing is good or does it suggest something more reflective, a self-conscious and carefully wrought decision that something is good? This does not seem likely, as our most carefully thought-out decisions are often the ones we are the least confident about. Most people are not so strong and confident in their own judgment that they are *always* inclined to follow through on their most considered, most difficult, decisions about what is good or best.

Moore is also silent about what it is to have a *special* attitude of will or feeling. Does "special" here just mean *positive* or does it refer to something more unique? If he is speaking of something more unique, his view is *greatly* qualified. The connection hardly ever breaks down within a special, limited class. And how much of a qualification to the stipulation of a connection between the thought of good and an act of will is brought about by the addition of the phrase "or feeling"? Are they just feelings or do they also contain a conative element? If there is a conative element, would the importance not then lie in it rather than in the feeling? If they do contain a conative element, what prevents them at times from issuing in action? If there are just feelings, do *they* necessarily lead to action if they reach a certain strength? How much would that possibility weaken the connection between the *thought* of good and the will? What importance would these feelings have if they *do not* lead to action?

Similar questions arise for this sentence from Section 82: "It may be admitted that when we think a thing good, we generally have a special attitude of will or feeling towards it; and that, perhaps, when we will it in a certain way, we do always think it good." If there is an airtight connection between only a *certain* kind of willing and a thought of good, the Socratic element of the theory is in danger of being so qualified as to be nullified. And how are we to characterize this kind of willing independently of its issuing in action? Is Moore in danger of giving a tautology the status of a profundity, saying that when we will something in a certain way – the way following upon a perception of its goodness – we do always think it good? These sentences show Moore to be uncharacteristically hesitant in stating his views on these matters. No doubt it is a difficult subject about which we need to tread very lightly.

We must also recognize that at least one passage in another part of *Principia* cannot be made consistent with the view he suggests here. In a discussion whose conclusion is that the virtues lack intrinsic value, Moore writes, "There is no doubt that a man's character may be such that he habitually performs certain duties, without the thought ever occurring to him, when we wills them, either that they are duties or that any good will result from them."[11] He says that these actions are "like many of the operations performed in the putting on of clothes." The best way to deal with this passage is to argue that he fails to see to the bottom of the situations he is describing. Because "a great economy of labour is effected when a useful action becomes habitual or instinctive," the virtuous person learns not to *have to* rehearse to himself, before he performs the action, the good it brings about. Still, if he is asked why he performs these actions, he can easily cite that good. To use Moore's own example, for reasons of health, sexual comportment, and aesthetics, it is quite easy to explain the good that comes about from the putting on of clothes. In fact, one of the reasons such actions become habitual is that the good they effect is so obvious.

Putting aside the qualifications and dealing with the contradictory passage, we have the following model for the natural history of the connection between the will and the cognition of good. At first, we just pursue, "make for," the things we want. Given what he says in his discussion of psychological egoism, Moore could say that originally, we just pursue those things the thought of which create a pleasure in us. We pursue them without any thought about receiving pleasure from them, let alone any thought that they are good.[12] Becoming more reflective as we grow up, we begin to take account of the following facts, which have not yet become truisms. Sometimes we get what we want and sometimes we do not; sometimes getting what we want satisfies us and sometimes it does not. Some things we desire for ourselves and some we desire for others; some things, perhaps, we want for no one in particular. We also notice that

---

[11] Ibid., p. 175.   [12] Ibid., pp. 69ff.

other people have desires that can either be aligned with or clash with ours, and that different desires *we* have may clash. In short, we realize that we need to make many distinctions about our desires and the actions we take in their service if we are to get about in the world.

At the same time that we are learning to make these distinctions, we also learn to judge things from the point of view of others. Finally, we begin to develop the ability, quite limited in most of us, to make decisions from an impartial point of view, what Sidgwick calls the "point of view of the Universe." At a certain level of moral and intellectual maturity, we realize the need for an overarching distinction, that between good and bad, to provide a completely satisfactory schema that not only classifies but *guides* the actions we and others perform. Because we have not yet (fully) discovered the property good, we cannot articulate to ourselves what exactly we are looking for. But the observations and distinctions we have already made give us some sense of what we need. They encourage us to look to a less immediately personal, more abstract level than we have hitherto used; we begin to move into the realm of the nonnatural. At first, perhaps we just postulate that there are the properties good and bad that make the ends of actions more or less reasonable. Perhaps it is only after postulating good that we come fully to "observe" it in particulars, although it is likely that moments of recognition of good have guided our journey into maturity. Having in some sense observed good, we now begin to act in ways we consider to be in accord with it.

Although the description of the growth of our awareness of good has been put in individualistic terms, much of it is as a result of training by those who raise us and the culture at large. This training is neither very orderly nor intellectual, but is more in the way of "propaganda." Its primary purpose is not to get us to observe a property or to accept a theory on intellectual grounds, but to get us to *behave* in certain ways. Most important for this task is its getting us to assume in some small degree a standpoint of impartiality. Although this is perhaps most successful if there is some intellectual component to the training, if we get *some* glimpse, however fleeting, of the property that is to guide our action, it is not necessary that we see good isolated from all else (even assuming it can be so isolated) in order to reach the requisite level of impartiality. As far as we can tell, the reach of the vast majority of our actions is quite limited. Thus it is usually enough, safer even, just to focus on a good that is near to one and engaging than on a more distant greater good that is not so immediately engaging. So our everyday awareness of good can be "selfish" to some degree, tangled up in our own individual desires. To anticipate, this can help Moore explain why the realization of ethical egoism's contradictoriness has been so long in coming.[13] The limited contact that

---

[13] Ibid., pp. 97ff.

develops in the ordinary course of life between the will and the cognition of good by no means guarantees our achieving a fully reflective, philosophical understanding of value.

This general theory must face the question, When do we become aware of the properties good and bad? Two different answers can be given to this question. As Moore states the position in Section 79, we are not even unreflectively or subconsciously aware of good when we will originally. We rather achieve an awareness of good at some unspecified point in time. Surely, it is not a matter of our waking up one day and finding ourselves aware of the property; the awareness dawns on us gradually. As children, we may have a deep awareness of the goodness of cookies while being blissfully unaware of the goodness of tact. The second answer is that we have always at some level been aware of the property good, have had an innate idea of it. Willing is then a cause of our recognition that we *already* think things good, not of our actually thinking them so. To mature is to become self-conscious about what we have already been conscious of. This view requires that we make nondrastic changes in three sentences of Section 79. The sentence beginning with "But so far" must have the ending of its first part changed to "it is only because we will or feel things in a certain way, that we ever *come to recognize* that we think them good." We change the end of the last sentence to "that willing is a necessary condition for *the recognition of* the cognition of goodness" and make a similar change in the first sentence of the second paragraph.

Our reading of Moore's view on the relation between perception and truth varies according to the two different possibilities on the time when we become aware of good. According to the first interpretation, we originally perceive without having any awareness at all of the properties truth and falsity. Our perceptions leave us with expectations and beliefs, some of which are met and some of which are not. In order to explain this most important difference, we *postulate* that there are the properties truth and falsity. It is only after we have come to feel the theoretical need for these properties that we look for and discover them. On the second interpretation, we read the comparison in this manner: Insofar as we instinctively trust our perceptions, we *already* think them true, even though we are not explicitly aware of ourselves as using the concept truth. Reflection on the fact that perceptual experiences sometimes guide us correctly and sometimes mislead us makes us explicitly aware of the properties of truth and falsity we have already been calling upon.

One might use features common to goodness and truth to support the first interpretation. Since these properties are insubstantial and atemporal, it likely takes a certain amount of conceptual sophistication on our part even to be subconsciously aware of them. Since goodness and truth are logically independent of the properties that make a thing good or true, we can think of those properties without in any way thinking of their goodness or truth. Others might find those who hold this view to be guilty of failing to distinguish between consciousness and self-consciousness. Despite the fact that it does not know that this is what it thinks, even a fox thinks that it is *true* that there is a chicken about and that it will make *good* eating. Some might object to this view as being too Kantian in spirit. It makes the deepening of our moral awareness a matter of uncovering a priori modes of thought – just the sort of view Moore is opposing here. If we think of ourselves as having such an a priori awareness of good, it becomes too tempting to say that good is a category of the understanding we "impose" upon the world, and that we must look to ourselves rather than to the world for enlightenment. But as difficult as it might be on this account not to fall into it, one *need* not fall into the trap of conflating good with our awareness of it, just as, assuming the same sort of view to be true for mathematical consciousness, one need not deny herself the right to think about numbers themselves rather than her innate awareness of them.

There may be a very important general philosophical reason for holding the second view, despite its difficulties. For the purposes of providing a unified philosophical account, one might find it necessary to embrace a Socratic theory of the will for the entirety of our lives and for all conscious beings. One might hold that such a universal law must be invoked in order to account for the action-guiding character of good. It becomes difficult or impossible to account for the fact that we generally will in accord with our perception of good if we do not become aware of good until we are some years along in life. Without explicitly realizing it, we must have felt the tug of goodness all along if we are ever to be self-consciously guided by it. Why else does our late self-conscious discovery of it come to engage us so deeply? Turning to a question that is crucial to Moore, why, unless we already have some implicit awareness of good, would he consider us to be able to recognize so immediately that ethical accounts in terms of other properties are lacking?

Before moving to a discussion of our awareness of good and its growth, let us take one more look behind. The point we have labored long to make – that Moore is mistaken in thinking that we have a deep and ineradicable awareness of the simplicity, indefinability, and nonnaturalness of good that somehow we lose sight of when we philosophize – holds on either of these versions of the history of the development of our ethical awareness. In order to be attracted by good and get about in everyday life, we do not need to have a conception of it of such a clarity that we can simply *see* it to be simple, indefinable, and nonnatural. Again, we are able to see the naturalistic fallacy in a new light, one making the errors of earlier philosophers much more reasonable. On neither version does the fallacy consist of philosophers making the bizarre error of conflating two properties they have already recognized to be distinct. Rather, the fallacy follows from the fact that philosophers have just never completed the difficult conceptual investigation that is necessary for seeing that good is utterly distinct from such properties as being pleasurable or desired or willed. Philosophers fail to see that any property other than good will fail to ground a *complete* ethical system. Because there is a great deal that one can do without being complete, we can still treat the efforts of earlier philosophers with respect. What Moore thinks he can establish at the beginning of his investigation can only be established at the end.

But at the same time that we see how our commonsense awareness of good is provisional, we also see that by the time we come to perform more distinctly philosophical reflection, we have a vast store of material upon which to work. We inherit from our elders an elaborate, if disorderly, casuistical system and theoretical understanding of good before we ever begin self-consciously to philosophize. The very richness of our commonsense moral awareness makes for the philosophical difficulties Moore so pitilessly dissects. There is much that must be gotten right and many ways to go wrong even before we can begin to clothe our thought in reflective philosophical dress. Many conflicting intuitions need to be made consistent, requiring detailed examination of the ethical concepts of everyday life. The thoughtful *nonphilosopher* must work very hard to achieve reflective equilibrium! Moore offers a couple of very valuable tools to help us achieve a more deeply satisfying state of equilibrium, the isolation test and the doctrine of organic unities. Many confusions will be ameliorated by their judicious application, more perhaps than will be ameliorated by rigorously following his strictures against committing the naturalistic fallacy.

Saving Common Sense

Having some sense of how one's unrefined moral awareness is shaped during maturation by humanity's common understanding of good and bad, we now have the resources to deal with the second stage of Alasdair MacIntyre's argument against Moorean ethical theory. MacIntyre sees in Moore the culmination of a movement that opposes all appeals to tradition, whether by philosophical theory or common sense. On MacIntyre's view, Moore's is a radically individualist theory making each of us her own supreme moral judge. We each decide "for ourselves" what things are good and bad.[14] MacIntyre has it that in order that our moral opinions be "our own," Moore finally *requires us to turn our backs on* common moral opinion, as well as on previous philosophical attempts to articulate the moral notions. This dismissal of tradition in the shaping of moral thought

[14] As we saw in the introduction, Regan has similar views about Moore on these matters, but unlike MacIntyre, he approves of them.

carries a steep price. MacIntyre seems to suggest that by appealing to pu-
tatively universal intuitions that are yet inherently of the individual,
Moore merely enshrines the views of his own class, the "aesthetic rich,"
as *the* views correct for all times and places. By refusing to make a place
in ethics for sociology and history, Moore manages the well-nigh impossible feat of joining nihilism to a stultifying provincialism.

We have already argued in Chapter 4 that a Moore who is more generous to the distinctly philosophical tradition can be brought to life and
have also seen how often he appeals to *common* sense. There are other
places in *Principia* in conflict with this portrait of one who is a foe of all
tradition. He offers a sketchy but interesting account of the different ob-
ligations the individual has toward different kinds of societal rules that
we shall argue is very respectful of tradition.[15] On the penultimate page
of *Principia,* he says that though his results may seem strange to philosophers, they will not appear so to common sense. Still, it must be admitted that in one place in *Principia,* he seems to hold that commonsense
moral thought is beset by errors so profound as to require its complete
abandonment. If we cannot soften or even eliminate this particular argument of his, not only will MacIntyre be right about the radical nihilism
of Moore's ethics, it will be that Moore's thought is in its own terms deeply
and obviously incoherent. There will be no sound, if inarticulate, judgment for him to return us to upon his exposure of the distinctly philosophical mistakes of the past. But if we can excise this radical argument,
we will not only save, but improve upon Moore's ethical theory. We will
be able to present a Moore whose eyes are opened wider to the fact that
there are many more intrinsic goods and a much richer interplay between them than he officially allows for in his "Ideal," a Moore who can
make better on his claim that the ideal contains many goods of vast complexity and who can show more convincingly that we have a deep native
awareness of this vast realm of good.

If he had not brought forward his questionable argument, Moore
might also have achieved a deeper insight into the methodology of the
validation of common moral insight. He might have seen more clearly
how our original, instinctive knowledge of the goodness of certain complex wholes guides us in our analysis of these complexes as well as in our
attainment of a richer awareness of good. In many cases, we know
prephilosophically that a certain complex is good, even though we do not
know what exactly the complex in question is or, for that matter, what
good is. We use our knowledge of the goodness of such complexes to help
ourselves to a more exact philosophical knowledge of them *and* good.
The operating thought is that the analyses of such ordinary notions as
health and happiness must have it that they are good. Any analysis deny-

---

[15] The argument is found in Chapter 8.

ing the goodness of these things may be dismissed out of hand. This provides the most convincing demonstration of the place of common sense in ethics. Most of ethics lies in the sharpening of insights whose origins are in our ordinary awareness of good and bad.

The argument, the more reasonable portions of which come unacknowledged from Sidgwick, forbidding this line of thought begins in Section 27 of *Principia*.[16] Its conclusion is a denial that we can have knowledge of a nontautologous proposition that health is good, but his introductory remarks show that he considers it to apply to all approaches that "point to a vague notion that there is some such thing as natural good; to a belief that Nature may be said to fix and decide what shall be good, just as she fixes and decides what shall exist." He denies the following supposition: "that 'health' is susceptible of a natural definition, that Nature has fixed what health shall be: and health, it may be said is obviously good; hence in this case Nature has decided the matter . . ." Such an appeal to nature annuls the logical autonomy of ethics. It makes it the case that "we have only to go to her and ask her what health is, and we shall know what is good: we shall have based an ethics upon science."[17]

Moore says that originally, such a proposition as "Health is good" is empty because originally "health" just means a certain natural complex that is good. Later, when it comes to mean a different complex, the proposition is false. He writes:

It may be true, indeed, that by 'healthy' we do commonly imply 'good'; but that only shews that when we so use the word, we do not mean the same thing by it as the thing which is meant in medical science. That health, *when* the word is used to denote something good, is good, goes no way at all to shew that health, when the word is used to denote [what he claims is the scientific definition!] something normal, is also good.[18]

Thus according to Moore, anyone who proceeds by trying to refine our rough-and-ready evaluative concepts in the manner we have suggested, who tries to use their goodness to pin them down more firmly for analysis, is guilty of equivocating: "We might just as well say that, because; bull' denotes an Irish joke and also a certain animal, the joke and the animal must be the same thing."

In this discussion, Moore turns the defense of common sense we have suggested on its head. If we are wrong about the goodness of health, what are we ever going to be right about? More generally and more deeply, on the matter of the methodology of analysis, by Moore's lights there is little or no possibility of our being able to start with a somewhat imprecise understanding of a complex and refining it as we go along so that our judgment continues to be about the same thing. "Refinement" leads rather to the judgment's being about something else entirely. This calls

[16] See *Methods*, pp. 80–3.   [17] *Principia*, p. 42.   [18] Ibid., p. 43.

into being an extremely revolutionary methodological principle that clashes with his own optimism about the prospects for philosophical progress. New discoveries cannot build upon and add to old ones, but can only overthrow them.

If this dismissal of common sense is right, then the profound impasse MacIntyre considers to beset the moral thought of this particular age pervades moral understanding at all times. MacIntyre fears that all that is available to the moral understanding of this age are bits of flotsam from previous competing traditions and ethoses. Upon their detachment from the larger social contexts that gave them life, they have become not merely anachronistic, but unintelligible to us. The problem bringing one nearly to despair is that the different traditions from which they have come are incommensurable with each other. Hence we cannot construct a new and coherent large-scale theory by a reenlivening historical synthesis of the different traditions. "Dialogue" between proponents of these incommensurable and now inadequate theories creates rancorous gibberish instead of consensus. But by the lights of *Principia*'s Section 27, the impasse would be even more extreme than this. It would have it that this is how things are for *each individual person*. One's *own* previous opinions are not built upon but razed, with the rubble providing the materials for later futile efforts at construction. Presumably, since one will not fully realize that the different stages of understanding she has reached are incommensurable with each other, the moral code of each individual will consist of "a series of fragmented survivals" from her own past. Each person talks past herself!

Even though it seems to take only a few childhood bouts with illness to grasp the very important distinction between health and sickness and their respective values, Moore holds that our thought that there is such a *good* as health is the product of hallucination. He does not tell us where we get such a profoundly misguided idea or how we can continue to have any confidence in our everyday judgments upon the exposure of its emptiness. Obviously, this claim is very much at odds with the confidence he expresses in the reliability of our ordinary judgments in other places. It is certainly in striking opposition to his claim that when many people profess to find beauty in something, they are likely to be right.[19] Despite his appeals to the initial superiority of common sense to philosophy, Moore now has us at sea when it comes to the commonsense awareness of value. This radical conclusion might have given him pause about the standing of his own judgments of intrinsic value. How can he be so sure, for example, that his conclusions about the goodness of friendship and aesthetic appreciation would survive his becoming a theist?[20]

---

[19] Ibid., pp. 200–201.
[20] Ibid., pp. 195–8. Also, see Chapter 9 for a discussion of Moore on friendship and religion.

It seems that Moore is unaware of just how radical an argument he is offering in these pages. He lifts most of the argument verbatim from *The Elements of Ethics,* which ends with the extremely conservative defense of common sense we noted in Chapter 3.[21] If he had fully understood this argument's implication that there is no possibility of our having *any* native awareness of natural goods, he could not have been any more sanguine in that work about common sense than he was about philosophical theory. His remark near the end of the long passage we subsequently quote, "But it does not follow, except by virtue of the naturalistic fallacy, that those things, commonly thought good, are therefore bad," might suggest that he takes his argument to be iconoclastic concerning theory but anti-iconoclastic concerning common sense. To support the claim that he let himself go too far in this discussion, we note that it occurs at the very beginning of his critical history of ethical theory. Having grand revolutionary designs upon that subject, he starts with the most grandiose of proclamations: *Everybody has been wrong about everything.*

We can begin the task of rescuing Moore from his disastrous argument by pointing out that he just cannot be right in thinking that the ordinary person and the doctor do not mean the same thing when they talk of health. Grant that when a lay person speaks of health, he does not have exactly in mind the doctor's much more precise understanding of it. But if the doctor is not just refining, but actually replacing the lay notion, we cannot make sense of the communication between doctors and patients. It would then be the case that when a doctor gives a patient the news that he is healthy, they only *appear* to understand it in the same way. Their both considering it to be *good* news would then be an incredible coincidence. In actuality, doctors are in a position no different from zoologists who talk to the laity about horses or sociologists who discuss friendship. Although the ordinary person defers to these experts on what the details of these complexes are, the experts are still responsible to the ordinary notions as they go about refining them.[22] This point goes back at least as far as the *Republic.* Remember Plato's concern at the end of Book IV to assure the reader that his account of justice is in accord with the everyday understanding of it.[23]

Immediately preceding the passage about equivocation quoted previously, Moore writes:

But what is this natural definition of health? I can only conceive that health should be defined in natural terms as the *normal* state of an organism; for undoubtedly disease is also a natural product. . . . When therefore we are told that health is natural, we may presume that what is meant is that it is normal; and that

---

[21] *Elements,* pp. 31–3.

[22] Field argues on pp. 85–7 of "The Place of Definition in Ethics" that the ethicist has even less leeway than the scientist in offering definitional revisions.

[23] Plato, *Republic,* 442e–3b.

when we are told to pursue health as a natural end, what is implied is that the normal must be good. But is it so obvious that the normal must be good? Is it really obvious that health, for instance, is good? Was the excellence of Socrates or of Shakespeare normal? Was it not rather abnormal, extraordinary? . . . Yet it may be said that nevertheless the normal is good; and I myself am not prepared to dispute that health is good. What I contend is that this must not be taken to be obvious; that it must be regarded as an open question. To declare it to be obvious is to suggest the naturalistic fallacy: just as, in some recent books, a proof that genius is diseased, abnormal, has been used in order to suggest that genius ought not to be encouraged. Such reasoning is fallacious, and dangerously fallacious. The fact is that in the very words 'health' and 'disease' we do commonly include the notion that the one is good, and the other bad. But, when a so-called scientific definition of them is attempted, a definition in natural terms, the only one possible is that by way of 'normal' and 'abnormal.' Now, it is easy to prove that some things commonly thought excellent are abnormal; and it follows that they are diseased. But it does not follow, except by virtue of the naturalistic fallacy, that those things, commonly thought good, are therefore bad. All that has really been shewn is that in some cases there is a conflict between the common judgment that genius is good, and the common judgment that health is good. It is not sufficiently recognised that the latter judgment has not a whit more warrant for its truth than the former; that both are perfectly open questions.

In this passage, Moore runs together many problematic claims that we shall consider in turn. To begin, it only takes a moment's reflection to see the falsity of his claim that the only plausible candidate for a scientific definition of health is of that which is normal. Such a definition prevents us from saying what we would sometimes need to say, that most of the members of a certain group are or were unhealthy. In making meaningful statements unutterable, *Moore* commits the equivalent of the naturalistic fallacy on the complex natural property health. He accepts this inadequate definition of health because he thinks that the only other candidate for it is of that which is natural. He finds this definition to fall by the wayside because disease is also natural.

It is certainly useful to note that because the word "natural" is slippery, it is open to a great deal of abuse and must be used with extreme care – Moore himself is not wholly innocent on this count. But he fails to consider that because of the different senses "natural" has and because of the different things it can be applied to, there can be definitions of *both* health *and* disease in terms of what is natural, in different senses of the term. With a modicum of care, the different senses can be sorted out with the conclusions being nothing very shocking. In one sense of the term, for a single organism to be healthy is for it to develop in accord with the standard set by the laws of development for members of its species. It is for it to flourish, to reach its potential, to fulfill its *telos*. To be diseased is to be impeded in this development. In this sense, health is natural and disease unnatural. From larger perspectives, where we consider what is natural for an entire species or some larger unit, including nature as a whole, it is perfectly natural that some individuals be healthy and others be unhealthy. For reasons of increasing the diversity of the gene pool, it might be healthier for the entire species that some individuals be unhealthy. We can grant Moore's point that in this sense of "natural," disease is also natural, while denying that this precludes a definition of health for an individual in terms of what is natural in the other sense. If a definition of health in terms of what is natural equivocates, so does a definition of it in terms of what is normal, as normality is similarly relative.

In "The Conception of Intrinsic Value," Moore expresses more clearly than he does here the fear that the sorts of views he is discussing jeopardize the possibility of a thing's intrinsic value being fixed solely by its own nature rather than by its relations to other things. Since it is possible for the laws of nature to be different from what they in fact are, it is possible for something that is healthy by the actual laws of nature not to be so. Thus the conclusion that the state of its health cannot be an intrinsic natural property of a thing. To allay this worry, we note that the property of being healthy is similar to the property of being true that we discussed in Chapter 2. As its truth is a "part" of a belief without the facts that make it true being a part of it, so is its health a "part" of an organism without the external facts upon which its health depends being a part of it. So it is possible for the state of its health to be an intrinsic natural property of an organism.

Moore also rejects the claim that we know health to be good because he thinks that it commits us to the view that nothing unhealthy, or abnormal, can be good. Thus his rhetorical question about the excellence of Socrates and Shakespeare. But a number of points can be made that allow one to ward off this unpalatable consequence. First, one is committed only to the claim that health is *a* good among possibly many other and greater goods. Moore thinks that the view he is opposing forces one to "hold that there is only *one* kind of fact, of which the existence has any value at all," that there is a "sole good." He seems to think that the acceptance of natural goods requires one to *define* good in terms of one of them! If this is so, then this is the only place in *Principia* where he underestimates the importance of his discovery of the naturalistic fallacy. Even if many philosophers, including the ones he proceeds to attack, have made this particular error, his exposure of the fallacy should have enabled him to see how it is possible for others to follow his strictures against it, while also showing how our natural awareness of many goods such as health provides the foundation for our more sophisticated value judgments.

Moore also fails to see how his own doctrine of organic unities can save one from the unpalatable conclusion that an unhealthy Shakespeare writing his plays is not good. Even though Shakespeare's being diseased is bad, the larger whole of a diseased Shakespeare writing his plays is far better than the whole consisting of a healthy Shakespeare not writing them.[24] Curiously, he also ignores what can be done with the distinction between ends and means. Shakespeare's being diseased would have been bad as an end, but good as a means to his writing his great work. Perhaps even more surprisingly, he fails to remember that it is his own view that it can be both *obvious* and an *open question* that something is good. At the heart of his work is the distinction between a platitude and a tautology, which those who try to define good confuse.

It is also odd that Moore objects to the claim that "Nature may be said to fix and decide what shall be good." His entire approach seems to require that in some sense Nature does "fix" what is valuable. Value is part of the "natural order" and we must be guided by it. It is not an *arbitrary* "decision" by nature that health is good. As is made clear in Section 30, the "modern vogue of 'Evolution'" feeds Moore's recurring fear that any concession at all to biology or any other science as being relevant to casuistry will lead to its taking it over completely. But rather than stand our ordinary notions of good and bad on their head, biology is in service to them. We already know before we ask about its details that health is *a* good. We use our knowledge of its goodness to characterize it more precisely. Without knowing the details of health, we can all usually distinguish, usually by nothing more than their look, healthy plants and animals from unhealthy ones. We certainly know, from the time we are children, when we "feel good" and when we do not. The sophisticated reflections of the scientist remain comfortable in these humble abodes. If there is subsumption of one science by another, ethics subsumes biology, the science of the great good of life.

This last point also speaks to the fear that any appeal to evolution must make us fatalistic and close minded. Many fear to this day that since there is a sense according to which everything happens in accord with nature, views taking evolution seriously force the conclusion that "Whatever evolves, is right." But our sense of what is good and bad in nature need not be so strongly tied to the contingent course of evolution. It is certainly possible for a species to deteriorate over time and for us to think that this has happened and is bad. Those who presently fear the course of the evolution of the environment do not thereby abandon evolutionary theory. It is also not the case that we are somehow locked in completely by our original views about what health and natural goodness are. In the face of experience, we can decide that a definition is inadequate and change it as well as any other view we happen to hold. Small changes in definition do not make for equivocation. If there is a danger of equivocation when definitions undergo such change, it plagues all inquiry.

Moore wishes to oppose any view that has the proposition "Health is

---

[24] Butchvarov, *Skepticism in Ethics*, p. 15. Butchvarov speaks of an unhappy Wittgenstein rather than a diseased Shakespeare.

good" or any other proposition containing good as being analytic. At the beginning of inquiry, an answer to the question "What is the good of health?," being rather general, vague, and uninformative, does come close to being analytic. But even at its vaguest, the proposition that health is good must have health be the good that has to do with one's living a long and vigorous life, being physically comfortable, and so on. So there is never a time when "Health is good" just means "That which is good, is good." Although our opinions will change as we advance in our study, it is hard to envisage our changing our understanding of health to such an extent that we decide that it is not, after all, something good.

Moore should not object to a procedure that starts by decreeing health to be good and then uses its goodness to keep it pinned down for further study. He would have to do the same with friendship were he to go into more detail in his discussion of it. We have already noted that he leaves himself open to the charge that he makes it a tautology that friendship is good. He holds friendship to be similar to aesthetic appreciation but with an additional element: "the object [that is being appreciated, the *friend*] must be not only truly beautiful, but also truly good in a high degree." To give a nontautologous account of this good, he must say what the features are that make an "object" – a person – truly beautiful and truly good. Without this, the statement that friendship is good is completely uninformative: "Those relations between good people that are good, are good." What he can say is that *originally*, almost all that we know ourselves to mean by friendship is that many of its instances are complexes involving good personal relationships. However far we go in our study of friendship, we never leave this thought behind.

Even while acknowledging the possibility of there being bad kinds of friendship, it remains a part of our human heritage to feel quite strongly that friendship is a natural social good. Young children who suffer the misfortune of being in the care of adults with sordid personal relationships realize that they are being cheated and yearn for decent personal relationships around which they can center their lives. Our concern then is to uncover those natural social kinds, to formulate nontautologous true propositions of the form "Personal relations having conditions X, Y, and Z instantiate a kind of friendship that is good." Quite likely, one of the conditions of a kind of friendship's being good is that the relations comprising it be healthful and the result of and conducive to virtuous behavior. Thus the reason that our understanding of greater goods is dependent on our understanding of lesser goods is that the very natures of the greater goods are dependent to some extent on the lesser goods. The greater goods are organic unities having lesser ones as parts.

If this discussion has been well taken, we can make Moore much more consistently friendly to common sense than his own discussion would indicate. We can thus allow the flexible, democratic, and generous Moore who lurks in *Principia*'s shadows to come out further onto center stage. This Moore is open to the insights of previous philosophers and ordinary persons alike. However deeply mistaken in detail were earlier naturalist philosophers, even they had focused on a part of the world having real value. The judgments of humble people about certain humble values are also vindicated. Although it may pale in the face of great art and the friendship of the high-minded, there is much to be said for "enjoying and appreciating the lesser goods which do and will exist."[25] Life is worth living not just for the happy few. The limitations of Moore's personal moral insight need not plague his overall theory.[26] When we separate Moore's theory from the limited and fallible statement and application of it in *Principia*, fill in some of its details, remembering that after all he considered it to be a prolegomenon,[27] we find it to be very rich indeed. We also find it to be more down to earth than earthshaking. This all adds a most attractive conservative flavor to his theory.

---

[25] *Principia*, p. 195.
[26] In *Essays and Sketches*, p. 254, Keynes, who admired Moore greatly and defended his overall ethical conception, writes that "there are many objects of valuable contemplation and communion beyond those we knew of" from *Principia*.
[27] *Principia*, p. ix.

6

Moore's Argument Against Egoism

Introduction

In the next two chapters, we discuss Moore's argument against ethical egoism – the view that each person ought only to be concerned with and pursue his or her "own" good. This is his one argument that makes Moore incontestably revolutionary not just against philosophy, but also common sense. He argues not merely that ethical egoism is wrong, but that it is *ir-rational* – egoists contradict themselves when they try to state their view. From this the conclusion follows, despite Moore's efforts to avoid it, that the distinction enshrined by common sense between one's interests and the interests of others, between goods that affect oneself and others that do not, is *illusory*. The changes in the understanding of ourselves and our fellows wrought by recognition of this fact are so momentous that what remains seems hardly human.

In the first part of this chapter, we examine assumptions about the nature of the self that lurk in the background of Moore's argument against egoism. In the second part, we first consider how his presentation of his argument against egoism sheds further light on the tension between his conservative and his revolutionary impulses, and then examine and evaluate the argument. In the third, we consider more exactly what his argument commits him to by examining his critique of Sidgwick's view that egoism is rational. In the first part of Chapter 7, we explore his attempt in his critique of Sidgwick to explain and weaken the psychological hold that egoism has on us. In the second part, we do two things. First, we examine more exactly the features of human life his argument threatens. Second, we look at his explication, in a later section of *Principia*, of a notion of self-interest that, if successful, would weaken the revolutionary force of his argument. We argue that because that explication does not stand up, the force of his argument remains extreme.

Against a Metaphysical Self

Let us turn now to the brief remarks Moore makes in *Principia* on the nature of the self. Although they are nowhere close to being fully worked out, his argument against egoism does seem to be informed by a view of the self that is suggested by these remarks. Every step away from the notion of a perduring, substantial self is a step away from the thought that there is anything capable of "having" "its own" good. So the dismissal of egoism fits more comfortably with looser than with tighter views of the self, and most comfortably with a Humean view of the self, a view quite inimical to common sense. This point is brought home nicely by Sidgwick. He writes:

It undoubtedly seems to Common Sense paradoxical to ask for a reason why one should seek one's own happiness on the whole; but I do not see how the demand can be repudiated as absurd by those who adopt the views of the extreme empirical school of psychologists, although those views are commonly supposed to have a close affinity with Egoistic Hedonism. Grant that the Ego is merely a system of coherent phenomena, that the permanent identical 'I' is not a fact but a fiction, as Hume and his followers maintain; why, then, should one part of the series of feelings into which the Ego is resolved be concerned with another part of the same series, any more than with any other series?[1]

Sidgwick does not pursue the matter, as it is not his concern to challenge commonsense notions of the self and self-interest. But since Moore chooses him as his foil, it is odd and perhaps troubling that *he* does not address it more directly in his attempt to remove egoism's surface plausibility. Perhaps it is because he is very unsure about the nature of the self. Thomas Baldwin observes that although he once claimed the problem of the self to be one of the two he was most interested in, he wrote very little on the subject. He did, however, flirt with Humean views of the self at different times in his career.[2] We may say with confidence that *Principia* rejects a number of "metaphysical" conceptions of the self, as well as the thought that any such conception could be relevant to ethics. His remarks on the self in *Principia* are part of a larger attack on the general notion of *substance* as something it is necessary or even possible for any kind of property to inhere in. This attack informs his act-object view of consciousness, which in its denial that there are any such things as mental "contents" needing something to "contain" them, perhaps fits most easily with a Humean view of the self.

Moore's rejection of metaphysical notions of the self follows directly from what he means by calling a notion metaphysical. Metaphysical philosophers are distinguished from naturalist philosophers by their recognition of nonnatural objects: "I call those philosophers preeminently 'metaphysical' who have recognised most clearly that not everything which *is* is a 'natural object.'"[3] But after we credit the metaphysicians for advancing beyond the naturalists in recognizing the being of such objects, we must remember that they misunderstand the nature of

---

[1] *Methods*, p. 418–19.
[2] Baldwin, *G. E. Moore*, pp. 54–5. Baldwin's discussion, pp. 50–5, *Consciousness and the Self*, is most helpful on this subject.
[3] *Principia*, p. 110.

these objects quite badly. The deepest symptom of their misunderstanding is that they find it necessary to provide "metaphysical underpinnings" or "foundations" for them. Instead of taking these objects simply for what they are, objects that do not exist in time, that depend on *nothing*, they allow themselves to become puzzled by them. To ease their misguided puzzlement about them, metaphysicians employ roundabout strategies to characterize them finally in terms of existent, temporal properties. They do this by appealing to what Moore calls *super-sensible objects*, objects that although "beyond" ordinary temporal objects, maintain enough of a conceptual connection to temporal objects that temporal objects ultimately become the ground of nonnatural objects' intelligibility. So as we have seen, instead of recognizing numbers to be atemporal objects that *are* independent of all other things, metaphysicians attempt to explicate them as quasi-temporal objects that *exist eternally* in the mind of God or as an a priori form of human understanding, etc.[4] Metaphysicians think that this lets them have their cake and eat it too. They grant these objects the eternality and necessity that is their due, but in ways they presume to be less mysterious than they would otherwise have to credit. But according to Moore, philosophical notions of super-sensible existents are just notions of ordinary existents tarted up. So the metaphysical philosophers make no real advance beyond the cruder, straightforwardly existential explications of nonnatural objects that naturalist philosophers proffer.

Moore's account of metaphysical explications of the self is complicated by another of those throwaway elaborations that make his accounts richer than they would be were he to stay within the bounds of his official view. In the continuation of the passage quoted previously, he writes:

'Metaphysicians' have, therefore, the great merit of insisting that our knowledge is not confined to things which we can touch and see and feel. They have always been much occupied, not only with that other class of natural objects which consists in mental facts, but also with the class of objects or properties of objects, which certainly do not exist in time, are not therefore parts of Nature, and which, in fact, do not *exist* at all.

This passage suggests that what distinguishes metaphysicians from naturalists is not their correctly upholding as the most fundamental ontological distinction the one between natural and nonnatural properties, but in their incorrectly upholding as most fundamental the distinction between one of the *subsets* of natural properties – the *spatio-temporal properties* – and all others. This way of accounting for the distinction between metaphysical and naturalist philosophers enables Moore to differentiate more accurately the three fundamentally different ways of doing philosophy he considers there to be. Naturalists do philosophy in the crudest way possible. They attempt to reduce all of reality to a single space-time

---

[4] Ibid., p. 110.

grid, to turn the three most basic kinds of being into one – matter. We may thus call these philosophers *naturalist-materialists*. Metaphysical philosophers recognize a reduction this heroic to be impossible. Still, since they cannot get themselves to fully credit nonnatural properties, they embrace a program that seeks to reduce all of reality to *two*, the natural-material and the natural-mental. We may then call them *naturalist-dualists*. Finally, the much too infrequently inhabited third class of philosophy that Moore practices makes both distinctions properly. We may call these lonely figures *nonnaturalist-dualists*.

Although metaphysical philosophers are to be credited for resisting materialism, Moore considers their incorrect categorical placement of the mental to cause them to make a terrible hash of the self. Given that he officially finds their basic error to be the explication of the nonnatural in terms of the natural, one might expect him to find their treatment of something mental and thus natural, even if turns out to be incorrect, at least to be in the proper sorts of terms. But although he does not state this outright, his account has them committing the further error of characterizing the *mental* in terms of the *nonnatural*. Since they lump these two kinds of thing into one category, this error is not unreasonable. Still, it creates an extraordinarily vicious circle: the natural is used to explicate the nonnatural at the same time that the nonnatural is used to explicate the natural.

Almost always, an impossible temporal notion is considered to be the glue that holds the different parts of a metaphysical object together. The logic behind the impossible appeal to time lies in this: Nonnatural properties are eternal in that they have no relation to time. Their having no relation to time is the gnat metaphysicians find themselves straining at. They thus misconstrue the being *out of* time of nonnatural objects as infinite duration *in* time. Since they realize that nonnatural objects are nothing "we can touch and see and feel," they seek to turn them into *mental constructs* of infinite duration. This creates in philosophers a sense of a realm of being much grander than that of ordinary temporal objects. They feel that if any ordinary temporal objects are to be invested with value, they must somehow be made to be part of that super-temporal realm. Natural objects are thus turned into *super*-natural objects, profound in the seeming but empty in the actuality.

There is yet another and more damaging level to the confusion that metaphysical philosophers bring to ethics. Applying the same misguided dialectic to good, they come to believe that its very *being* depends on one of the objects of their fancy. This goes a great distance toward explaining one of the subjects of *Principia*'s last chapter and our last two chapters, the deep-seated sense of disappointment with the world so many philosophers suffer from. Unable to shake completely their awareness of the nonbeing of the objects upon which they purport the nature of good to depend, they sense the world in its present configurations not only to not contain any value, but to be *incapable* of containing any value. They thus come to believe that the world requires a profound transformation if its existence is to be justified. Alas, the nature of the objects upon which good is purported to depend makes the required transformation impossible.

As an example of a metaphysical view, Moore considers the one held by "modern writers" according to which "the final and perfect end is to realise our *true* selves – a self different both from the whole and from any part of that which exists here and now in Nature."[5] One who accepts with perfect consistency all the implications of this view is forced to accept ethical fatalism. As we have seen, the realm occupied by such an "eternally real"[6] self should properly be understood as being out of time rather than as having infinite duration in time.[7] But if this realm out of time is what is real, then "nothing either has been, is now, or will be real in time. . . ." From this, the conclusion follows "that nothing we can do will ever bring any good to pass. For it is certain that our actions can only affect the future; and if nothing can be real in the future, we can certainly not hope to make any good thing real."[8]

Because it is easier to believe a contradiction than a plain piece of philosophical nonsense, metaphysicians continue inconsistently to maintain "that there is some reality also in the temporal. . . ."[9] But *really* to allow reality to the temporal, they must grant what puts their theory on the rocks, "the distinction between a real subject and the character which that real subject possesses."[10] Since the "real subject" to which they look originally for value is out of time, its valuable characteristics must be separable from it if there is to be anything good in temporal reality for us to aim at. But the separability of these characteristics insures "that the eternal reality cannot possibly be the sole good."[11] What is good is good whether it is attached to something eternally real or to something that passes into and out of existence. Once one is no longer mesmerized by the thought of the eternally real as being the sole good, looking there for *any* good ceases to be plausible. And once it is granted that good can be found elsewhere than in the eternally real, it becomes implausible to suppose that the *nature* of good depends on anything there. Good is what it is and we find it where we find it.

Moore's argument can be made to range beyond the bounds to which he here confines it. It provides the means by which to separate *all* properties, value and nonvalue properties alike, from *all* subjects, personal or impersonal. In short, it threatens even the least pretentious of metaphysical accounts of substance. Let us note first that nothing in Moore's argument hinges on the eternally real subject being personal or on its

---

[5] Ibid., p. 113.   [6] Ibid., p. 120.   [7] Ibid., p. 115.
[8] Ibid.   [9] Ibid., p. 116.   [10] Ibid., p. 120.   [11] Ibid.

separable properties being value properties. So the metaphysician who attempts to account for the universe's infinite temporal duration by appealing to an "eternal" impersonal subject or substance must grant that its modes are separable from it as soon as he grants sense to the thought that it is possible for the universe to undergo change. But it is then no longer the case that the sole reality is eternal, and so the eternal subject is again threatened with superfluity. Anything temporal that appears to be part of something eternal is a philosophical illusion – the gulf between the temporal and the eternal is unbridgeable.

Now suppose someone to try to account in metaphysical terms for the permanence and change of things while lowering the metaphysical flame. In an attempt to make one thing both permanent and subject to change, the subject having the properties is no longer held to be eternal, but is invested instead with a less elevated nontemporal dimension as well as a temporal dimension. The problem with this is that there is nothing to give the subject a temporal dimension but the temporal properties it is supposed to *have*. These properties are once again separable from the subject and thus this subject is again threatened with superfluity. When it is realized that the properties had by the different-in-kind "subject" must always be able to sheer off from it, the grip of the thought that there is a need for such a subject to "have" them begins to loosen. Literally, there is *nothing* that remains the same while changing: What is in time are *just* collections of instantiated properties. Accounting for the *relative* permanence of things through change is the fact that the properties of collections do not go into and out of existence at the same time. It is no surprise then that in *Principia,* Moore rejects a substance ontology for natural objects.

A separation problem also haunts the egoist, who needs to be able to make sense of the thought that good is something that can be had by a single subject. For the egoist to be able to think that there is something that one ought to do, the thing that is good has to be separable from the subject that has it on the lines of thought rehearsed in the preceding argument. But it then follows that the nature and value of that thing is utterly independent of the subject it is "had" by. If the egoist tries to say that even though the thing is separable from the subject, the thing does not become valuable until it is had by that subject, she must explain why that subject's having any one thing is more valuable than its having any other thing. This will not be easy to do. If the characteristic only becomes good upon its being had by that one particular subject, then its being had by that subject is what *makes* it good. But from this it follows that *whatever* that subject has is good. The egoist thus falls into a trap similar to the one the metaphysician of the "eternally real" falls into: As long as one keeps oneself alive, it is indifferent how one acts, as any action one performs brings about an equal amount of good.

This discussion clears the way for the view that what brings value to the

world is not the "having" of certain characteristics by any particular subject, but the existence of certain characters or properties taken alone or
in combination. The possibility is slipping away of *any* kind of subject playing a role in the exemplification of value in the world. Because good is a
separable property, there is no place where it can be hoarded or hidden.
Even if each of us comes to have a sense of an "inner" self whose development in one direction rather than another has value, this development, as anyone who has ever loved another knows, is available to others
to take an interest in. There is nothing in the notion of *a* self to give the
notion of *one*self enough depth to make for a distinction of fundamental
ethical importance between one's interest and the interest of others.

The Contradiction of Egoism

Moore begins his discussion of egoism with some remarks on Sidgwick,
the philosopher he chooses as his foil. In them, he situates his argument
in relation to common sense and philosophy. As he does elsewhere,
Moore sees himself as a protector of the instinctively sound, though
rather unreflective moral thought of the "plain man" from philosophical
depredation. Sidgwick claims that the basis of ethical egoism lies in a distinction between oneself and others that common sense recognizes to be
of great ethical import. Moore can either accept Sidgwick's claim and say
so much the worse for common sense, or he can dispute it. Without being completely explicit about it, he mostly disputes it. He also scolds Sidgwick for accepting a hedonistic account according to which one's own
good or one's own interest consists of one's own pleasure or happiness.
He claims that this is not the view of the plain man – in fact, the plain
man does not even consider his pleasure to be a *part* of his interest – and
makes much of Sidgwick's failure to note this.[12]

Moore seems to be saying that although it is natural on reflection to
profess that one's interest consists of one's happiness, it is, as with the theory of psychological egoism, only natural to profess this on *first* reflection.[13] These initial theoretical forays leave one farther from the truth
than when he started. (Once again, errors such as these threaten to make
ethics a dangerous activity.) Moore insinuates that there is something almost willfully primitive about Sidgwick's identification of one's interest
with one's happiness, as ancient philosophers had already noted that
these things were not identical. Sidgwick gives an incorrect account of
why the ancients did not identify them, based on his confusion concerning the notion 'my own good', and thus allows himself to continue in his
mistake. So he ends up being doubly damned. He gets wrong what the

---

[12] Ibid, p. 98.   [13] Ibid., p. 68.

ordinary person gets right and gets it wrong despite the warnings of philosophers who had trod the ground before him.

This brings us to a troubling point that must be acknowledged. There is an unseemly note of meanness and contempt in Moore's discussion of Sidgwick. Since he does give Sidgwick credit for being the first philosopher to recognize the naturalistic fallacy and since he also borrows a great deal from him, one might expect him to see himself as building upon the great, albeit flawed, insights of his great teacher.[14] But after giving him credit for exposing the fallacy, Moore carps at him, even ridicules him, on other occasions. If one may be allowed to speculate, there are probably extraphilosophical reasons for this. There are first the usual Oedipal reasons; strengthening them is the fact that Moore seems to have disliked Sidgwick.[15] These combine with the fact that although he sees himself as a conservator of ordinary moral thought, he has the temperament of a revolutionary. As we saw in previous chapters, he prefers to see himself as breaking new ground through his own efforts rather than as engaging in a cooperative effort to build upon the work of others. Although Moore was an Apostle, he was no disciple. In any case, his discussion of Sidgwick on egoism is marred by an excess of rhetorical zeal.

He certainly gets carried away when he claims that the plain man does not normally include his pleasure even as *part* of his interest. It seems plain that we do not consider such things as "my own advancement, my own reputation, the getting of a better income, etc., etc.," as intrinsically in 'my interest'.[16] It is the commonest of commonplaces that those who consider wealth to be intrinsically in their interest are woebegone. However valuable as a means wealth may be, it is valuable *only* as a means. Were one asked what made any of the things on Moore's list in one's interest, he would be likely to reply with only the briefest of hesitations that it is because they lead to pleasure or happiness. So even if he is not a thoroughgoing hedonist, the plain man certainly considers his pleasure to be one of the things in his interest. Although this is by no means a decisive point against Moore, it does make one less confident that hedonists, including Sidgwick, are completely out of touch with the thought of their fellows. So if the egoist makes her case with a hedonistic conception of one's own interest, she is not employing a notion of good that is utterly foreign to everyday thought.

We turn now to Moore's argument. In introductory remarks, Moore makes a distinction between two different versions of egoism. According to the first, egoism "is apt to denote merely selfishness. In this sense, a

---

[14] Besides failing to acknowledge Sidgwick in his discussion of the goodness or lack thereof of the "natural," Moore also fails to acknowledge him in his discussion of chastity in *Principia*, pp. 158–9; see pp. 328–31 of *Methods*. His discussion of the different kinds of ideals, pp. 184–7, also seems to borrow from *Methods*, pp. 18–22.

[15] *The Philosophy of G. E. Moore*, p. 16.   [16] *Principia*, p. 98.

man is an egoist, if all his actions are actually directed towards gaining pleasure for himself."[17] The second version of egoism tells *each* person what she ought to do, namely, pursue her own interest. This anticipates a distinction made years later by Brian Medlin between *individual* egoism and *universal* egoism.[18] The individual egoist is indifferent about how *all* people should act. He offers no standard for all people to follow, but just does what he wants. He could not care less whether he is "rational" or not; whatever he has of a "code" is purely individual. According to Medlin, argument cannot touch this kind of egoist, but that is not philosophically problematic, as he puts forward no argument himself. He is "vermin" upon whom philosophers need waste no time.[19] The universal egoist, however, is caught in a logical impropriety, as she does offer an argument. By doing so, she appeals to standards, accepts some condition of impartiality.

Moore also wishes to be concerned only with the egoist who argues. According to him, the flaw haunting the egoist's argument is found in the notion 'my own good'. He notes that the conception 'my own good' or 'my own interest' is a common one, being one of the first people come upon when they start to reflect on ethical matters. But even though he says later in the text that there is a notion 'my *interest*' that does make sense, the sense in which the egoist must employ the notion 'my own *good*' is incoherent. There is no way for something to be good just *for me*, for its goodness to be *mine*. When I say that something is good for me all I can mean is that the thing *I get* is good or that *my* getting it is good. And:

In both cases it is only the thing or the possession of it which is *mine*, and not *the goodness* of that thing or that possession. There is no longer any meaning in attaching the 'my' to our predicate and saying: The possession of this *by me* is *my* good. . . . In short, when I talk of a thing as 'my own good' all that I can mean is that something which will be exclusively mine, as my own pleasure is mine (whatever be the various senses of this relation denoted by 'possession'), is also *good absolutely;* or rather that my possession of it is *good absolutely*. The *good* of it can in no possible sense be 'private' or belong to me; any more than a thing can *exist* privately or *for* one person only.[20]

Because there is no way for something to be good just for me, the notion 'my own good' just collapses into *good*. Given this fact, the argument runs as follows:

The only reason I can have for aiming at 'my own good,' is that it is *good absolutely* that what I so call should belong to me – *good absolutely* that I should *have* something, which, if I have it, others cannot have. But if it is *good absolutely* that I should have it, then everyone else has as much reason for aiming at *my* having it, as I have myself. If, therefore, it is true of *any* single man's 'interest' or 'happiness' that it ought to be his sole ultimate end, this can only mean that *that* man's 'interest' or

[17] Ibid., p. 96.
[18] Brian Medlin, "Ultimate Principles and Egoism," *Australasian Journal of Philosophy*, Vol. 35 (1957), pp. 111–18.
[19] Ibid., p. 114.   [20] *Principia*, pp. 98–9.

'happiness' is *the sole good, the* Universal Good, and the only thing that anybody ought to aim at.[21]

The conclusion that one person's happiness or interest is the sole good in the universe is silly enough to be laughed out of the court of philosophical appeal. But however silly it is, it does not contain a contradiction. The contradiction arises from the egoist's requiring *each person* to go through the same line of reasoning. This eventuates in the claim that each person's good, on the hedonistic conception, each person's happiness, is the sole good: "What Egoism holds, therefore, is that *each* man's happiness is the sole good – that a number of things are *each* of them the only good thing there is – an absolute contradiction! No more complete and thorough refutation of any theory could be desired."[22]

Let us lay out the argument in order to examine it more closely:

1) The good of a thing can in no sense be private or belong to me alone.
2) Therefore, the only reason I can have for aiming at 'my own good' is that it is good absolutely.
3) If it is good absolutely that I should have a thing, the reason that holds for my having it also holds for everyone else.
4) If it is true of 'my good' that it ought to be my sole ultimate end, the only thing I have a reason to pursue, then it is the sole good, the only thing *anyone* has a reason to pursue.
5) Egoism holds that for each person, 'his good' is the sole ultimate end, or the sole good.
6) According to Egoism, many different things are the sole good.
7) Egoism is absurd.

In our discussion, we shall be concerned with the argument's first four steps. If these can be established, the rest of the argument, which establishes the absurdity of applying the egoist's individual line of reasoning to every person, falls neatly into place. We can come to grips with the first premise by noting the failure of fit between the property good and the metaphysical notion of privacy. Moore has a fairly deep distrust of this notion even though in 1911, in "The Subject Matter of Psychology," he speaks of the property some mental items have of being "mine."[23] In "The Refutation of Idealism," remember, he claims that merely to have a sensation is to be outside the circle of sensations. Similarly, to have a perception of good is to be outside the circle of one's own perceptions and in contact with good itself. This view is also in the spirit of the Moore who wrote in "The Nature of Judgment" that truth does not depend upon the relation of our ideas to reality. Clearly, Moore is uncomfortable with the

---

[21] Ibid., p. 99.   [22] Ibid.

[23] Moore, "The Subject Matter of Psychology," *The Proceedings of the Aristotelian Society*, Vol. 10 (London: 1909–10), p. 41.

view that there is a realm of "one's own" private thoughts; what is "in" our thoughts are the very things the thoughts are about.

But Moore does grant that at least some mental items are private. The pleasure I feel is in *some* way mine and no one else's. Good, however, is not something that can be mine in that way or any way related to it. This would seem to follow from its being nonnatural, or even just from its being nonmental. Being nonnatural, good does not exist in time, as mental items do. Among temporal items, only mental ones have the requisite privacy. (Because of their conflation of nonnatural and mental properties, we might expect egoism to have a peculiar attraction to metaphysical philosophers.) The thought that good is private is thus on a par with the thought that numbers or physical properties are private. The notion 'my good' makes no more sense than the notion 'my two' or 'my green'. Another theme prominent in Moore's discussion of Sidgwick is that just from its being a universal, good is one and indivisible, and hence something incapable of being parceled out.

Although it is not a point he raises here, as we have seen from the previous section, Moore would also dismiss the thought that something can become good merely by its becoming mine. What makes good *my* having something rather than someone else's having it are properties I just *happen* to have. For instance, it might be good that a father, a daughter, or a citizen have something that it is not good for others to have. But even if such good-making properties can be had by only one person and that person is me, the goodness of my having it depends on the goodness of its being had by the person with the relevant property, not the "property" of being had by me. The special feeling and perspective I have about myself plays no role in giving things their value. The properties upon which value depends must be *thoroughly* transpersonally characterized.

2) is a conclusion drawn from 1). Since there is no sense in which good can be mine (and adding the point just mentioned, no sense in which something can become good just by becoming mine), my reasons for pursuing what is "my" good' must connect to *good* – period. It follows from this, as stated in 3), that there can be no reason for pursuing this or any good that holds for me alone. Since the properties upon which the goodness of anything depends are in the most important sense available to everyone, even if it is the case that not everyone can instantiate them, the reasons for acting they provide are also available to everyone. Everyone has the same reason to pursue any instance of good as I have (recognizing that they may have overriding reasons to bring about a greater or more likely to be realized good). Thus from 4), if "my" good is the only thing *I* have reason to pursue, it is the only thing *anyone* has reason to pursue. The contradiction comes when we repeat the same argument for every single person. Upon repetition, many different things become the sole good.

The immediate worry is that in its formality, the argument wins victory too cheaply; without further elaboration, it is not psychologically compelling. Good is supposed to provide a reason for *action* and from this purely formal perspective, it is difficult to see what that reason could be. We can see this point by noting that instead of accepting 2) as it stands, one could accept a conditional version of it while leaving it open whether one accepts the antecedent: "*If* I have a reason to pursue 'my own *good*,' it is because it is good." This would also suggest a twist for 3) that Moore could not accept. Everyone has as much reason for pursuing (just) absolute good as I do – no reason at all. If good need not provide one with his reason for acting, it would appear that the egoist could put her point in terms of one's own *interest* rather than one's own good. Moore's slide from talk about one's good to one's interest or happiness suggests that he does not think this is possible. Indeed, he must finally maintain that one's reason for acting must necessarily be provided by good.

In response to the ontological claim that Moore's view simply follows from the fact that good is an indivisible and "public" universal, one can argue that no matter what the ontology of the matter is, even though one cannot distinguish "parts" of the universal *qua* universal, one can still distinguish between the universal and the different particulars exemplifying it. One's attention and concern is not drawn ineluctably to the universal good that is one and the same in all its instantiations; rather, one can distinguish and concern herself with the instantiations that *concern her.* When asked why she concerns herself only with those particular manifestations, the egoist answers, "Because they are *mine.*" To give her answer metaphysical respectability, she can appeal to the sense of "I" noted by Sidgwick and taken up further in subsequent discussion.

To try to make the fact that good is indivisible and "impersonal" less mysterious, Moore's defender might wish to make a comparison between goodness and truth. Despite the protestations of intellectual faddists, everyone recognizes that *no* sense attaches to the notion 'my truth'. If something is true, it is true and that is the end of the matter. *Qua* epistemic agent, the only relevant consideration for accepting a belief is its truth. This is so even though we all grant our epistemic limitations, that each person is in a better position to ascertain some truths than others, and our epistemic imperfections, that sometimes we resist believing what we do not want to be true. Nor do we let the epistemic fact that we cannot distinguish between what we *think* is true and what *is* true affect our understanding of *truth itself.*[24] Similarly, we recognize that facts about our own particular situation do not affect what *is* good. As impartial reason requires us to believe only what is true, so does it require us to seek only what is good.

[24] *Principia,* pp. 132.

But this is where the egoist is going to find an important difference between truth and goodness. Even assuming what both the ethical egoist
and Moore will find debatable, that indivisible truth is the only criterion
for gauging the ultimate rationality of belief (sometimes the exigencies
of a situation make it better for one to believe what is not true), there appears to be a criterion other than goodness for measuring the rationality
of action. It is a truism not to be taken lightly that we are more affected
by certain goods than we are by others. It is implausible to think that we
are *required* to ignore this fact when we make our decisions about what we
ought to do. If from the standpoint of pure good or impartial reason it
makes no sense to note to whom the good "belongs," that just shows a de-
ficiency in having human beings, with the full panoply of their inclinations and desires, look at things solely from that perspective. If it is
granted that an instance of good does not become good just because it is
one's own, then one's reason for pursuing it is not only that it is good.

Moore's defender might reply that once one recognizes good as the ultimate source of value, it is irrational not to base one's morality on it completely. But this is just the point at issue. *Why* is this supposed to be so? Is
it held to be necessary to insure the accepting of a requirement of impartiality? If so, the egoist replies that she *does* offer a standard everyone
can follow. She allows herself nothing she refuses to others. Competition
is an ineluctable fact of life and it is a "fair" competition the egoist advo-
cates: Each person is to try to better *his own* life and let the chips fall where
they may.

In defense of her argument, the egoist can offer a thought experiment
similar to the one Moore offers in his Beautiful World Argument.[25] The
experiment is best performed in the first person: Imagine two worlds containing an equal amount of good. The first world consists of many beautiful objects containing a great deal of good and my living a bad or unhappy life. The lesser value accruing to the second world by its having a
smaller number of beautiful objects is balanced perfectly by the extra
good that comes to it from my living a good or happy life. Since by hypothesis, the amount of good in the worlds is equal, from Moore's point
of view, there is no reason for me to choose the second world rather than
the first. But to the egoist – and the person of plain sense – I would be
crazy if I failed to choose the world in which I live a happy life. That world
is better *for me* than the other. This suggests that there is a quasi-
indexical character lacking in epistemic reasons for believing that is had
by reasons for acting. Different instances of good attach more intimately
to different people, giving them reason to pursue some goods over other
equal or even greater goods. If it turns out not to be possible for each person to pursue his own *good,* the egoist can shift her position slightly by ig-

[25] Ibid., pp. 83–5.

noring good and putting her point in terms of one's interest or one's happiness instead. Even if we do not agree with the egoist, we know what she means.

To sum up so far, the fear is that in order to defeat egoism, Moore has desiccated good. To guarantee the heroic impartiality he thinks good requires, he has made it too impersonal. There must be some sense in which different goods attach more intimately to different individuals if anyone is to have any reason to pursue good. This is not to say that egoism must view good as a purely private item. It does not require some sort of value solipsism where every instance of good gives a reason to *no more than one* person to pursue it. It is to say rather that it is not a requirement of rationality that we view things from a deeply metaphysically neutral perspective, from Sidgwick's "point of view of the universe." Such a perspective, being one in which everyone is completely "outside himself," is one in which there are no interests – is one in which it is impossible to understand anyone as *living*. Rather than its being a perspective in which each "I" is equal, it is one in which there are no "I"s.

Moore on Sidgwick

To investigate further the commitments of Moore's argument, we turn to his critique of Sidgwick's defense of the rationality of egoism. Sidgwick claims that our ability either to distinguish between parcels of good that affect different people or to delineate spheres of private concern that do not have to do with good is connected to our ability to delineate a sense of self that separates our concerns from the concerns of others. This is the burden of a sentence Moore does not quote, although it follows one he does quote. Moore's failure to deal clearly with the issues raised by this sentence haunts his entire discussion and keeps him from seeing the extent of the ethical revolution he effects:

It would be contrary to Common Sense to deny that the distinction between any one individual and any other is real and fundamental, and that consequently "I" am concerned with the quality of my existence as an individual in a sense, fundamentally important, in which I am not concerned with the quality of the existence of other individuals: and this being so, I do not see how it can be proved that the distinction is not to be taken as fundamental in determining the ultimate end of rational action for an individual.[26]

It is because of this fundamental distinction between oneself and others that, as Moore quotes Sidgwick, The egoist "'may avoid the proof of Utilitarianism [Sidgwick's rational alternative to Egoism] by declining to affirm,' either 'implicitly or explicitly, that his own greatest happiness is not merely the ultimate rational end for himself, but a part of Universal

[26] *Methods*, p. 498.

Good.'"[27] Moore quotes Sidgwick further as saying, "It cannot be proved that the difference between his own happiness and another's happiness is not *for him* all important."[28]

We can read Sidgwick as providing the egoist with two ways of "declining to affirm" any important connection between his own greatest happiness and Universal Good. The first even grants that his well-being is good and that its goodness gives him his reason to pursue it and also makes it a part of Universal Good. Still, he "declines to affirm" that its being a part of Universal Good is what gives him his reason for his acting as he does. His reason for acting is that it contributes to *his own* good, in *disregard* of the fact that it is a part of Universal Good. This allows a theory according to which rationality requires the pursuit of good, but not the pursuit of all good. This version of egoism would be consistent with Sidgwick's claim that both egoism, which he calls Rational Prudence, and an ethic of impartiality, which he calls Rational Benevolence, are rational. Rational Benevolence is rational only if there *is* such a thing as Universal Good to care about. We can get some sympathy for this position by shifting the emphasis in one of Moore's statements: "that it is truly good in itself means that it is a *part* of Universal Good." So long as one can distinguish "his good" as a distinct part of Universal Good, he will violate no canon of rationality if he concerns himself with *only* that part of it. We have a sense of self strong enough to ground the thought that different things come out better and worse for oneself and others, that makes it reasonable for one to pursue only those instances of good that concern oneself.

The second option is just to ignore the thought that something is part of one's own *good* and to use instead some such notion as one's *happiness* or one's *interest* to make one's point. Again, it is a sense of self that enables one to spell out such a notion. Whether it is good "universally" or "locally" or not at all, it is rational to bring happiness to oneself, to enable one's own interests to flourish. On this interpretation, Sidgwick enables one to deny Moore's claim that "By no possible meaning, then, . . . can the Egoist escape the implication that his own happiness is absolutely good. . . ."[29] One would put forward this view if he agreed with Moore that the recognition of such a thing as Universal Good would require one to care about it, but who also thought that the notion of Universal Good had no purchase. Moore does not worry enough about this version of the egoistic argument, but what he says can be extended to cover it.

Moore seems to waver between weaker and stronger responses to the egoist in his discussion of Sidgwick. The weaker response begins by granting the possibility of one's carving out spheres of private concern. The stronger response is that it is not possible for one to do this. To attempt to carve out spheres of private concern is to operate under a deep and

[27] *Principia*, p. 99.   [28] Ibid.   [29] *Principia*, p. 101.

lasting illusion. The only thing, finally, we are even *capable* of being concerned about is good. There is just good and bad as it redounds to the *whole world*. Although in this discussion Moore is not very explicit about it, given the first part of his argument concerning the notion 'my good', this must finally be his position.

That Moore wavers in his response can be seen by investigating a lengthy piece of his reply to Sidgwick. Moore analyzes two phrases used by Sidgwick, (that the egoist's happiness can be his) "ultimate rational end" and "the difference between his own happiness and another's is *for him* all-important." Moore claims that no analysis of these phrases enables the egoist to make his case. We begin with his discussion of the first phrase:

> Is there any sense in which a thing can be an ultimate rational end for one person and not for another? By 'ultimate' must be meant at least that the end is good-in-itself – good in our indefinable sense; and by 'rational,' at least, that it is truly good. That a thing should be an ultimate rational end means, then, that it is truly good in itself; and that it is truly good in itself means that it is a part of Universal Good. Can we assign any meaning to that qualification 'for himself,' which will make it cease to be a part of Universal Good? The thing is impossible: for the Egoist's happiness must *either* be good in itself, and so a part of the Universal Good, *or else* it cannot be good in itself at all: there is no escaping this dilemma. And if it is not good at all, what reason can he have for aiming at it? how can it be a rational end for him? That qualification 'for himself' has no meaning unless it implies '*not* for others'; and if it implies 'not for others,' then it cannot be a rational end for him, since it cannot be truly good in itself: the phrase 'an ultimate rational end for himself' is a contradiction in terms.[30]

In this passage, Moore does say that if one is concerned with any "part" of good, one must be concerned with all of it, that if the egoist uses good to delineate the spheres of private concern, he will inevitably be swept up by Universal Good. Let the egoist waive this and put forward the second position, saying that he does not care then whether his happiness or self-interest is good. His happiness or interest is *his* end in any case; let other people have their own happiness or interest as *their* end. Moore attempts to fend off this response with a pair of rhetorical questions: "And if it is not good at all, what reason can he have for aiming at it? how can it be a rational end for him?"

What does Moore mean by "reason" and "rational" in these questions? Does he mean just that there cannot be a *moral* reason that fails to connect to Universal Good, or does he mean that there cannot be *any* kind of reason that fails to connect Universal Good? Is an end irrational merely for its failing to lead to good or irrational in a more coldly logical sense that it cannot really be willed despite initial appearances to the contrary? If Moore means only that there can be no moral reason that does not connect to good, the egoist will just continue to recommend to each person that she pursue her own end (even if he is not allowed to use the word

<hr />

[30] Ibid., p. 100.

"ought" to make his recommendation) and just not worry about whether he is "moral" or not. Following Philippa Foot, if this is all that is meant by the claim that the egoist is irrational, we do not in any way show the ego-ist to be inconsistent when we call him this.[31] As long as sense can be made of personal benefits and harms, egoism is a code that can be stated and followed and that is what interests the egoist. He will cheerfully agree that he is not rational in Moore's sense because he is confident that every-one still understands what he means.

In the discussion of the second phrase, "the difference between his own happiness and another's is *for him* all-important," Moore says some things that suggest only the weaker claim and some others that suggest the stronger. He offers four possible analyses of this expression. The first of these is "that his own happiness is the only end which will affect him" and the third is "that it is only his own happiness which he cares about."[32] Ini-tially, these analyses seem to allow the possibility of someone being con-cerned with or caring about the way in which things redound to one in disregard of their universal goodness. If the egoist uses the third analysis, she is recommending that each person pursue what is important to him without any concern for its universal goodness.

Moore writes immediately after offering the four analyses:

And none of these propositions, true as they may be, have the smallest tendency to shew that if his own happiness is desirable at all, it is not a part of Universal Good. Either his own happiness is a good thing or it is not; and, in whatever sense it may be all-important for him, it must be true that, if it is not good, he is not jus-tified in pursuing it, and that if it is good, everyone has an equal reason to pur-sue it so far as they are able and so far as it does not exclude their attainment of other more valuable parts of Universal Good.[33]

So far, Moore could still just be saying that one is not morally justified who chooses not to bring about the greatest good. To this, the egoist re-peats what we had her say previously. But against Moore's stipulative analysis of justification, she also pushes her point that there is a sense we all recognize in which she *can* justify herself. Moore himself implicitly recognizes this when he distinguishes between what is important for one and what is good. The egoist can justify herself because her pursuit of her own ends, her pursuit of what is important for her, *makes sense,* is expli-cable to impartial observers, whether it leads to Universal Good or not. So is her recommendation to others to do the same, even if they happen to think that to act in accord with it is *wrong.* This sense of "justify" con-nects to explanation. To explain an agent's action is to connect it to the agent's thoughts about good *or* to her own ends. What would be inexpli-cable is action that has nothing to do either with what one considers to be required by Universal Good or with what one considers to be impor-

[31] Philippa Foot, "Morality as a System of Hypothetical Imperatives," p. 161.
[32] *Principia,* p. 101.   [33] Ibid.

tant for oneself – that is, perfectly haphazard action – and a recommendation to others that they be equally haphazard. Thus Sidgwick's conclusion that egoism and altruism are both rational.

But in the very next sentence, Moore seems to claim that the thought that something can be important for one independently of its universal goodness is *contradictory:* "In short, it is plain that the addition of 'for him' 'for me' to such words as 'ultimate rational end,' 'good,' 'important,' can introduce nothing but confusion." If, as seems necessary, this is to be connected in the strongest way possible to the argument against egoism, Moore must mean that it is just as much of a confusion to think that something can be important for one as it is to think that something can be good for one. The phrases "ultimate rational end for me" and "important for me" are "confusing" because "for me" is either senseless or superfluous. For "important for me" to have sense, it must reduce without residue to "important" and that must reduce to "good". This makes it an analytic truth that for something to be important for one is for it to be good and thus to contribute to Universal Good.

If this is so, then Moore is making a stronger claim than that morality requires one always to be concerned with Universal Good. There is a *contradiction* and not merely a mistake in the thought that something can be important for one without contributing to Universal Good. Notice that Moore claims that one of the possible meanings to be had by the thought that something is an end for one is "that the thing is what he desires or thinks good."[34] The context pretty clearly requires Moore to consider that to desire something and to think it good are one and the same thing. Using that point to give life to the strongest claim about the connection between thinking something important and thinking it good: If we think that we are thinking about something other than a thing's contribution to Universal Good when we desire it or think it to be important, we are wrong in the same way as when we think that the very same thing is both a square and not.

This interpretation requires that the next two sentences also be read in the strongest way possible: "The only *possible* [emphasis added] reason that can justify any action is that by it the greatest possible amount of what is good absolutely should be realised. And if anyone says that the attainment of his own happiness justifies his actions, he *must mean* [emphasis added] that this is the greatest possible amount of Universal Good which he can realise."[35] Even though his use of "justify" suggests that he has not yet fully confronted his own point, Moore has finally got to be saying that it is not just that other sorts of justifications for action fail to measure up to the high standards set by morality, but that *they cannot even be offered.* To make the words of the egoist contradictory, it must be the case that to jus-

[34] Ibid., p. 100.   [35] Ibid., p. 101.

tify our actions and to make sense of them are the same thing. To do that one thing, we must connect our actions – with no qualifications whatsoever – to good. So the egoist who thinks of herself as recommending that we not concern ourselves with Universal Good is thinking of herself as recommending something she *cannot*.

On this interpretation, Moore's claim is stronger than that the egoist issues a recommendation that makes sense but necessarily cannot be followed. That claim would hold if it were a synthetic necessary truth rather than an analytic truth that for something to be important for one is for it to be good. If it were a synthetic rather than an analytic truth, it would be possible for one to think that what is important for one is not what is good, just as it is possible for one to think the necessary falsehood that a triangle that has the property of being equiangular does not also have the property of being equilateral. We can think this of this pair of properties because even though whatever has the one property also necessarily has the other, the properties are different. Similarly, if being important and being good were different although necessarily connected properties, the egoist would not be contradicting herself, but "merely" recommending something impossible. If we are to take Moore at his word about what we *must* mean, we *must* see him as embracing the stronger of these views.

7

The Diagnosis of Egoism
and the Consequences of Its Rejection

Why Egoism Seems Plausible

The stronger view is something very difficult to accept. To get into a position to accept it, one will have to engage in a great deal of psychological and anthropological reflection to wean oneself from the thought that there is sense in such notions as 'my own good' and 'important to me': *Why* do such notions lodge so deeply within us if finally they make no sense? Moore's attempt to engage in these reflections and answer this question in the rest of his discussion of Sidgwick is disappointing.

Sidgwick's concern has been to come to grips with the felt conflict between duty and self-interest, between what he calls Rational Benevolence and Rational Prudence. He holds that because it is rational to act in accord with either of these opposing positions, there is a "contradiction" in ethics. He suggests a way to resolve this contradiction by reconciling the two positions. If there is a Deity who insures that actions done in accord with the dictates of Rational Benevolence are the same as those done in accord with Rational Prudence, there would never be any difference in what the two principles require. Thus the contradiction would evaporate. Moore argues that this suggestion is misguided on a number of different counts. First, Sidgwick's view that there is a contradiction in ethics is born of his failure to realize that *egoism* is contradictory. Second, if there were a contradiction in ethics, nothing Sidgwick could say or God could effect could make it disappear. After disposing of Sidgwick's false reconciliation, Moore attempts to pinpoint the real nature of the difficulty Sidgwick has misidentified.

On the first point, Moore is overcome by his mean-spiritedness. He says that when Sidgwick calls upon the Deity to insure that what gives pleasure to others also gives pleasure to oneself, "he overlooks the fact that even this exercise of Divine Omnipotence would leave in Ethics a contradiction, in comparison with which his difficulty is a trifle – a contradiction, which would reduce all Ethics to mere nonsense, and before which the Divine Omnipotence must be powerless to all eternity."[1] Moore is not here criticizing Sidgwick for failing to deal adequately with the problem Sidgwick thinks *he* has identified, but for failing to deal with the real problem *Moore* has identified. The use of "overlooks" is particularly

---

[1] *Principia*, p. 103.

vitriolic and inappropriate. Recalling for the reader the paradox of ethics and indulging in a bit of vitriol ourselves, if his scolding of Sidgwick for "overlooking" something is well taken, then his own argument against egoism cannot have been all that pioneering.

This is not to say that we should not ourselves be troubled by Sidgwick's "solution." Although his own tone suggests that he is perfectly capable of looking at the world with a cold eye, many who try to "change the facts" to make self-interest and duty coterminous simply cannot accept the fact that people are often harmed by their goodness and rewarded by their badness: we should not believe in God simply to brush a harsh fact under the rug. Consider how Sidgwick's proposal looks to one who, after considering the conflict fully, comes to accept one or the other of these conflicting principles. First, take the attitude of one who accepts the principle of Rational Benevolence. She thinks that Sidgwick loses sight of what is most moving about people – that they have the capacity to and often do sacrifice themselves for others. She finds that in his fear of self-sacrifice, Sidgwick embraces the morality of a pinch-penny accountant. Meanwhile, the egoist admires those with the courage to put themselves above others. Their principled indifference is hard-won. It is an *achievement* to see through the herd morality of the Sunday school teachers and go out and get for oneself. (The universal egoist may well share Medlin's disgust with the individual egoist.) In the eyes of these antagonists, Sidgwick's solution is most hollow, as it deprives human beings of the issue in life upon which they can take their deepest stand, or if that is too existential and antiintellectual a way of putting it, as it removes from life that fact about which their disagreement can be most profound. But Moore too threatens to take that away from us.

The rest of Moore's response to Sidgwick is confusing and unconvincing. By his own lights, he is right to consider it a "mere fact" and not a contradiction "that our own greatest happiness and that of all do not seem always attainable by the same means."[2] But he then grants a great deal more to Sidgwick than he should. He says, "This fact [that one's own greatest happiness and the happiness of all are not always attainable by the same means], if Happiness were the sole good, would indeed be of some importance; and, on any view, similar facts are of importance."[3] This signals a recognition that *if* good could be parceled out, there *would* be a conflict between duty and self-interest. It also seems to grant that the thought that good can be parceled out is reasonable on the supposition that happiness is the sole good. His argument seems to be this: If happiness were the sole good then since it can be parceled out, so too could good. If good could be parceled out, there would then be a conflict between bringing good to oneself and bringing it to the whole world. This

<hr/>

² Ibid.   ³ Ibid., pp. 103–4.

interpretation of Moore's claim is consistent with his earlier criticism of Sidgwick for failing to note that ordinary ethical thought does not identify 'my own interest' with 'my own pleasure'. Moore claimed there that Sidgwick's failure to note this was due to his confusion about the notion 'my own good'. The notion 'my own interest' seems less easily separable when its meaning contains "my own advancement, my own reputation, the getting of a better income, etc., etc," but not my pleasure or happiness. He had brought the matter up there because he thinks that if Sidgwick had realized that 'my own interest' is not (so easily) separable, he would have come to realize that 'my own good' is also not separable.

But Moore just seems to be inconsistent with his own deepest principles when he says that this fact about the relation between one's own happiness and the happiness of others would be important if happiness were the sole good. Even if happiness were the only thing to *have* the property of being good, it would remain that happiness and good are different properties. The logical point that there is no sense in the notion 'my own good', depending as it does *solely* on the indivisible property good, would remain completely unaffected by the fact that happiness happened to be the only thing to have that property. By Moore's argument, the goodness of a thing would then lie in its being an instance of *happiness,* not in its being an instance of *my* happiness. 'My own good' would cease to be an incoherent notion only if good and happiness were *identical.* But to accept this identity is, of course, to commit the naturalistic fallacy. In his confusion, then, Moore commits the very same fallacy as the "characteristic fallacy of Empiricism" he scolds Sidgwick for committing. Just as the empiricist thinks that a change in facts could make a contradiction disappear, so too does Moore. But if Moore's argument against egoism is well taken, changing the facts to make happiness the only good thing leaves the contradiction of egoism completely untouched.

Moore goes further astray when he says that on any view, "similar facts" are of importance. He does not give any example of such facts, but seems to be suggesting that on any view, there are facts suggesting that good is divisible, that it is something different people can have more or less of. But if this is what he means, he had no prior right to consider it to be a major matter that Sidgwick misidentifies one's interest with one's pleasure. He is now saying that Sidgwick could reasonably have been tempted to embrace egoism on *any* ethical view he held.

Moore does grant that we *feel* there to be a conflict between duty and self-interest. No matter how badly he smudged it, Sidgwick had put his finger on a crucial point. He tries to identify "the one important fact" Sidgwick was after but did not capture. That fact is:

that in this world the quantity of good which is attainable is ridiculously small compared to that which is imaginable. That I cannot get the most possible pleasure for myself, if I produce the most possible pleasure on the whole, is no more *the* profoundest problem of Ethics, than that in any case I cannot get as much pleasure altogether as would be desirable.[4]

The first thing to note about this reply is that no matter how much more goodness we imagine the world as having, as he had previously recognized, it will still be "ridiculously small" compared to other larger amounts we can imagine it as having.[5] The fact Moore has pointed out is simply one of mathematics and lacks the poignancy of the fact that so troubles us. A thought experiment similar to the one employed by Moore in his Beautiful World Argument shows the inadequacy of his characterization of the problem. We can imagine that the universe contains worlds of great beauty and hence great goodness. (Such a thought is not at all fanciful to an astronomer lost in the beauty of the universe's starry reaches.) This makes the world's value seem less "ridiculously small" without at all easing our problem. This "faraway" goodness does nothing to allay the fact that *here* some people get a great deal of good and others get too little. Bringing the point closer to home, consider that innumerable people are creating works of great beauty on earth. We will still remain troubled for as long as some people are getting good and others getting bad. It is not then just the amount of the world's goodness that troubles us, but its *distribution*. Meanwhile, in a world without much good, the egoist who has many good things will remain untroubled by its overall scarcity.

Moore seems to think that if there were more good in the world, we would no longer have to compete for it. There would then be enough for everyone to get as much as she needed. But this, of course, is not a thought he can really endorse. Depending as it does on the thought that good is something different people can have or lack, it is senseless on Moore's view, no matter how much or how little of it the world contains. Thus his substitute thought must fail to pinpoint where the real worry lies. To see to what lengths Moore will go to glide over the facts of competition and maldistribution, consider his next sentence: "It only states that, if we get as much good as possible in one place, we may get less on the whole, because the quantity of attainable good is limited."[6] First, we note that good is not the sort of property that Moore can really allow to be in a place. The thought that good can be in a place is as contradictory as the thought that people can have it. Even if we could give some sense to the notion of good being in a place, it is not its place we worry about, but the fact that not everyone can be "at" that place.

We hope we shall not be accused of cruelty to a dying horse if we point out that the last sentence of Moore's discussion is also suspect: "To say that I have to choose between my own good and that of *all* is a false an-

[4] Ibid., p. 104.   [5] *Elements of Ethics*, p. 186.   [6] *Principia*, p. 104.

tithesis: the only rational question is how to choose between my own good and that of *others*, and the principle on which this must be answered is exactly the same as that on which I must choose to give pleasure to this person or to that." Given his argument against egoism, the reason that this is a false antithesis must be that the notions 'my good' and 'the good of all' make no sense: *There is just indivisible good.* But this is not what he says here. He suggests by his use of italics that the falsity of the antithesis has rather to do with the fact that it is set up between oneself and all rather than oneself and others. But since 'the good of others' also makes no sense, that antithesis is false on the very same grounds.

If these antitheses were to be real, that is, if there were to be a way of making a point about a conflict of interests that does not fall prey to a contradiction, the more important one would be the one that sets oneself against all rather than against others. Duty does not require of one that he not consider the consequences of his actions on himself, but that he not consider only those consequences. Thus one who dutifully wonders what to do considers himself to be one among *all* of those who will be affected by his action. Perhaps what Moore is not quite clearly asking is that each person pretend for a moment not to be affected by his actions in order to avoid the temptation of special pleading. That this is the weight he is asking his distinction to carry is suggested by the last independent clause of the sentence: "the principle on which this must be answered is exactly the same as that on which I must choose to give pleasure to this person or to that." He is suggesting that upon the removal of oneself from the picture, it is easier to see that good alone provides the reason for deciding what to do. But removing oneself in this way need not remove the temptation for special pleading for the egoist. He can argue that it is reasonable for him to weigh the scales in favor of the people he *likes* – egoists do leave wills. If he is asked to imagine himself as so far removed from the world as never to have been or be in it *at all*, the egoist will say that he then has no reason to choose according to any principle. Perhaps he will choose in accord with good or perhaps he will favor those with brown eyes or blue, or perhaps those with freckles. Most likely, he will refuse to choose, explaining that it is idle to consider choosing for a world in which one has never existed nor ever will exist.

The general problem with Moore's discussion of Sidgwick is that his own argument against egoism makes his strategy misconceived. He grants that a certain line of thought has a psychological hold over us, even though it ultimately turns out to be illogical. But his substitute line of thought just does not capture what we worry about, nor could any that fails to make distribution and competition fundamental matters. He has a great deal more work to do, both excavational and therapeutic, if he is to expose the deeper philosophical mistakes that *seem* to give sense to the contradictory notions behind egoism. Until he does that work, we

are unlikely to escape the grip of thinking that Sidgwick is on to something.

Perhaps we can best encapsulate Moore's difficulty by noting that at the
very beginning of his argument, he states that the confusion of the notion 'my own good' "has, perhaps been more clearly perceived by Plato
than any other moralist."[7] Despite his scathing comments about other
philosophers and his claim that not until *Sidgwick* did any philosopher
clearly recognize the naturalistic fallacy,[8] Moore avoids criticizing Plato
anywhere in *Principia*. And is there any philosopher to whom he is closer?
Is there anyone else who emphasizes so strongly that Good is part of "the
furniture of the world." But the reference to Plato as offering an antidote
to the confusion regarding the perceived conflict between Good and Self-
Good is puzzling. In the *Republic*, Plato takes as his charge showing that
justice is in the interest of the just person, that justice is good *for him*. So
Plato's most famous work seems to rest on the very confusion he was supposed to have seen so clearly.[9]

No doubt leavening this fact is the thought running throughout the
Republic, culminating in the comparison of The Good to the sun, that the
person who becomes absorbed by The Good loses that narrow sense of
self that wears so heavily on the unenlightened. But still, Plato considers
the losing of that sense of self to be good *for* the one who loses it. In the
third proof in Book IX of the superiority of justice to injustice, where he
suggests that not even pleasure can be measured or understood in purely
interior, "private" terms, Plato continues to maintain that the superior interior life of the just person is a benefit *to* that person. Remember also
that he insists that philosophers must *sacrifice* by taking their turn and
reentering the cave. At no point in the *Republic* then does Plato express
the thought that for the philosopher, the thought of good things happening to one becomes completely chimerical. Nowhere is a concern for
one's own good shown to be *contradictory*. It appears then that Moore is
all alone in having seen with complete clarity the confusion lying behind
egoism. Given this fact, one does not know whether to be dismayed by the
superior air he takes toward all the rest of us or to be dazzled by his innocent boldness in thinking that he could dispel such a deep illusion in
such a small number of pages.

Moore's Greatest Revolution

As even Hume recognized, even if it is without philosophical depth, we
all do still have a very strong sense of self. So strong is this sense of self

---

[7] Ibid., p. 98.   [8] Ibid., p. 17.

[9] In this regard, see H. A. Prichard's "Does Moral Philosophy Rest on a Mistake?," in *Moral
Obligation* (Oxford: Oxford University Press, 1968), p. 2, for his criticism of Plato for attempting to justify morality by an appeal to self-interest.

that we might call it inalienable. Intrinsic to it is our feeling that we are each self-contained and separate from our fellows. With this sense of the separateness of self comes "selfishness" in all its variegated forms. Although this is not to justify selfishness or egoism, its philosophical spokesman, it is to say that they are attitudes or points of view that can be taken without contradiction. Let us recall Sidgwick's observation that a sense of self grounds the egoist's claim that rationality does not require one to be concerned about others. Although he does not fully realize it, in arguing against the rationality of "I" having a special concern for myself, Moore attacks this sense of self. Upon the success of this attack, he must change the explications of many notions crucial to human life. By making partiality rest upon a confusion, he does not allow for it to be appealing or even plausible to one who is fully clearheaded. He has it that anyone with a correct understanding of the matter will recognize impartiality to have no cost to oneself. With no sense attaching to the notion of good accruing to one person rather than another, a fully rational person realizes that she does not ever sacrifice anything by bringing about the greatest good.

Let us start with the point, recognized by Moore in "The Subject Matter of Psychology," that, whatever its correct philosophical explication happens to be, there is some sense in which pleasures, pains, and other feelings are "one's own." Although we all feel pleasure and pain, each of us feels only a very tiny subset of the world's total. These are the pleasures and pains in which our most immediate perceptions of good and bad are rooted. It is also through them that the connection between the perception of value and the will is made. At least originally, without the words to state it, we consider good and pursue that which gives us pleasure and consider bad and avoid that which gives us pain. However subtle the properties good and bad happen to be, however abstract and intellectual a way of cognizing them we eventually come to have, the primal connection between our perception of these properties and our own pleasures and pains is never completely severed. We never turn into, nor ought to turn into, affectless value-calculating machines.

The original connection of the perception of value to pleasure and pain contributes to our self-regard. This is not originally a matter of "selfishness," even if it provides the basis for the theory of egoism; our self-regard preceu:\~ our having any articulate sense of self. It is a brute fact that because we feel our own pleasures and pains, we are moved by them immediately, whether in conjunction with a perception of good and bad or not. The good and bad that arises from our own inner life is by necessity more intimately connected to us than the rest of good and bad. The fact that we take our own feelings so seriously is as brute as the fact that we have them; as they are a part of us, we cannot help but be moved by them. So our tendency toward self-partiality, stemming from the way we are constituted and not from faulty logic, does not make us irrational. Because it is rooted in our nature, argument and insight cannot wash it away.

One might reply for Moore that he does not consider this original *unreflective* partiality to be irrational. We become irrational only when, after becoming more self-conscious and more deeply aware of good, we philosophically defend our partiality and hold on to it in the face of our awareness that good ranges far beyond the small concerns of self. What is irrational is to assume an impersonal point of view in order to defend what is ineluctably personal. But even if Moore grants that our original unreflective behavior is *arational*, it still follows on his view that we must change if we are to become *rational*. This is enough to make his theory troubling. As we become more reflective about good, we also develop a more reflective and sophisticated sense of self. With this sense of self and a subtler conception of what constitutes its well-being, we stand up to the larger sense of good and continue to see ourselves as receptacles of value. It thus continues to make sense to suppose that each person's life can go better or worse *for him or her.* Even if we grant that morality requires us to sacrifice our own concerns for the sake of the greater good, it follows from its being a sacrifice that we clearly recognize our not doing so to be a real option. So we are with Sidgwick at least to the extent that we find two opposing ethical theories to make sense, even if one of them turns out to be wrong.

One may say for Moore that this is just to point out that the head fails to persuade the heart, that the hold of an incoherent moral conception is very strong. But it is more plausible to say that if the head cannot change the heart, there is something wrong with its argument. Even if one cannot pinpoint the flaw in the argument, if he remains unable to live in accord with it, he does not really find it compelling after all. This is analogous to what Moore says concerning the naturalistic fallacy and in his later defenses of our commonsense knowledge of physical objects. No argument, however powerful it originally seems to be, can stand up to the facts that we know good to be unique and know there to be physical objects. Similarly, we know that value does connect in some way to individuals.

One might find that in separating good from the original source of its cognition in what is "one's own," Moore is simply fighting on one more front the tendencies toward idealism and monism. Even if the perception of value is clothed originally in pleasure and pain and keeps a personal flavor throughout, we must, as we do with all other notions of philosophical interest, clearly distinguish value from everything it is not. As Moore tells us many times, we must not commit the naturalistic fallacy. But as the poet tells us, we must be careful not to murder what we dissect. If we lose sight of the personal flavor of good and bad, we are left with a distorted picture of how we actually think about ourselves and others.

Among other problems, we fail to capture what makes becoming impartial such a difficult achievement. By the terms of Moore's argument, impartiality is no more than a matter of thinking clearly and performing the proper logical operations upon a concept. This is despite his admission that most of us are utterly incapable of complete impartiality, that we are moved more by the instances of good and bad affecting us than by those affecting others.[10] That admission should have provided him with the clue that something more than an intellectual cramp explains egoism's appeal.

In claiming that no sense attaches to the notion of 'my good', Moore is forced to give unsatisfactory accounts of the notions of benefit and well-being, as well as of such negative notions as suffering and harm. The point is put more dramatically in the negative. It would seem that the most plausible account of suffering includes the fact that something bad happens to the one who suffers. But because he rejects the notion of good and bad being had by anyone, Moore cannot say this. Although he would agree that something bad happens, he must say that the badness redounds no more to the one who suffers than to anyone else. This claim sounds draconian and preposterous, even insane, on its face. It makes it wrong to say that a person just struck by a car, lying in a pool of blood and moaning in agony, has had something bad happen *to him*. Nor can we say that a mother who loses her child suffers because of *her* loss. But if there is no sense in which good or bad can be had by anyone, this extreme conclusion forces itself on us.

It seems that Moore must say something like this: Even though the bad of the suffering is no more one's own than anyone else's, one cannot help but have her attention absorbed by what she mistakenly comes to consider her own. This suggests that Moore is committed to saying that our views about the "suffering" one undergoes or the state of "well-being" one achieves are based on an illusion brought about by attention too narrowly focused. With a properly wide philosophical understanding of good and bad, we see that that which is really good or bad is either everyone's or no one's. But if the badness of suffering is everyone's, then if we are rational we must all be equally moved by its different instances. If it is no one's, we must be equally *un*moved by them. We deny the facts of suffering on either alternative. It is part of the very concept of suffering that it is personal, that it especially attaches to one or some but not others. If we do not see what is special for the one who suffers, we do not see the *suffering*. Without an allowance for *some* kind of "selfishness," Moore's account becomes not just inhumane, but incoherent.

A plausible psychology must recognize that if we did not each have our own brute concerns, there could be no possibility of our extending sym-

[10] Ibid., pp. 166–7.

pathy to others. To extend sympathy to someone is to show concern for his well-being – and not just as this contributes to overall good. A similar recognition of brute personal concern is necessary for a proper understanding of the great good of friendship. Analyses are incomplete that account for a person's special concern for her friend solely in terms of its being a means to the greatest good. On such accounts, the special concern is justified on the grounds that it is wiser for each of us to concentrate on certain goods that, for whatever reasons, are easier than others for us to bring about. Having accepted such an account, we may then resolve in reflective moments to cultivate friendships because of the great amount of good they enable us to bring into the world. But even if our long-standing motive is then just to bring about the most good overall, we must at times lose sight of that justification for friendship and concern ourselves with our *friends* or else remain bereft of them.

Moore does not explicitly consider suffering, but he does employ the notion of sacrifice. He tells us in Section 102 in the chapter "Ethics in Relation to Conduct" that not only does the notion of sacrifice make sense, but that sacrifice is *required*. He spells out the notion of sacrifice in terms of what is in one's interest. Because of his earlier argument against egoism, he must be a very adept juggler in his discussion of sacrifice and interest. He must somehow connect the notion of one's interest to good because without such a connection, the notion of interest is irrelevant to ethics and indeed, action. But he must do this in a way that does not allow the egoist to reargue her case. To see how difficult his task will be, we note that at the beginning of his argument against egoism he writes, "The conception which is, perhaps, most closely associated with Egoism is that denoted by the words 'my own interest.'"[11] Clearly, if this association cannot be severed, his later discussion must fail.

He starts the later discussion by saying:

When we ask the question, 'Is this really to my interest?' we appear to be asking exclusively whether its *effects upon me* are the best possible; and it may well happen that what will affect me in the manner, which is really the best possible, will not produce the best possible results on the whole. Accordingly, *my true interest* may be different from the course which is really expedient and dutiful.

Immediately, this seems to give the egoist a chance to make his case. Even if he had been wrong to put his point originally in terms of a good he could have, he will happily put it in terms of a good that affects him. To forestall this response by the egoist, Moore rehearses his earlier argument:

To assert that an action is 'to my interest,' is, indeed, as was pointed out . . . to assert that its effects are really good. 'My own good' only denotes some event affecting me, which is good absolutely and objectively; it is the thing, and not its

[11] *Principia*, p. 97.

goodness, which is *mine;* everything must be either 'a part of universal good' or else not good at all; there is no third alternative conception 'good for me.'

This shows that Moore recognizes the temptation to see the notions 'my interest' and 'my good' as the same. But he claims that there is a different way of understanding 'my interest' that keeps it from falling prey to his original argument. He writes, "But 'my interest,' though it must be something truly good, is only one among possible good effects; and hence, by effecting it, though we shall be doing *some* good, we may be doing less good on the whole, than if we had acted otherwise." Only after this remark does he go on to speak of sacrifice, saying that:

Self-sacrifice may be a real duty; just as the sacrifice of any single good, whether affecting ourselves or others, may be necessary in order to obtain a better total result. Hence the fact that an action is really to my interest, can never be a sufficient reason for doing it: by shewing that it is not a means to the best possible, we do not shew that it is not to my interest, as we do shew that it is not expedient.

Moore takes these remarks to contain the insight upon which adequate notions of interest and sacrifice can be built, that enable him to spell out the way in which one's own interest can be good and yet in conflict with the greatest overall good. The challenge is to get clearer on this unreflective notion of interest in order to see whether it withstands philosophical scrutiny. Moore does not take great pains to demarcate the distinction with complete clarity, but it seems that it stems only from a conflict in points of view. When I think of "my own" interest, I am thinking of a part of the world that consists *just* of me and the effects of things upon me. This part of the world holds the good that, epistemically speaking, is closest to me. When I think about a good extending beyond my interest, I think about the larger world that contains more than me and the things affecting me. Since many of the items in the larger world are far from me, I do not know them easily. The good or bad of them does not *seem* to affect me and thus is of less concern to me. Even though the good of the smaller world is less than the good of the larger world, everything in it, including the good of it, seems to flow toward me. Because the good of that world is in this sense greater *for me,* it is in my interest to bring this world about.

Moore must be careful in using this notion of interest. Certain wholes of which a person is a part would by his lights be good even though they seem not to be in that person's interest. For instance, Moore finds the sorrowful and sympathetic awareness of another's plight to be an intrinsic good.[12] Obviously, we are very reluctant to say that this state is in the interest of the sorrowful person. But note that the good of this state depends on what it is about. Following the way of distinguishing between different wholes containing belief that was explored in Chapter 2, we can

[12] Ibid., p. 217.

specify a smaller whole that has nothing to do with what the state is about
that connects more intimately to the person – *just* the sorrowful state. *Qua*
sorrowful state, that smaller thing is bad and not in the person's interest.
Conversely, the pleasure one feels in another's pain is bad, but *qua* pleasure it is good, and thus can be considered to be in one's interest. For the
sake of our discussion, we shall assume that there is always some intrinsically good or intrinsically bad whole, however tiny, that can be found to
be in accord with our intuitions about whether something is in a person's
interest or not.[13]

Spelling out the notion 'my interest' in this manner seems to provide
the most plausible sense according to which the good of things can be
mine, or alternatively, a sense according to which the things comprising
this smaller world affect me to the exclusion of other things. With myself
as the only person in this world, the good is not "mine" in any illicit metaphysical sense, but only in the sense that there is no one else affected by
it. This also insures that the conflict between the smaller and greater
good does not have any deep metaphysical foundation. There is no conflict in *good* as it is exemplified in the two different worlds (because the
universal good cannot be "in conflict with itself") but conflict only in that
the two worlds cannot both be the *entire* world. Immediately, it seems that
from the point of view Moore has explicated, I can concern myself with
the smaller good and remain rational. Although I am irrational if I try to
concern myself with one good to the exclusion of other goods, in the
world I envisage, there is no other good I exclude. So this one good I envisage is no different to me than any other. I thus think exclusively of the
good that redounds to me without violating any canon of rationality by
thinking of it in opposition to other goods.

But however ingenious this conception of 'my interest' may initially appear to be, it finally falls apart. When I consider the larger world in which
I *actually* exist, I cannot distinguish sharply enough between those things
that have an effect upon me and those that do not. The crucial difference
between the smaller whole whose good seems to have a greater effect
upon me and the larger whole whose good does not seem to have so
strong an effect is that I know more readily about the smaller one and its
effects. But if I am a rational agent, the good of *all* things, whether I know
of them or not, is of concern to me – all things affect me *qua* rational
moral agent. Finally then, there can be no real clash between my own interest and overall good on this conception. As a rational agent, I see that
I do not lose anything at all if I "give up" what from a *mistaken* perspective
appears to be my interest. Because I cannot as a rational agent stand in
some personal and philosophically respectable relation to the limited

[13] We do not imply that there will be unanimous agreement on what whole is relevant for
determining this in any particular situation.

good of the first world in which I do not also stand to the greater good of the larger world, the smaller good does not hold any special benefit for me. This is just to say that the good in that smaller world must obey the dictum Moore cites in his argument against egoism. The good is still not my own in any sense that from a rational perspective makes it more worth pursuing than other goods. If we wish to use the notion of benefit at all, we must say that the larger world, since it contains more good, is actually more beneficial to me. The benefit of something can be very difficult to know, as it can be difficult to observe. But a benefit is *good* – not good *for me* – whether I see it or not.

It is only if the good I bring about in the smaller world were the most good I could bring about that it would be in "my interest." But this is not the world I actually find myself in; the smaller whole is *contained* by the larger one. This fact gets finessed in the original description of the two conflicting points of view. The smaller world is, as it were, set off to the side of the larger one. Setting it aside, I momentarily forget or pretend that if I choose to bring that limited good about, I do not also bring about the rest of what I bring about outside of it. But, of course, I cannot keep this pretense up. Once I give it up, I must strive as a rational agent to do what brings about the most good. By doing this, I do what benefits me, what is in "my interest." When it comes to good, the effects of all things upon me are relevant in direct proportion to the amount of good they bring to the *world*. We must refuse then to accept in any form whatsoever the notion of people having separate interests. What is in the interest of everyone is the very same – the creation of as much good as possible.

To see more clearly that this is what Moore is committed to, let us return to his claim that "To assert that an action is 'to my interest' is . . . to assert that its effects are really good." He wishes this to be the assertion of the principle that it is a necessary condition of a thing's being in my interest that it be good. Stating *only* a necessary condition, it allows something besides a thing's goodness – for Moore, its "proximity" to me – to contribute to a thing's being in my interest. But if something besides its goodness contributes to a thing's being in my interest, it would seem that if it obtains to a great enough degree, something could be in my interest even when its overall effects were *bad*. The small change from the least good to the least bad should not have such epochal consequences as to make in my interest a whole containing a good for me and the least good overall, but not in my interest another whole containing a much greater good for me and the least bad overall. So Moore's claim contains the seeds of the stronger principle that a thing is in my interest in *direct proportion* to its overall goodness.

That nothing but its goodness contributes to a thing's being in my interest is also supported by the claim, "hence the fact that an action is really to my interest, can never be a sufficient reason for doing it. . . ."[14] If there were other factors that contributed to a thing's being in my interest, they should, if found in great enough degree, provide *me* with a sufficient reason for performing an action even when that action did not bring about the greatest good. If they cannot, in no matter how great a degree they are found, weigh more heavily than the tiniest amount of overall good in giving me a reason to act, then they do not form any part of my reason for acting. Something's being in my interest provides me with only a *provisional reason* for acting. To say that it is in my interest to perform a certain action is, whether I fully realize it or not, only to say that *so far as I have been able to determine,* the action brings about the most *overall* good. Because the effects of the action upon me are the easiest to see, they are the ones I note most readily. True, I often fail to examine the further effects of an action after I determine it to be in my interest, but this does not mark a difference of philosophical significance. So 'my interest' really has nothing to do with the effects of the action upon *me* – has nothing to do with *my* interest.

At the end of the section, Moore comes close to recognizing the emptiness of his own notion of interest. He writes:

And the chief distinction conveyed by the distinct words 'duty' and 'interest' seems to be not this source of possible conflict, but the same which is conveyed by the contrast between 'duty' and 'expediency.' By 'interested' actions are *mainly* meant those which, whether a means to the best possible or not, are such as have their most obvious effects on the agent; which he generally has no temptation to omit; and with regard to which we feel no moral sentiment. That is to say, the distinction is not primarily ethical. Here too 'duties' are not, in general, more useful or obligatory than interested actions; they are only actions which it is more useful to praise.

Moore tells us here that two different things can be meant by the distinction between duty and interest, the one he has just finished explaining and the one he now mentions. He also calls the distinction he now mentions the "chief one." This is quite odd. Why discuss at length the distinction that is not responsible for the more important conflict and only mention in passing the one that is? But actually, there are not two sources of conflict, but one. The distinction he describes in passing, which "is not primarily ethical," that is, which does not have to do with the ontological explication of good, is the same one he has been describing all along. When I try to spell out 'my interest' in terms of a thing's effects on me, I am actually spelling it out in terms of the obviousness of its effects on me. But the obviousness of effects, obviously enough, is not sufficient to make for a distinction that carries ontological weight, even if, as does the egoist, I think it does. It merely has epistemological and, from that, psychological weight.

[14] *Principia*, p. 171.

In November of 1900, Moore read his final original paper to the Apostles, entitled, "Is It a Duty to Hate?" In that paper he wrote:

For good is not a private thing, like pleasure and pain, of which you can say, "So much belongs to each man". . . . Thus it may quite well happen that to put your enemy to the most excruciating tortures, ending in death, even though he is perfectly innocent, and without any chance of a future life, may be to do him the greatest possible good.[15]

Although he attempts to avoid this appalling conclusion in *Principia,* he is finally unable to do so.

To finish, we speculate about what motivates Moore's attempt to give sense to the notion 'my interest'. Obviously, it is due to his recognition that for each one of us, some goods carry more weight than other equal or greater goods. Moore tries to make this fugitive thought respectable – but not too respectable. If he had seen all the ramifications of his argument against egoism, he would have given up the attempt. This leads us to pose a dilemma for Moore. Either the notion 'my interest' makes sense or it does not. If it does make sense, then his argument against egoism fails. But if it does not make sense, he is a much greater radical than he ever acknowledges in *Principia.* Far from returning us to common sense, he stands on its head one of its most fundamental presuppositions – that as a brute matter of fact, different people really *do* have different interests.

[15] Levy, *Moore and the Cambridge Apostles,* pp. 220–1.

8

Moore's Practical and Political Philosophy

Introduction

In this chapter, we consider Moore's views on practical and political philosophy, which he presents in *Principia*'s fifth chapter, "Ethics in Relation to Conduct." Our focus will be on his discussion of the proper attitude to take toward the vast array of moral and social rules we confront as we make our decisions about what we ought to do. As we have elsewhere, we will find his thought to manifest both conservative and revolutionary impulses, with some of the things he says bespeaking a great deal of respect for rules and others sounding as though he considers most of them to be quite unimportant to morality and perhaps even an impediment to it.

To resolve this tension, we must explore the distinctions he makes between three broad, rather vaguely delineated classes of rules: 1) Rules found in all societies that must be widely followed if there is to be the civilized life necessary for there being much or anything at all of value. 2) Rules in place in various societies that are not absolutely necessary for there being civilized life. 3) Rules not in place in a society that some philosopher or philosophically minded reformer wishes to impose on it or perhaps even on *all* societies. It is uncontroversial that Moore is conservative with respect to the first and the third of these classes of rules. He argues that we ought always to obey the necessary rules and he opposes attempts by philosophers to persuade us to impose new rules on ourselves. His argument for universal compliance with the first class of rules can be seen to stem from his defense of common sense as a primary source of ethical insight. The plain person understands perfectly well that whatever slight exceptions or small refinements we allow, the fundamental importance of such a rule as "Thou shalt do no murder" makes it applicable to *everyone*. His rejection of the innovative, finely honed rules of philosophers is born of the same suspicion toward moral monism as he displays in his rejection of the naturalistic fallacy. Human nature, especially as it undergoes different patterns of acculturation, is just too varied for the one-size-fits-all conception of morality that philosophers appeal to in proposing their new rules.

There is, however, controversy over Moore's attitude toward the second class of rules. Is it more like his attitude toward the rules of the first or the third class? This issue has recently been explored by Tom Regan in his book *Bloomsbury's Prophet*. Regan wishes to supplant what has been the received view, given early expression by Bertrand Russell in a letter to Moore upon publication of *Principia*. According to this view, Moore is, to use Regan's word, an "insipid" conservative completely in thrall even to those of society's rules that are not necessary for the maintenance of civilization.[1] But according to Regan, a reading that pays sufficient attention to the "details and subtlety" of Moore's argument, which follows it in all its "rigor, precision, and analytical power," reveals him to be not a hidebound conformist to "the moral status quo," but something akin to a 1960s radical.[2] According to Regan, Moore wishes to protect the individual from the "moral imperialism" of rule makers.[3] His "mission is to liberate his readers from those chains of lies by which both preachers and would-be scientific moralists would keep them in bondage"; he aims to enable them to achieve "a liberation of the self from the habitual drudgery of conventional morality, heavy with the burdens of conforming to a proliferation of rules of duty. . . ."[4] Regan maintains that Moore holds the number of rules in the first class to be very small. Further, Moore applies to the second class of rules the argument that the received view considers to apply only to the third class. He thus concludes that Moore's view is that we "almost always must decide what we ought to do independently of what moral rules prescribe."[5]

Pending a more detailed and theoretically reflective discussion than Moore provides in *Principia* of the exact nature of common sense, one might plausibly argue that either the role of attacker or defender of such rules is in accord with it. One might argue from common sense in opposition to nonuniversal, or nonnecessary, rules that our plain ability to detect instances of good and bad and act upon them is hindered if we allow our thinking to get tangled up in a vast array of rules. But another might reply that it is plain that a well-functioning society requires a great many rules to help people get about in their interactions with each other. Common sense thus puts the onus on those who wish us to ignore or overthrow those rules. Moore seems to hold the second of these opinions about what the view of common sense is, as he speaks of both the necessary and the nonnecessary rules as being within the province of commonsense ethics.[6] So if Regan's interpretation is correct then by his own lights, Moore's defense of common sense in *Principia* is diminished another little bit.

We disagree with Regan's interpretation and shall use it as a foil for our own. But we concede that any answer to the question of Moore's position on rules of this type must be tentative. His discussion is very sketchy and he does not always provide much guidance on how to flesh out his sketch.

---

[1] *Bloomsbury's Prophet*, p. 221.   [2] Ibid., pp. 228, 234, 236.   [3] Ibid., p. 227.
[4] Ibid., pp. 223, 240.   [5] Ibid., p. 259.   [6] *Principia*, p. 158.

This sketchiness is combined with the rhetorical overkill that mars *Principia* in other places. Certain of his pronouncements lead one to think that he is going to blow down the walls of Jericho, until he mutes his trumpet with the qualifications that make his views both less dramatic and more respectful of society's established ways. Regan often fails to note Moore's qualifications and so gives some of his stronger sounding pronouncements more weight than they deserve. By giving a more nuanced account of the psychology of rule following than Regan's articulation of the dichotomy between conservative and liberator would suggest, Moore actually closes much of the gap that Regan supposes to lie between following a rule and following individual inclination. He thus goes no little distance toward synthesizing views that appear originally to be in dramatic opposition. Still, after acknowledging the nuances, Moore remains recognizably conservative. The best interpretation sees him as suggesting that although by definition, no rules of the second class are absolutely necessary for the maintenance of society, many of them play an important role in preserving one member of a (likely open-ended) class of social arrangements or practices, one of which must be instantiated if there is to be much at all of value in a society. There can thus be great presumption in favor of obeying such a rule, with the strength of the presumption depending on how important a role the rule plays in preserving such an arrangement or practice.

Necessary Rules

Given the view that he argues for twice, that 'ought' means productive of the most good, one might expect Moore to be deeply skeptical about the possibility of our ever coming to know what we ought to do.[7] Since the most innocent of actions might turn out some day to have disastrous consequences, not only can we never know of any possible action that it is the one having the best consequences, we can never even know that it is not the one having the worst. But Moore is no skeptic. He says that we can first conclude that, in general, we ought to obey certain rules. Although at first sight this conclusion appears to be rather weak, as it does not seem to enable us to know on which particular occasions we ought to obey them, he argues that it actually leads to the strongest possible conclusion – that we ought *always* to obey these rules.

His statement of this position is found in Section 95, where he takes the rule prohibiting murder as his example of a rule found in all societies. Although his argument appears germane only to this particular rule, he says that a similar argument can be constructed for all the necessary rules. He begins with the striking claim that the rule against murder is useful even

---

[7] For Moore's arguments, see *Principia*, pp. 24–7, 147–8.

though the contention of the pessimist that human life is bad has not been proven wrong. If human life is bad, ought we not commit murders in order to contribute to humanity's demise? He responds that since most peoples' desire for life is too strong for them to acquiesce in the actions required by such a project of extermination, the actions committed in its furtherance would only serve to increase life's misery. So in general, acts of murder are bad. From this it follows that there is always a presumption in favor of obeying the rule prohibiting murder. Considerations must be brought forward to override this presumption in any particular case. The uncertainty of our knowledge of both the effects of our actions and their value makes it highly unlikely that we shall ever be able to do this.

Two further general facts appear to Moore to clinch the argument that we ought never to break any of the necessary rules. First, our concluding in a particular case that we ought to break one of them is likely to be the result of bias in our own favor. Second, the example we set by breaking such a rule when there is justification for doing so will be overly encouraging of ourselves and others to break it when there is not justification. He concludes his discussion thus:

It seems, then, that with regard to any rule which is *generally* useful, we may observe that it ought *always* to be observed, not on the ground that in *every* particular case it will be useful, but on the ground that in *any* particular case the probability of its being so is greater than that of our being likely to decide rightly that we have before us an instance of its disutility. In short, though we may be sure that there are cases where the rule should be broken, we can never know which those cases are, and ought, therefore, never to break it.[8]

Note how uneasily these two sentences sit with each other. According to the most natural reading of the first, all we need to justify breaking a rule in a particular case is the knowledge that breaking it will probably bring about the most good, not a guarantee that it would, whereas the second sentence suggests that we do need such a guarantee. But however implausible we take the claim to be that we need a guarantee of better consequences before we can be justified in breaking certain rules, his accepting that claim explains his accepting what is also implausible, that we are *never*, on utilitarian grounds, justified in breaking them.

Although Moore does not say what exactly are the rules covered by his argument, he does say that "A similar defence seems possible for most of the rules, most universally enforced by legal sanctions, such as respect for property; and for most of those recognised by Common Sense, such as industry, temperance and the keeping of promises." He suggests that a rule falls under his argument if it passes two tests: 1) its general observance is good as a means in *any* known state of society, from which it follows that 2) obedience to it can be defended independently of our hav-

---

[8] Ibid., pp. 162–3.

ing correct views on the primary ethical question of what is good in itself. If these conditions are met, then whatever happens to be intrinsically good, we can be sure that we are fostering it by following those rules.

A host of questions centers around the claim that if there is to be anything of value in a society, there are certain rules its people must always follow. Consider Moore's own example of a rule that is followed by all societies, the one prohibiting murder. It is certainly true that all societies strongly prohibit many acts of homicide and that there would be little or nothing of value in a society in which homicide was rampant. But it is also true that different societies have different rules that allow for killing in different circumstances. There just does not seem to be any *one* rule concerning homicide that all societies follow, but instead a class of more or less sharply delineated rules, different ones of which different societies follow. If this is so then the claim upon which Moore rests the conclusion that we ought always to obey certain rules – that they are *necessary* for civilized life – is false. The point is even more obvious if we consider others of his "necessary" rules, for example, those enjoining respect for private property. While it is highly likely that societies that allow and encourage people to acquire and keep property have a better chance of flourishing than those that do not, there are obviously many different property rules with which a society can flourish.

Perhaps Moore wishes us to shift to a more Platonic understanding of rules in order to find the necessary ones: Different societies agree on the same rule forbidding *murder,* but disagree about which actions constitute murder and thus have different ways of implementing it. This would raise the immediate danger that the rules Moore has in mind are tautologous. If "murder" means "An act of killing which is bad, which ought not to be done," he is telling us no more than that we ought not to kill people when it is bad to do so. We then get none of the guidance such a rule is supposed to provide: When is an act of homicide murder and when is it not? Is it his view that one most effectively obeys the rule against murder by always obeying the version of it found in his own society? In support of this view, one might note that in the paragraph immediately following his discussion of this rule, he suggests that we ought to obey the "common legal rules" concerning private property. But in many cases the strategy of following the version of the rule found in one's own society would be problematic. For one, one's society may have set its standards too low (or too high). For another, it is based on a failure, which Moore's theory seems susceptible to in any case, to recognize that societies make rules with a sense of their imperfection. Rather than set them in stone, societies are more or less willing to revise their rules as they are found wanting. While it may be wise to be conservative in challenging a society on its rules, we would not wish for there to be *no* challenges to them. Finally, even if one decides that she ought to act in accord with her own society's

rules, in many difficult cases, she will have to decide what constitutes acting in accord with them. But she will not then be following her society's
rules so much as making a proposal, which the society may then either
ratify or reject, about what the rules *should be.*

At this point, one might object that to search for an overly refined understanding of Moore's view is to lose sight of the value of the crude tenac-
ity of common sense. Nitpicking too often provides us with the means of
shirking our duty. We must then be bullheaded enough to put subtleties
aside and obey the rules we *know* to be sound. Those rules are best that
encourage honesty over dishonesty, respect for property over disrespect
for it, kindness over cruelty, and so on. But granting that we appeal far
too often to subtleties to let ourselves off the moral hook, given life's
messy realities, in many cases we will have to engage in very subtle reasoning before we decide which complicated course of action is likely to
bring about the most good. Even at the most basic of levels, we will find
well-taken rules that call for conflicting courses of action: However wrong
in general it is to kill, civilizations that fail to defend themselves against
aggressors cannot survive long. Moore eventually came to accept the un-
tenability of the view that there are rules we ought always to obey. In *Ethics,*
without mentioning that he had once argued the contrary, he claims that
there are no such rules.[9]

The rather obvious problems with maintaining that there are any necessary rules raise the possibility that Moore finds it necessary in *Principia*
to tell a noble lie for the sake of morality. Perhaps he actually thinks that
there are rare occasions when even the most "necessary" of rules ought
to be broken, but that it would be dangerous to admit this even to the
readers of *Principia,* since even this small admission would lead to their
being broken too often. Although he had allowed himself in 1901 to admit to an elite audience that the belief in the intrinsic worth of virtues
and duties "is an illusion, which the preacher does well to encourage,"[10]
he thinks that the consequences of breaking the necessary rules are just
too grim to allow the illusion of their necessity to suffer *any* exposure –
even silent exposure to oneself.

Nonnecessary Rules

Given the depth of Moore's conservatism with regard to the rules he calls
necessary, one might conclude that he would have to be schizophrenic in
order to argue that there is no presumption in favor of obedience to a society's nonnecessary rules. There is certainly textual support for the view
that he argues for some presumption in favor of obedience to these rules.
Most strikingly, he says that although the utility of nonuniversal rules can-

---

[9] *Ethics,* pp. 111–12.   [10] Regan, *Bloomsbury's Prophet,* p. 162.

not be proved in exactly the same way as the utility of universal rules, they *can* get a "defense valid for many conditions of society."[11] He even thinks that *bad* rules, such as certain ones enjoining theft, can have some presumption in their favor.[12] He is maddeningly reticent about the nature of the defense of nonuniversal rules, but since he classifies rules by degree of universality (however he understands that problematic notion), it seems that the strength of the presumption in their favor is at least partly a function of their closeness to that mark. To defend obedience to a rule on the grounds of its near universality, one would argue that its near universality is a sign that the rule plays an important preservative role in the societies in which it is found. The rule is likely to concern matters lying very deep in the thoughts and desires of many or most of the people of those societies. So in the absence of evidence that it is actually detrimental, in most cases the rule ought to be obeyed. With a rule less frequently found, one argues that it still plays some preservative role in the societies having it. Because the people have gotten used to obeying the rule, there will be some social dislocation on its annulment, which makes for a smaller presumption in favor of obedience.

This argument would be strengthened by being explicitly joined to an argument in the spirit of Moore's defense of obedience to universal rules: Even though the particular rules guiding a society's behavior in a certain realm of life are not necessary, it is necessary for there to be some rules regulating behavior in that realm. To take Moore's own example, although it is "not difficult" to imagine a society raising its children effectively in the absence of a particular set of chastity rules, it is difficult to imagine a well-functioning society having *no* rules concerning what sexual relations its members, especially its parents and prospective parents, may enter into. As strong as they no doubt often are, parental bonds can still corrode in those whose sexual attention wanders. In order to defend obeying the actual rules in place in a society, one need not decide what things are intrinsically good (this will be important in contending Regan's view), but can argue instead that since a society must have some rules if it is to manifest the level of civilization necessary to bring about any of the great intrinsic goods, social inertia favors obeying the rules already in place. Because it is difficult to replace rules successfully, the presumption in favor of the actual rules remains even if we believe that things would have worked out better had different rules been put in place originally. We thus do not allow the best to be the enemy of the pretty good. This defense of nonuniversal rules would actually be the strongest that could be provided for *any* rule if there are no universal rules.

These lines of thought take very seriously the fear of special pleading that Moore expresses in his discussion of universal rules. We may, in fact,

---

[11] *Principia*, p. 158.   [12] Ibid., p. 164.

be even more susceptible to special pleading when a rule is not universal than when it is. We can tell ourselves that since the rule's nonuniversality guarantees that society will not collapse upon its falling by the wayside, it cannot "really" hurt to allow ourselves a small exception to it. In order to combat the possibility of special pleading, we add enough extra value to obeying the rule to lead to the conclusion that we ought to obey it even in some of the situations in which our best attempt at honest, impartial calculation calls for *dis*obedience. Still, since that which would be left in the wake of the demise of a nonuniversal rule would have some value, we do not conclude that we ought always to obey it.

One who confronts Tom Regan's view of Moore on rules of this type faces the same problem as one who confronts Moore's view directly. There are many passages, such as the one following, in which it is difficult to weigh the fervor against the qualifications: "Just as the Science of Morals cannot rationally justify general adoption of a *new* set of rules, so it cannot rationally defend uniform conformity to the *old* set of rules that define the conventional morality of one's society. . . . Moore's fundamental point is that in the vast percentage of cases the individual does – and should – get along just fine without trying to conform to *any* rule, *old or new.*"[13] The second sentence must be an overstatement – Moore simply thinks that there are rules we ought always to conform to. But conforming to, or obeying, these rules does not require "uniform conformity." Rules may leave a great deal of leeway about *how* they are to be obeyed. There are many different ways of being temperate or faithful, for instance. Having no interest in turning rules into straightjackets, a conservative will also cheerfully agree with Regan that many, even all, of a society's rules admit of some exceptions and are thus to be observed *generally* rather than *uniformly.* But he will put his foot down against Regan by insisting that from the fact that a society doing without a certain rule ought not to implement it, it does not follow *at all* that a society whose members' desires and expectations have been shaped by that rule ought to jettison it.[14] The law of social inertia works in different directions in the two cases.

Regan's central claim is that it is Moore's view that since those who defend obedience to a nonuniversal rule cannot argue that it is necessary to preserve civilized life, their only recourse is to show first, what the great intrinsic goods are and second, that the rule in question leads most efficiently to the creation of those goods. This is a task Moore thinks no one has even really tried to do, let alone succeeded in doing.[15] Because no

---

[13] *Bloomsbury's Prophet,* p. 227.

[14] So the decisions we would imagine any group of ur-humans to make about the rules in their society are of little or no relevance to the rules that ought to be adopted by other societies.

[15] *Principia,* p. 166.

defense of obedience set within these narrow parameters is likely to suc-
ceed, it follows that people ought not to consider the effects of their actions upon such rules, but instead just ought to do some good directly.

Regan's argument that this is the only defense available for obedience
to such rules is based primarily on a misreading of a single passage in *Principia*. In this passage, Moore considers chastity rules as an example of
ones not necessary for all societies. Since it is important to place Moore's
discussion in context, we shall quote the full paragraph in which it appears, which comprises the entirety of Section 96, and place within single quotes that part of it which Regan quotes:

But not by any means all the rules commonly recognised combine these two characteristics [of concerning desires which *all* people can be presumed to have and
of being defensible without a knowledge of what things are intrinsically good].
The arguments offered in defence of Common Sense morality very often presuppose the existence of conditions, which cannot be fairly assumed to be so universally necessary as the tendency to continue life and to desire property. Such
arguments, accordingly, only prove the utility of the rule, so long as certain conditions, which may alter, remain the same: it cannot be claimed of the rules thus
defended, that they would be generally good as means in every state of society: in
order to establish this *universal* general utility, it would be necessary to arrive at a
correct view of what is good or evil in itself. This, for instance, seems to be the
case with most of the rules comprehended under the name of Chastity. 'These
rules are commonly defended, by Utilitarian writers or writers who assume as
their end the conservation of society, with arguments which presuppose the necessary existence of such sentiments as conjugal jealousy and paternal affection.
These sentiments are no doubt sufficiently strong and general to make the defense valid for many conditions of society. But it is not difficult to imagine a
civilised society existing without them; and, in such a case, if chastity were still to
be defended, it would be necessary to establish that its violation produced evil effects, other than those due to the assumed tendency of such violation to disinte-
grate society.' Such a defence may, no doubt be made; but it would require an examination into the primary ethical question of what is good and bad in itself, far
more thorough than any ethical writer has ever offered to us. Whether this be so
in this particular case or not, it is certain that a distinction, not commonly recognised, should be made between those rules, of which the social utility depends
upon the existence of circumstances, more or less likely to alter, and those of
which the social utility seems certain under all possible conditions.

Regan's gloss on the part of the passage he quotes is this:

Not all moral rules, certainly not even all those claimed on behalf of Common
Sense, are so firmly rooted in desires at once so strong and universal. Many human desires are alterable in a variety of ways, and any rule that is connected with
a malleable desire may itself change without posing any threat to the stability of
society. Whether such a rule *should* remain in force thus depends on which things
are great goods, which great evils. If the general observance of such a rule does
produce the most good, then the Science of Morals, having been properly reformed and assigned its "humbler task," can offer its defense; if not, not. Moore,
in short, is so far from offering a blanket endorsement of conventional morality
that he assigns to the practitioners of the Science of Morals the task of ferreting
out those rules that *are* generally observed but that are *not* productive of good

consequences. Ethics *does* have a role to play in the effort to reform the existing rules of society, by using its principles to either modify or to abolish them.[16]

From a conservative point of view, the line of reasoning rehearsed by Regan is quite untenable. To start, the second sentence expresses much too shallow an understanding of some of the "malleable" desires and is thus too blithe about the consequences that follow from changes in the rules regulating them. It seems, for instance, to consider one's switching the object of one's sexual interest to be of no greater moment than one's switching one's brand of breakfast cereal. But however malleable sexual desires may be, however often their objects may change, their *depth* is something a society can ill afford to take lightly. In fact, it is just the combination of malleability and depth in these desires that makes it necessary for societies to have some rules to guide the behavior of parents and prospective parents. If the entire array of rules involved in the implementation and perpetuation of a society's familial arrangements were to change quickly, the society would have no guarantee that it would be able to institute new arrangements for the care of its children before it collapsed or had its stability undermined to a very dangerous extent.

In order to justify a concern about the effects on societal stability of the breaking of such rules, one need have no more refined an awareness of the great intrinsic goods than is needed to justify concern about the effects of breaking the universal rules (assuming there to be any). In this regard, note that Moore says only that the nonuniversal rules do not *combine* the two conditions of concerning desires all people can be presumed to have and of being defensible without knowledge of what things are intrinsically good. Since he is discussing rules he considers not to meet the first condition, it is possible that he does consider them to meet the second. Certainly, it takes no great understanding to conclude that whatever happens to be intrinsically good, children must be fed and clothed and loved if a society is to harbor any of it. Regan's argument also misses the fact that because of the malleability of desires, rules can help shape desires as well as rein them in. Moore seems to endorse this point in a sentence we shall examine again for other reasons. He says that when we say that something is a moral rule, we mean that it is such that "*almost everybody can* observe by an effort of volition, in that state of society to which the rule is supposed to apply."[17] It seems obvious that what makes people capable of obeying a rule in one state of society but not another is the conditioning their desires have undergone.

It does not follow from what has been said that all rules need to be enforced with an iron hand. The ideal is to minimize the friction between inclination and rule by having peoples' inclinations so shaped by rules that they do not feel them to be a burden. There can be many rules that

---

[16] *Bloomsbury's Prophet*, p. 234.   [17] *Principia*, p. 160.

gently encourage people to develop their natural affections for their children and that reward them for staying in marriages. If people are raised from childhood to find marital fidelity important, most will embrace monogamy or failing that, put some limits on their wanderings. One might protest that by doing these sorts of things, society imposes a kind of false consciousness on people that keeps them from exploring all the goods the world has to offer, that prevents them from discovering all available avenues to happiness. But one can reply that the imposition of this kind of consciousness is necessary, since children need so much care. Further, since desires and attitudes are subject to shaping whether by rules or other means, there is *always* going to be "false consciousness." Societies might just as well make intelligent use of this fact.

Having examined and found wanting the argument of Regan's Moore, we must now consider whether the argument *is* Moore's: It is not. Regan fails to take seriously the second sentence he quotes, which states that a defense of chastity "valid for many conditions of society" may be offered. This sentence, along with the second and third he does not quote, support an interpretation according to which there are defenses of rules that follow their gradations in universality. Moore is saying that although before much reflection we mistakenly take certain rules to be *universally* defensible, they are actually defensible only for as long as certain facts – which may last a *very* long time – obtain.

What leads Regan astray is his failure to note that in the passage, Moore indulges in another of those startlingly casual additions to his official view. Although everything Moore has previously said has prepared the reader to think that he will offer two different ways of defending rules, the passage actually offers three different ways of defending rules – two ways of defending them when they have "universal validity" and one way of defending them when they do not. The first universally valid defense is the one concerning rules all societies can be presumed to have. The second universally valid defense is offered for rules like those concerning chastity, which all societies cannot be presumed to have. It is because all societies cannot be presumed to have these rules that Moore envisages their defense as taking place in "a civilised society existing without them." Using different senses of the word, this is a universal defense of a nonuniversal rule. This defense is conflated by Regan with Moore's nonuniversal defense of nonuniversal rules. But these two defenses must be different. The first of them always holds, being based on universal truths about what things are intrinsically good and bad, while the second holds "only so long as certain conditions" obtain. Because he fails to separate these two different defenses, Regan pays insufficient heed to what Moore says concerning rules whose defense "*depends* upon the existence of circumstances, more or less likely to alter."

That Moore is considering three and not two defenses of rules is made

clearer by the summary of the argument he provides in the first paragraph of Section 98. The last sentence of that paragraphs reads:

Others [rules failing to meet the first test of universality] seem to be justifiable
solely by the existence of such more or less temporary conditions, *unless we abandon the attempt to shew that they are means to that preservation of society* [emphasis
added], which is itself a mere means, and are able to establish that they are directly means to good or evil in themselves, but which are not commonly recognised to be such.

Although Moore is skeptical of there being many instances where one
can successfully defend the introduction of a rule to a society that does
not already follow it, he might be suggesting that the defense of chastity
rules provides one such instance. Although such a defense "require[s] an
examination into the primary ethical question of what is good and bad
in itself, far more thorough than any ethical writer has ever offered to us,"
he might think that *he* provides the groundwork for that examination in
Principia's last chapter, where he cites "the love of love" as one of the
world's two greatest goods and "lascivious behavior" as one of its greatest
evils.[18] Although Moore's remarks about love and lasciviousness are too
brief for any interpretation to be defended with great confidence, it is not
unreasonable to read him as saying that monogamous sexual relationships provide by far the greatest instances of the good of romantic love.
Thus rules requiring monogamy can be defended for all societies.

Let us note also that this interpretation would remove an important
piece of evidence from Alasdair MacIntyre's brief charging Moore with
provincialism and bias in favor of his own class, the "aesthetic rich." According to MacIntyre, Moore's view is that socialists are not to complain
about the accumulation of private wealth, as it is essential to the Bloomsbury way of life, and prudes are not to say a word about the Bloomsberries' licentious mores, as they bring into being that love of love whose
value is beyond their paltry comprehension.[19] Although it is worth pointing out that Moore shows little interest in some of the most interesting
moral and social criticism of his time, we might reasonably conclude that
one has been overcome by animus who reads him as saying that while others may not covet *his* neighbor's goods, his neighbors may covet *their* wives.

We turn now to Regan's reading of Moore's claim that there are many
situations in which we ought just to do some good directly without wor-
rying about the effects of our actions upon rules. Does it follow that in
most situations we ought not to consider the effects of our actions on nonnecessary rules? As Regan notes, at one point Moore says the following:
"It seems, therefore, that, in cases of doubt, instead of following rules, of
which he is unable to see the good effects in his particular case, the individual should rather guide his choice by a direct consideration of the

<hr>

[18] Ibid., pp. 203–5, 209–10.   [19] *After Virtue*, pp. 16, 107.

intrinsic value or vileness of the effects which his action may produce."[20] In defending the view that Moore thinks that such cases arise often and are in fact the norm, Regan makes much of a statement found in the preceding paragraph: "The extreme improbability that any general rule with regard to the utility of an action will be correct seems . . . to be the chief principle which should be taken into account in discussing how the individual should guide his choice."[21] But the context of this remark appears to make it more of a firecracker than a firebomb. In the sentence immediately following it, he writes, "*If we except those rules which are both generally practised and strongly sanctioned among us* [emphasis added], there seem to be hardly any of such a kind that equally good arguments cannot be found both for and against them." And the sentence after that, in which he complains about "the contradictory principles which are urged by moralists of different schools as universal duties," suggests that his concern is more to oppose philosophers' *new* rules than society's *old* ones.

The paragraphs containing these remarks are the second and third of Section 100. In the first paragraph of that section, Moore announces that he will discuss "the method by which an individual should decide what to do with regard to possible actions of which the general utility cannot be proved." Immediately, he sounds quite conservative. He writes, "According to our previous conclusions, this discussion will cover almost all actions, except those which, in our present state of society, are generally practised." Then he becomes ambiguous: "For it has been urged that a proof of general utility is so difficult, that it can hardly be conclusive except in a very few cases. It is certainly not possible with regard to all actions which *are* generally practised; though here, if the sanctions are sufficiently strong, they are sufficient by themselves to prove the general utility of the individual's conformity to custom."

On one reading, the second of these remarks is quite a bit less conservative than the first: There are cases where the only reason to conform to rules is to avoid various kinds of punishment. But another reading of this remark also seems plausible. In the first sentence, Moore has partly in mind the necessary rules, the only ones whose general utility can be proved conclusively, that is, shown *always* to hold. This gives the qualifying function of "all" in the second sentence, where his attention is more fully on nonnecessary rules, a more conservative flavor. Also, since this sentence immediately precedes a reference to the only available strategy for arguing in favor of rules not already in place, the emphasis on "are" suggests again that his skepticism is directed more toward the third class of innovative rules than toward the second class of rules already in place. Moore can thus be read as saying that if we cannot even defend *all* of a

[20] *Bloomsbury's Prophet*, p. 238. *Principia*, p. 166.
[21] *Bloomsbury's Prophet*, pp. 237–8.

society's *actual* rules, we can hardly be expected to defend very many merely *possible* rules. We shall return to these important paragraphs after looking at the rest of Moore's discussion. We hope to show that when placed in their widest context, these passages are part of a very conservative attitude toward nonuniversal rules.

Moore's Conservatism

What seems clearest in the murk so far is that Moore's opinion about the number of nonnecessary rules to which we ought to show deference and the extent of the deference we ought to show them depends on what he thinks it is for a rule to be "generally practised and strongly sanctioned." The more relaxed he is about what it is for a rule to meet these conditions, the greater the number of rules he would require us to take account of when deciding what we ought to do. The more stringent he is, the fewer the rules he would think we need to defer to. Unfortunately, he makes us tease out his views on these matters, although he is perhaps a bit more direct on what constitutes a rule's being strongly sanctioned than he is on what constitutes its being generally practiced. Recall that by sanctions, he does not mean only legal sanctions. He has already stated in Section 95 that the universal rules enjoining promise-keeping, industry, and temperance ought to be obeyed even though they are not legally sanctioned. In Section 97 he speaks of the "sanctions of legal penalties, of social disapproval, and of private remorse." It is true that he states that by themselves, sanctions are not a sign that obeying a rule has utility independently of the fact that those who break it suffer by being punished. He recognizes the possibility of a society's being wrong in disapproving of and punishing certain actions and thus the possibility of a person's being wrong in feeling remorse upon performing them. He might well think that some or all societies ought to loosen the grip of at least some of their rules. But these passages do not by any means suggest that the only reason to obey a nonuniversal rule is to avoid getting into trouble.

We must next ask what Moore considers to constitute a rule's meeting the standard of general obedience. It is unlikely that the only thing required for a rule to meet this standard is that most people follow it most of the time. Considering only the percentage of the time a population follows a rule fails to capture the importance it attaches to following it. A rule might count as being generally obeyed even if it is broken by many or even most people on some occasions, if many or most of the people who do occasionally break it think that they and others *ought* to break it less often than they do, and if they feel remorse on some of the occasions when they break it. Almost certainly, these are the conditions to be met with in rules requiring honesty. Almost all of us have failed to be honest at times when we thought we ought to have been; perhaps like St. Peter, we felt ashamed almost at the moment of our failure. One must beware, of course, of severing too sharply the general observance of a rule from people's actual behavior in particular situations. The fact that many or most people "break" a rule in a certain situation (as when they tell a "little white lie" to spare someone's feelings) is often a sign that a consensus has arisen that the rule does not apply there. But we must also be careful about how many exceptions or refinements to a rule we consider a society to allow. Would we want to say that if almost everyone who can get away with these things skims a bit on taxes or pads insurance claims, then society has reached a consensus that these are legitimate exceptions to the rule forbidding theft? Would we go so far as to say that these are examples of the kinds of theft there is a presumption in favor of *performing?*

Moore's brief discussion of temperance, which, as tolerance is, is open only to incomplete assays, encapsulates the difficulties to be encountered in steering through the shoals of strictness and laxity. At first glance, one might think that Moore considers the obligation to be temperate to be extremely demanding. Since temperance is enjoined by a universal rule, we ought *always* to be temperate. But what would it be always to be temperate? Is it temperate *never* to leave work early or take one drink too many, or, following Aristotle, is such unyielding behavior one of temperance's extremes, the one toward which most of us do not incline? Moore says of temperance that it "merely enjoins the avoidance of those excesses, which, by injuring health, would prevent a man from contributing as much as possible to the acquirement of those necessaries [of civilization]."[22] The expressions "merely" and "avoidance of excesses" suggest that he is rather relaxed about the requirements of temperance – just avoid having *too many* nights in a bar. But then one wonders whether even *one* night out keeps a person from contributing "as much as possible" to the necessaries. To follow Aristotle again, negotiating these sorts of difficulties requires good judgment, which one develops only by acting temperately: Do your work while also enjoying the fruits of civilization your work has contributed to.

At this level of generality, such recommendations are neither objectionable nor interesting. Controversy arises only when we consider different strategies of implementation. Does Moore think that people ought to decide for themselves on such matters as the right proportion between work and play or does he think that they ought to show some deference toward the standards set by their society? The quick answer is that he argues for deference. The place to start looking at how he uses a sense of what a society generally observes in order to determine what an individual ought to do is in his discussion of moral rules found in Section 98. He claims there that it is very important for societies to have rules that

---

[22] Ibid., p. 157.

most people are capable of observing. Too much moral exhortation consists of advocating actions that "are very commonly such as it is impossible for most individuals to perform by any volition," requiring as they do, a "peculiar disposition, which is given to few and cannot even be acquired." In order that too much not be asked of people, "it should be recognised that, when we regard a thing as a moral rule or law, we mean that it is one which *almost everybody can* observe by an effort of volition, *in that state of society* [emphasis added] to which the rule is supposed to apply." Still, even though a rule ought to be such that it is possible for most people actually to follow it, it seems that it should demand of people a little bit more than they would give if there were not a rule – otherwise, why have it? The phrase "by *effort* of volition" helps capture the thought that we use rules to demand and get that little bit extra from ourselves and others that it is possible to give. Although one wants to leave the office early, one recalls the rule to get a certain amount of work done every workday and thus polishes another paragraph. One who respects a general rule requiring honesty decides not to cheat on an insurance claim even though "no real harm" is done by the theft of a few dollars. Even if most people do steal in such situations, they could easily refrain from doing so if they made the small effort to follow a rule forbidding it; thus they too can be forbidden to steal.

This strategy avoids the futility of acting in accord with rules whose general observance would be beneficial, but whose observance the individual can do little or nothing to help implement. As Moore notes:

> The question whether the general observance of a rule not generally observed, would or would not be desirable, cannot much affect the question how any individual ought to act; since, on the one hand, there is a large probability that he will not, by any means, be able to bring about its general observance, and, on the other hand, the fact that its general observance would be useful could, in any case, give him no reason to conclude that he himself ought to observe it in the absence of such general observance.[23]

We avoid these difficulties, which much beset the philosophical innovator, by noting that since most people already generally observe a closely related rule, they only need to extend a little more effort to obey the slightly more stringent rule that oneself already observes and lobbies for.

Having considered how not to pitch rules too high, we now consider how not to pitch them too low. A danger we must consider is that in order to get general compliance from those least inclined to give it, rules will have to be such that many, perhaps even most, people will find them requiring less than they would be naturally inclined to give. If we ask people only to meet minimum standards, standards will wane; to use Senator Daniel Patrick Moynihan's memorable phrase, we will begin to "define

---

[23] Ibid., p. 161.

deviancy down." To deal with this problem, we need to make a small adjustment to Moore's theory and then to bring another feature of it out further into the light.

The adjustment is to Moore's statement that those with the "peculiar disposition" enabling them to obey the more demanding rules proposed by reformers ought to obey them. Although he speaks here of a single disposition, there are surely a great many virtuous dispositions. Further, they are not such as to be had completely by such people as Mother Theresa and not at all by the rest of us, but are such that the graphs representing the different degrees in which they are instantiated make bell curves. Saints and heroes have one or more of them to a very great degree, most of the rest of us bunch up in the middle with them, and a few others are extremely deficient in them. (Perhaps the curves are imperfect, as the number of those significantly bereft of a virtue is greater than the number of those significantly endowed.) With this adjustment, Moore can be seen to recommend that rules be pitched to the particular abilities of *each individual*. Rather than think of rules as asking for a little bit more from one than what the least impressive among us is naturally inclined to give, one sees them as asking for a little bit more from one than *oneself* is naturally inclined to give, and also as asking for a little bit more from others than *they* are inclined to give. Thus do Moore's compromises with the crooked timber of humanity attempt to avoid the pitfalls of complacency.

Further guidance in setting rules is provided by the observation that any large society is actually comprised of many different smaller societies and subcultures, each of which has its own rules that members are expected to follow with greater or less rigor. Since peoples' characters are shaped to some extent by the rules of the groups and subcultures in which they find themselves, the strengths and weaknesses of the members of a variegated society can be expected to differ widely. So rather than have rules that demand uniformity from an entire society, let peoples' different group memberships play a role in determining the proper expectations to be placed on them. This highlights Moore's suggestion, which appears in a paragraph we have already discussed, the second of Section 100, that we further explore the viability of the principle of the ethical division of labor, according to which different people are encouraged to follow different rules and exemplify different virtues. In this passage, which seems to have been foreshadowed by his early discussion of the perilous state of casuistry,[24] he writes:

The most that can be said for the contradictory principles which are urged by moralists of different schools as universal duties, is, in general, that they point out actions which, for persons of a particular character and in particular circumstances, would and do lead to a balance of good. It is, no doubt, possible that the

[24] Ibid., pp. 4–5.

particular dispositions and circumstances which generally render certain kinds of action advisable, might to some degree be formulated. But it is certain that this has never yet been done; and it is important to notice that, even if it were done, it would not give us, what moral laws are usually supposed to be – rules which it would be desirable for every one, or even for most people, to follow. Moralists commonly assume that, in the matter of actions or habits of action, usually recognised as duties or virtues, it is desirable that every one should be alike. Whereas it is certain that, under actual circumstances, and possible that, even in a much more ideal condition of things, the principle of division of labour, according to special capacity, which is recognised in respect of employments, would also give a better result in respect of virtues.

Moore does not then reject outright the attempt to formulate wide-ranging moral principles, but rather the attempt to formulate principles for people of all types of character in all circumstances. He does, of course, find there to be an important place for such universal principles as "Do no murder" and such virtues as temperance. But even one's attempt to delineate the universal must be played off against the moral understanding and resources he has inherited from his own particular tribe(s). Rather than bemoan the need to pay heed to what is more particular, Moore recommends to philosophers and leaders of ordinary moral opinion alike that they welcome the particular as a way of uncovering and allowing to flourish many *different* ways for people of different temperaments and circumstances to be good.

Moore's point about expecting different things from different people may be extended by noting that those who have the best sense of what can be expected of a person in a particular situation are the ones closest to her in *that situation*. This will usually consist of other members of the group who in that situation are most directly affected by her actions. If this suggestion is on the mark, then an interesting twist is to be given to the sentence immediately following the previously cited passage, which is another of those that Regan considers to be supportive of his interpretation of Moore as liberator: "It seems, therefore, that, in cases of doubt, instead of following rules, of which he is unable to see the good effects in his particular case, the individual should rather guide his choice by a direct consideration of the intrinsic value or vileness of the effects which his action may produce." What Moore is suggesting is that many cases of doubt arise because individuals are burdened by overly general rules that require them to consider distant consequences too difficult to measure. But if rules are made more specific, are drawn up with an eye on their more immediate consequences, individuals will suffer fewer cases of doubt, will more often be able to see the good effects of following them. Further, because the more immediate consequences are closer to the agent than the consequences that guide philosophers in the making of their rules, these rules will be easier for imperfect humans to abide by, being in accord with Moore's observation that egoism is superior to altruism as a doctrine of means. Desirable psychological consequences will also come from following this recommendation. Closing the distance between inclination and rule is crucial to the formation of well-integrated personalities capable of sustained, disciplined, and confident pursuit of various goods. So rather than posing a stark dichotomy between following rules and following inclination and siding with inclination, Moore suggests a way to make the distinction less troublesome by closing the gap between them.

In fact, Moore seems to imply that in the performance of *every* action, human beings of even minimal acculturation both pursue some good toward which they have an inclination (or avoid some bad toward which they have an aversion) and take some account of what rules in the circumstances it would be beneficial to follow. His discussion of necessary rules would seem to commit him to the truth of the second claim. Having been duly acculturated, it is so obvious that we ought to perform only actions that are in accord with the rule prohibiting murder that we hardly ever bother to note we are following the rule; still, we never rightly act in total disregard to it. But neither do we ever *just* follow rules, as rules never specify how *exactly* they are to be followed. Even a positive rule such as the one requiring us to tell the truth leaves open what our tone of voice should be when we take up the unpleasant subject, whether we should be frank or tactful, etc.

It is our blessing and our curse that since we think as we act, even as we perform the actions that satisfy our strongest, deepest desires, we are always subject to the thought that there is *something better* we could be doing. Offering the G-rated version of this: In going into the kitchen to get some ice cream, we notice the cookies that provide a lesser good that is easier to effect, and also the chocolate syrup and cherries that can with more effort be added to the ice cream to provide a greater good. In choosing among possible courses of action, we must decide, using the amount of time that seems appropriate, which of the available courses is likely to bring about the best consequences overall – *and then abide by that decision.* So even the most instinctive of our actions must be subject to some discipline, which seems to put them under the purview of rules. That the notion of totally pure spontaneity in the pursuit of good fails to hold up is perhaps at the heart of Socrates' argument against Thrasymachus. Some limits must be respected by anyone who is to enjoy *any* good. To reach for every good one glimpses, no matter how fleetingly, is to suffer from a self-defeatingly short attention span, is to make a course of action impossible – is finally to make one's life incoherent.

The flip side of the problem faced by the Thrasymachean is the one faced by the person suffering from Hamlet's syndrome. Rather than having one's actions constantly buffeted this way and that by every glimmer of good, one never starts a course of action because of his fear that there is always some greater good he could bring about if only he looked and thought a little more carefully. (Perhaps we can say that such a person's *thought* suffers buffeting.) One can suffer "paralysis by analysis" in one of two ways. One can be forever unable to start a course of action because he is never satisfied that he has weighed the different goods and the probabilities of their obtaining carefully enough, or one can be kept from acting because he is unsure whether or not an action is in accord with the most well-considered of rules. The person suffering the syndrome in its first manifestation will not order a martini for fear that a gimlet would taste better, or be easier on his liver, etc. The person suffering from it in its second form will never get a drink because of his inability to decide whether it is best to follow a rule that allows him to imbibe alcohol (or orange juice or soda or . . .) just before dinner or after, in company or alone. . . . The conception of complete indecisiveness in the face of good is as incoherent as the conception of complete spontaneity in the face of it, if for no other reason than that to postpone a decision is itself to take a stand on some good, is to decide that it is better to wait. We are never literally doing nothing.

Despite the incoherence of supposing that one could be guided by one of these poles exclusively, it is possible for one to set her course too closely to one relative to the other. The way to avoid doing this is to bring the poles closer together. It is easier to do this on Moore's account of rules than on some others because he does not make a sharp philosophical-psychological distinction between acting from inclination and following a rule. He offers nothing like a Kantian account according to which following a moral rule is distinguished from acting from inclination as the expression of both a priori moral insight and moral autonomy. For Moore, rules are simply tools that help us to maximize the amount of good we bring about in the face of both our epistemic and moral imperfection. Rules summarize calculations, performed when we are not under the gun and are thus less prone to error, about what actions are most likely to bring about the most good in different circumstances. Adhering to rules also makes it easier for us to act with consistency in the many different situations where, within a certain range, *what* particular course of action is adhered to is much less important than *that* one is.

At times when we must make difficult decisions about how to act, even if we sincerely mean well, we cannot always bring to mind the overall best consequences we have coolly summarized in a rule. Somehow, evoking the rule at the moment of decision gives motivational strength to our belief that a course of action is best, even if the full weight of the more distant consequences does not readily come to mind. It is as if we transfer the future good that comes from following the rule to the present by attaching it to *our just following the rule.* This helps us to close the motivational gap between the greater faraway goods and the lesser but closer-to-the-present goods that alternative actions have as consequences. If we were not able to use rules in this way, we would have to aim at even smaller goods than the ones we currently aim at. Further, rules help us to be more impartial between ourselves and others. Whatever philosophical account we give of this crucial fact, it is our common experience that we are all selfish to varying degrees, inclined to benefit ourselves at the expense of others. Somehow, by invoking rules, we manage, without extending our concern to everyone, to act less self-interestedly than we would were we just to pursue some good directly. We manage to succumb less often or to a lesser degree to the temptation of favoring ourselves and those closest to us.

To sum up, rules help us to maximize utility in the face of our various imperfections by enabling us to ignore lesser but more naturally attention-engaging goods for the sake of other greater goods. If this broad understanding of the nature and role of following rules is correct then, against Regan, it follows that there are no responsible human actions that do not fall under the purview of some rules. Importantly for our discussion, even though people are naturally differently disposed toward different goods, the formation of their characters must be understood in terms of their acceptance and rejection of various rules. Although Moore insists on the wisdom of respecting our different natural inclinations, these inclinations must be subject to some discipline by rules whether or not we are very aware of their being so. It is only by subjecting our inclinations to rules that we develop the characters that enable us successfully to pursue relatively settled sets of goods over other possible sets. Moore's general recommendation is that we lessen the tension between inclinations and rules by becoming more pluralistic and allowing different people to be subject to different rules. Since rules are to *shape*, not *stifle*, peoples' natural inclinations, there should be a great many different rules for all the naturally different types of people there are.

We begin to bring this conception of rules to life at a society-wide level by making rules more local than wide-ranging. Rather than have rules that require people to aid all of humanity, have ones that require them to aid their friends and neighbors. Anyone who has negotiated a snowy sidewalk with a bagful of groceries is confident that one who shovels her sidewalks and helps her elderly neighbors with theirs does more good than one who pickets about the plight of strangers in far-off lands. Although the cognitive and motivational gap between inclination and rule is never completely closed as long as we are epistemically and morally imperfect – and if we were perfect we would not need rules – such rules are formulated with an eye on the goods we know better and have a better chance of effecting. Because we know the people of our own groups and care more about their well being and their opinions of us, we have a better sense of what will do them good and are also more inclined actually to do it. Even heroic actions are more likely to be done for the sake of smaller and more immediate goods than for larger and more distant ones. Those who throw themselves on grenades do so to save their buddies in the foxhole, not their country or democracy. This conception gives us what Regan calls for, spontaneity in the pursuit of good, but with an increase in discipline and steadiness. Once we start on a course of action, our commitment to rules gives us the momentum that stifles for a time the natural inclinations that so often keep us from completing the course. It would also seem that this sort of policy enables us over time to extend the range of our concern. While not doing the impossible of manifesting a concern for everyone who will ever live, we do manage to extend our concern beyond family and friends to neighbors, colleagues, fellow citizens of town and nation, coreligionists, and others.

No doubt, a defense of this sort of particularist program faces a number of important objections. For one, it appears to be a prescription for draconian Balkanization. One wants to ask: Can a society afford to go without a large common space in which all its citizens interact with each other as members of a common polity? One begins a response to this question by asking a question of one's own: Is it really advisable to attempt to create such a space by formulating from on high a single set of standards that *all* people shall be expected to follow? Beyond the insistence that certain necessary rules of decency prevail, it is hard to see how standards appropriate to all the vastly different people of a large society can even begin to be formulated. It is much wiser to see a society's common space as being composed of many overlapping smaller spaces that different people carve out for themselves by creating their own rules and expectations.

This also suggests that the way to minimize the friction bound to arise between people of different groups and subcultures is to leave some space between the spaces. Much is to be said for *quietude;* one lives in one's own milieu and ignores without fuss or fume the rules that do not apply to him. But even though fences often do make good neighbors, it would neither be possible nor desirable to make our fences gateless. To get about successfully in all the different spaces we inhabit, we must play up or down the different sides of our character while heightening and lightening our different allegiances. It is worth noting that this is how all of us, except perhaps a tiny few whose single-mindedness makes them fanatics and boors, actually do behave. People do not find a certain amount of tact and discretion to be overly chafing or in bad faith. In fact, it is surely to the benefit of individual flourishing that there be different spaces in which one can emphasize the different sides of her character. So if to live in this way with an eye on the ways of one's fellows is to surrender authenticity and autonomy, then these are values that both society and the individual can well do without.

We have not yet confronted Moore's most difficult problem. Oftentimes, societies do not just require people to show "tact," but rather require them to stifle themselves to the edge of endurance, to live in various conditions of physical and spiritual blightedness. This will not occur in the ideal version of Moore's social-political conception, because of the way in which it allows for a steady stream of small adjustments to a society's rules. Because the adjustments are steady and small and negotiated by the people who are to live in accord with them, the shaping will not be a *misshaping*. At any particular time, it will be seen that most or all of a society's rules from an earlier period have undergone a great deal of change or have even been abandoned. But Moore should realize more than most that the most important criticism to be made against the universal rules of philosophers is also to be made against local rules – ideals and reality always collide.[25] It is a most culpable naïveté to think that there is any sort of invisible hand to ensure the course of small adjustments always being smooth. A series of small changes often leads to conditions far too horrible for anyone of good faith ever to have wanted. So societies cannot afford to focus only on the small and the specific, but must also develop a keen sense of their overall pattern of development. This will require them to look outside themselves, to engage in comparative casuistry that instills and keeps alive an awareness that there are other ways of doing things than their own. This is to grant that well-functioning societies must make room for reformist sensibilities and must occasionally allow for reform on a grand scale.

One might wonder how one can even speak of such reform in Moore's name, since he appears so troubled by innovation. The first thing to remember is that he does not require people *always* to follow the nonnecessary rules. Badly considered or badly functioning rules ought sometimes to be overthrown – even, if they are sufficiently threatening to the necessaries, at the cost of a great deal of social dislocation. As the defense of nonnecessary rules need not be grounded in deep or abstruse reflection on what things are intrinsically valuable, so may it occasionally be with the *critique* of such rules. In many instances, it will strike one that it is the defense of a nonnecessary rule that has become overly abstruse; common sense will then be on the side of its reform.

But, when great reform does become necessary, it is wise to undertake it in the conservative spirit of Moore. In order to lessen the amount of social dislocation brought about by reform, reformers are advised to tailor their efforts to local conditions. It does not appear to be too large a concession to common sense to assume that in most instances, the people of a culture can be trusted still to have within themselves resources to be utilized in the reform effort. Reformers should be willing to accept a steady

---

[25] We discuss this point about the clash between the real and the ideal in the next two chapters.

stream of input from the people of the society undergoing the reform, including even the people whose interests appear to lie in opposition. Such a course will often help to lower resistance to reform or at least to head off disaster. Reformers who trust too much in their own good intentions and sagacity are far too likely to miss the warning signals emitted by all failed experiments in living.

Adjusting reform efforts to local conditions in this manner is likely to make reform piecemeal. This might increase the risk of inefficiency, as momentum from a reform in one area is allowed to dissipate by a lack of follow-up in another. It might even happen that uncoordinated efforts will work at cross-purposes with each other. But smaller and more concentrated efforts are also less likely to be swallowed up into amorphousness and thus are more likely actually to do some good. Further, one small success can often breed another. As the affected people note the improvements that have been made in a certain area of society, they will often take it upon themselves to make similar improvements in others. Still, reformers must remember to be patient. Since people can only change their standards and their behavior gradually, reform will inevitably proceed in fits and starts. All of this is to say that reformers will have to trust, in the spirit of democracy, that a localized process, although often maddeningly slow and inefficient, is in the long run more efficient at bringing about good than is the process of reform by imperial edict.

In any case, the fact that the course of reform is often disastrous requires a great many impediments to be placed in the way of its totalizing impulse. A reform that does not reach into every nook and cranny of a society is far less likely to leave it devastated. In this regard, it is well to remember that the deformations wrought by the last century's – which is to history's – most murderous, tyrannous, and drabbest regimes were mostly in the name of universal reform, not parochial tradition. Reformers must learn then not just to be humble about the amount of positive good they can effect, but also to be even warier of themselves than they are of those they seek to reform. They must do what so many in the last century failed to do – resist the temptation to violate the necessary laws against murder and mayhem in the name of (allegedly) great and distant goods. And apologists who normally pride themselves on their skepticism must resist their impulse to be credulous toward reformers. When reformers do engage in wide-scale violations of the necessary rules, they must not close their eyes to it or pretend that it is simply a matter of breaking eggs.

Many are likely to be worried that doubts about reform are piling up almost as high as the doubts Moore piled up around the breaking of necessary rules. There is going to be a great deal of resistance to reform even when those who benefit from the old ways of doing things retain a modicum of interest in making things better. When such good faith is lacking, ceding so much to caution will give the resisters a permanent upper hand. We must accept that at times, reformers will have to resort to drastic measures and even bloodshed to bring about needed changes. But since blood more often waters the tree of tyranny than the tree of liberty, it is wise to sound notes of *extreme* caution before any of it is allowed to flow. Although it does not do to blink at tragedy and sounds unexceptionable to say that rigid societies ought to be made to ease up on those they oppress, reformers must honestly acknowledge that catastrophe often awaits those who simply barge in. Perhaps in most cases, in order to get a toehold that provides for a reasonable chance of success, outside reformers must wait upon the self-directed stirrings of those they would help. This might seem again to rig the argument in favor of stasis, as Moore does not counsel the dominated of a society to butt heroically against their unjust conditions. But perhaps he would respond that people in very difficult situations first need many small and local acts of resistance to pave the way for reform. If there has been little or no local resistance, it is unlikely that even the supposed beneficiaries of the proposed reform effort will look upon it favorably.

Let us conclude this chapter by again comparing Moore's views to Plato's. Both Plato and Moore recommend that there be strong communal ties among those bound together by rules. They also agree that if a society takes care of the big (the necessary) things, the little things will pretty much take care of themselves. But since Moore thinks that rules local in conception as well as enforcement work better than rules formulated and enforced from on high by philosophers, he is much more of a multiculturalist than a monoculturalist. His defense of common sense also makes him more of a democrat than an aristocrat. The moral insight captured by universal rules is available to everyone – it takes no expert to know that it is wrong to kill and steal and cheat. The more detailed knowledge a society requires, having as much to do with the nuances of local mores as with a systematic, universal psychology, is also suffused throughout the entire society.

Moore's great concern with the particular does make him amenable to the Platonic view of justice as doing one's own work and minding one's own business. It might even be that this conception of justice is taken further by Moore than it is by Plato, just because he would never approve of a society's having philosopher-rulers whose business it is to get involved in everyone else's business. As he resists the monistic strain that leads philosophers to commit the naturalistic fallacy, so does he resist the strain in Plato that finds it desirable for all societies to live according to the same blueprint. Moore's suggestion that philosophers make greater use of the ethical division of labor also seems to be a radical extension of Plato's tripartite division of labor. Everyone needs the virtues of temperance, courage and reason, but they and all the other virtues are best distributed nonuniformly *across* as well as within cultures. Finally, Moore's parochialism is one of great optimism and tolerance. Whatever be their rules and way of life, most cultures can be trusted to bring about, in the infinity of its manifestations, some *good*.

9

Moore's Cosmic Conservatism

The Dialectic of Innocence

In *Principia*'s final chapter, "The Ideal," Moore completes his project of revolutionary conservatism by responding to skeptical-philosophical challenges to commonsense *casuisitic* knowledge. He maintains that a fissure in the thought of philosophers similar to the one that causes them to lose sight of the truth about good also causes them to lose sight of the truth about *the* good. He attempts to provide philosophers with the means to repair that fissure so that they may once again fully trust their everyday judgments about the good things the world has to offer. Despite his warning against overestimating the value of unity in ethics,[1] this makes *Principia* the expression of a unifying vision and a special kind of moral prophecy. Moore's is a work of *cosmic* conservatism. For no one, least of all philosophers, is it possible to compartmentalize neatly one's way of understanding the world and one's way of being in the world. By exposing to them their tendency to falsify the *entirety* of moral reality, Moore gives philosophers the chance no longer to fall prey to their own subterfuge. Showing them that the *world as it is* has enough of value to make life worth living, he enables them to escape from the perpetual state of disappointment with the world they have considered to be the badge of their superiority.

Upon nurturing, the sense of disappointment philosophers suffer from becomes the fundament of profoundly reformist religious and political philosophies we shall call *ideologies*. Because ideologues come to radically underestimate the amount of value that is contained – that *could* be contained – by the world in its present configurations, they suffer from a deep-seated, ever to be frustrated feeling that it stands in need of a special kind of transformation, or that it must somehow be transcended, if human life is to be made worth living. The unique feature of the sought-for change is that it depends on a thoroughgoing *reconception* of the world. Their thought is that since the value of the things in the world as we presently conceive it to be is insufficient, we must conceive it wholly anew as the first step toward remaking it if we are ever to discover the things that would give it sufficient value.

---

[1] *Principia*, p. 222.

Moore responds to this not always articulate line of thought by arguing that such a reconception is not merely unnecessary and self-defeating, but the cause of great unhappiness. Whatever value is had by the things purported to be utterly new really results from their being one of the things human beings have known to be good from time immemorial. Thus to try to make any of these things into something never before beheld is to try to make something into what it is not. This attempt to make a contradiction true results in double frustration. We must become disappointed in those moments when we admit to ourselves that the new things we have posited to be are not. But because we also think we see these ever elusive new things lying unrealized within things that actually do exist, we cannot shake the thought that their reality is just one crystallizing transformation away. We are thus always looking at the world's truly valuable things with an eye toward their transformation. Our attitude toward them must then be one of denigration rather than enjoyment.

Although it is not always easy to do so in particular cases, logically, we must distinguish the sense of cosmic malaise Moore wishes to speak to from other kinds of large-scale disaffection. Most importantly, we must distinguish cosmic-political disappointment from more purely political kinds of disappointment. However much a person feeling purely political disappointment wishes for change, she wishes for it so that more of the good things the world already has to offer might be brought into being. Although it likely is true as a psychological matter that Moore's cosmic conservativism both influences and is influenced by his political conservatism (just as we find similar relations of influence in the thought of many radicals), these mutual relations are not inevitable. Logically, it is quite open to one to be a cosmic conservative and a political radical, to argue that the good things the world already has to offer are in insufficient quantity because political arrangements are in place which require very great change. Moore is speaking here only to those who wish to deal with the world's perceived inadequacies by bringing forth something they consider to be totally new.

To begin our investigation of Moore's thought on the nature and origin of philosophical disappointment with the world, we note something quite startling: He does not play up, or even seem to notice, the similarity between the urge of philosophers to reconceive the world and their urge to reconceive good. But if philosophers allow the nature of other things to leak into good when they philosophize, surely they are also going to be mistaken about some of the things whose natures they allow to leak. It is also plausible to suppose that a sense of disappointment with the world lies behind the attempt of philosophers to turn good into something other – something "more" – than it is in a desperate bid to fill a void. But just as philosophers never completely lose their sense of the uniqueness of good even as they try to turn it into something else, so also do they never completely lose their sense of the world's good things as they try to turn them into something else. So once again, Moore's aim is to return philosophers to a place they never completely leave.

However disappointed we might initially be at Moore's failure to explore the various relations between these impulses (more likely, one impulse with two ways of manifesting itself), it is of the utmost importance that we not understand it merely as something that could have been rectified if only the psychological currents of his thought had run a little more deeply. It is integral to Moore's vision that any psychological explanation he offers of the tendency toward philosophical disappointment be such as to be described from other vantage points as requiring him to "skim along the surface." But before we plumbers of the depths allow this fact to make us disappointed with *Moore*, we must recognize that this points us to what is finally most interesting and moving in his moral vision. Recall the observation of John Maynard Keynes that, especially in the sixth chapter, *Principia* is the expression of great innocence.[2] The final and greatest manifestation of Moore's innocence is that he does not think of himself as one who, following the lead of so many others, delivers to humanity the means of *redemption*. If he were to think of himself in those terms, it would be necessary for him to think that there is some inescapable and tragic feature of the world we need to be delivered from. But this is just what his cosmic conservatism is in denial of – what he wishes to "deliver" us from is the *thought that there is any such thing as, or need for*, redemption. And for it even to seem possible that this thought is what we need to be delivered from, it is necessary to think of it as resting on a simple, easily rectifiable, *innocent* misunderstanding of the world.

To understand this point more fully, it will be helpful to contrast Moore's vision to more familiar ones concerning innocence lost and redemption won he does not accept. (It will become clear shortly that he cannot be completely self-consciously *in opposition* to them.) Although thinkers who maintain that there is a state of either religious or secular redemption that human beings can achieve or have delivered to them recognize innocence to be of very great value, they finally accept that losing it is the price we must pay for the deeper and more satisfying understanding of and relation to the world that comes from achieving redemption. The paradoxical thought they embrace is that finally, the loss of innocence, the awareness of and acceptance of evil as being or having been a pervasive feature of the world, makes the world a better place than it would have been had it never been at all. So, for instance, will a Christian like John Milton find the fall of Adam and Eve to be "fortunate." So too, presumably, would many a Marxist find that the knowledge of past suffering it will embody will make the world of the classless society supe-

[2] "My Early Beliefs," p. 250.

rior to any world that never had the problems this one will have solved. Although views such as these may have us reaching something akin to a state of innocence upon our achieving redemption, they cannot have us returning to a state of innocence we had been in previously. At the heart of the new, *superior* state of awareness we achieve is the recognition that something had to have gone deeply wrong in the world, something had to have been irretrievably lost, for it ever to have been achieved. This is to say that it is required of our new awareness that it be chastened by the awareness of what was lost if it is really to manifest a deeper and more satisfying knowledge of the world and ourselves.

Moore's argument for the indivisibility of good leaves no room for regret upon the sacrifice of a smaller good for the sake of a greater good. More importantly, although his doctrine of organic unities leaves it open for him to say that the greatest of goods depends on something bad, this is a possibility he explicitly rejects.[3] Immediately, this is surprising, as he finds tragedy, the artistic representation of suffering and evil, to be a very great good. But he maintains that the actions and emotions that art displays for our wonderment in its presentation of the eternal struggle between good and evil can rest on make-believe rather than reflect anything real.[4] The world is at its best when it can be fully understood without the slightest sense of foreboding, when one's sense of the evil in it need not go any deeper than what a child feels in a game of cops and robbers. Moore's thought is thus an exercise in the dialectic of innocence rather than of lost innocence.

This probably locates the deepest source of the dissatisfaction that so many philosophers feel with Moore, even as they recognize his historical importance. Equating his innocence with tender-mindedness, they dismiss his thought as something an adult need not take completely seriously. They sense before they undertake a serious investigation of it that the world just cannot be as simple as he makes it out to be. But perhaps Moore is the one who is tough and all those who try to tell themselves that evil is somehow necessary, containing as it does the seeds of the world's transformation, tender. It is he who is strong enough to accept that there are no consoling tales to justify any of the world's ills, neither those that are of our own making nor those that are not. And at the level of personal morality, he fully accepts that there is nothing we need to wait upon in order to do a little bit better than we have been.

But however interesting and moving we find Moore's message to be, it finally appears to founder on paradox. For it even to occur to one to state that the perspective on the world from which it appears to stand in need of redemption is mistaken, it is necessary for him to make some sense of

---

[3] *The Elements of Ethics*, pp. 189–90. *Principia*, p. 220.
[4] *Principia*, p. 219.

the world from that perspective. But just to entertain thoughts of the world from that perspective violates the condition of innocence. To be completely innocent is to be unaware that there is any perspective or condition in opposition to which a case for innocence needs to be made – it is to be unaware even of the tricks of thought that lead the misguided to deny innocence. It follows then that anyone who attempts to diagnose those tricks of thought in order to make the case for innocence cannot be completely innocent. But if only someone who is no longer innocent can make the case for innocence, then to make the case is to guarantee its defeat. The paradox here anticipates and perhaps goes deeper than the one Wittgenstein faces at the end of the *Tractatus*. The possibility of innocence as a permanent condition of life cannot be said. But because it could only be done against a backdrop it requires to be impossible, it also cannot be shown.

For it even to occur to one to try to state Moore's message, he must consider that a simple and easily recoverable misunderstanding lies behind the thought of those who see the world or us as standing in need of redemption. If the impulse to see the world falsely in this way were to run at all deep in us, *it* would be the thing we need to be delivered from. To recall Moore's own example of ethical error, the impulse must be of the depth of a simple arithmetical mistake.[5] (But how could an error so egregious remain innocently unnoticed?) Moore is surely the last philosopher to think that something that philosophers have found to be problematic can be rendered unproblematic by the simple expedient of finding its origin to be "inside us" rather than "outside in the world." If there were something that caused us to stand in need of redemption, to harbor such a thought about it would be to make a mistake concerning it similar to the mistake Kantian philosophers make concerning the nature of good. Moore's "solutions" to philosophical problems concerning both the *real* property good and the *illusory* need for redemption involve showing that there are not really problems, but simply misunderstandings. But *his* problem is that it is much more in the spirit of his work to defuse a problem by getting us to accept that something is real than that something is illusory.

The paradox Moore faces here is not only of a piece with the one he faces in the earlier stages of *Principia* concerning the value of attaining the philosophical resources to refute skeptical challenges about the nature of good, but also with the one he faces later in his career over the value of attaining the resources to refute skeptical challenges about our knowledge of the external world. In other words, it is the great paradox upon which his entire philosophy turns. Perhaps it also explains why in *Principia* he does not claim philosophical understanding to be of very

---

[5] Ibid., p. 145.

great or even any intrinsic value.[6] For Moore, the highest kind of philosophical wisdom lies not merely in responding to skeptical arguments,
but in completely undermining their viability. There are certain doubts
to which nothing is to be ceded: Some things we just *know*. But if skepticism has no viability in these arenas, it would appear that there is nothing to be gained by taking it seriously. If this is so, a distinctively philosophical response to skepticism appears to give us no deeper an
awareness of the world than the one we would have had we never fallen
under skepticism's spell. It appears then that the highest wisdom is never
even to entertain skeptical-philosophical doubts. This creates a peril for
philosophy. If philosophy is born of a tendency to problematize reality
where it is not problematic, then *philosophy* is problematic. Moore's problem would not then just be that the reality of philosophy is the opposite
of its usual self-image, that in philosophy there lies not wisdom but folly –
it would be that there *is* something, namely, philosophy, we need to be
delivered from. As we have said, that this "thing" is in ourselves and not
the stars makes it no less problematic, nor we any less in need of deliverance from it.

   If philosophy is to be defended as a worthwhile human activity from
this perspective, its first task must be the delineation of the boundaries
beyond which skepticism cannot go and the putting to rest of the philosophical impulse to violate those boundaries. So Moore's statement in
Principia's preface that he means his work to be a prolegomenon in the
manner of Kant is no casual remark. But if philosophy is to make a positive contribution to human life, it must not simply dissolve upon the com-
pletion of these tasks. It cannot be that philosophy's only good is to put
to rest the impulse to philosophize. There must also be a domain inac-
cessible to other modes of thought that philosophy provides worthwhile
knowledge of. But Moore's strong philosophical realism makes finding
such a domain more difficult for him than it was for Kant. To chart the
manner in which the mind imposes order upon a world that is unknow-
able in itself is not to answer skepticism, but to surrender to it.

   One might try to argue that Moore succeeds in the task of outlining a
nonproblematizing philosophical program in *Some Main Problems of Philosophy* (a very nice title for the issue at hand!). According to Moore, the
most important and interesting task of philosophy is "to give a general
description of the *whole* of the Universe." This task is threefold: "mentioning all the most important kinds of things which we *know* to be in it,
considering how far it is likely that there are in it important kinds of
things which we do not absolutely *know* to be in it, and also considering
the most important ways in which these various kinds of things are related
to one another."[7] According to this program, philosophy begins by cata-

---

[6] Ibid., p. 199.   [7] Moore, *Some Main Problems in Philosophy*, p. 1.

loging the unquestionable judgments of common sense and confines its skeptical attitude to the second and third of its tasks. Although it is not his concern in this work to deal with the main problems of ethical philosophy, Moore mentions at the end of the first chapter that by following this program, "We get a means of answering the question whether the Universe is, on the whole, good or bad, and how good or bad, compared with what it might be. . . ."[8]

Further reflection suggests, however, that it will be enormously difficult to maintain the impregnable borders required by such a philosophical program between those things we know absolutely and those we do not. Moore notes in *Some Main Problems* that there have been changes over time in the views of common sense.[9] Even a single change raises problems if common sense is supposed to embody things we know. A line breached once can be breached again. If earlier peoples did not really know some of the things they thought they knew, then perhaps there are things *we* only think we know. One might argue further that just because we have no common sense beliefs about the world as a whole,[10] we cannot know beforehand whether or not a fully satisfactory holistic understanding of the world will require any changes to be made on them.

It might be most in the spirit of Moore's work both before and after *Some Main Problems* to argue that he was simply mistaken in thinking that any of the beliefs he cites as once having been a part of common sense ever really were. Some of these beliefs, for instance those regarding the number of people on and the size of the earth,[11] were, to use Moore's own vague word, not "important" enough to have been a part of common sense. However socially dislocating it might have been for different groups of people to have to become "accustomed"[12] to the fact that there were other peoples who lived at distances from them greater than any they had previously imagined, no changes had to be wrought upon the framework into which these new beliefs were placed. They were not, for instance, required to change any of their opinions about the nature of the earth as an object in space. It would have been no more conceptually disconcerting to these people to have learned these things than it would be for us to learn on the Internet about the discovery of intelligent life on a heretofore unknown planet. One might also argue that the animistic beliefs Moore considers to have been a part of common sense are best understood as religious in character, which makes them subject to the psychological-casuistic analysis that he proposes for religious beliefs.[13] Following the lead of his discussion in "The Value of Religion," one could say that these beliefs were never a part of common sense because, whatever the effects of them on people's happiness, they had no real effect on

---

[8] *Some Main Problems*, p. 27.   [9] Ibid., pp. 2ff.   [10] Ibid., p. 2.
[11] Ibid., p. 3.   [12] Ibid.   [13] Ibid., p. 7.

their understanding of how the things they knew to be in the world were causally related to each other.[14]

But preserving the timelessness of common sense is not all that is required by this manner of defusing skepticism. It is of the utmost importance that Moore not allow that we gain a richer understanding of the world by challenging common sense *even when we find those beliefs to stand firm*. *Nothing* is to be gained from the failure to breach an unbreachable line. To return to the issues of casuistry that are our main concern here, Moore cannot have it that by his defeat, the skeptic has a deeper appreciation of the world's goods than those who have never been skeptical. There is no special place in Moore's casuistry for the prodigal son.

Moore's Diagnosis

Because innocence is not cunning, it cannot be that Moore fully understands the dangers he faces and devises a strategy to deal with them. Nevertheless, he does manage to go a very long way on his very tight rope. To remind ourselves, he must satisfy two crucial conditions. One, no matter how deeply we find philosophy to alienate us from the world's good things, it must never lead us to lose sight completely of these things' great goodness. Two, the errors that lead to philosophical confusion must be the result of honest, good-faith attempts to understand the world and value as a whole. A by-product of meeting these two conditions will be that optimism about the chances of casuistry's being put on a sounder footing than it has ever been on before will seem much less unwarranted than it would otherwise be. Moore takes up the first of these conditions in the last of the chapter's four introductory sections. He says there that the question "What things are intrinsically good to a great degree?" "is far less difficult than the controversies of Ethics might have led us to expect." That "the pleasures of human intercourse and the enjoyment of beautiful objects" are the greatest goods is a "simple truth . . . [that] may be said to be universally recognised." To deal with the obvious problem posed by the fact that philosophers and nonphilosophers alike have not only questioned this truth, but explicitly denied it, he says, "What has *not* been recognised is that it is the ultimate and fundamental truth of Moral Philosophy . . . that it is they – these complex wholes *themselves,* and not any constituent or characteristic of them – that form the ultimate end of action and the sole criterion of social progress."[15]

Moore's view then is that we all have a prephilosophical awareness that friendship and aesthetic appreciation are the greatest of goods, but that

---

[14] "The Value of Religion," pp. 111–12.
[15] These particular truths of Moral Philosophy are the fundamental ones of casuistry, not ethical theory.

we misidentify these things when we undertake a more reflective inventory of value. Our attention gets lost inside these large and complex objects and we identify some smaller element of them, pleasure, say, as that
which contains the value we have found. This analysis does enable Moore
to maintain that we never completely lose our knowledge of the great
goods. At some level, we continue to acknowledge the things that are truly
valuable even as we think ourselves to be acknowledging the great value
of some other thing(s). So here as elsewhere, philosophy's failure to attain knowledge has been due to its failure to attain self-knowledge. As it
has been and will continue to be, Moore's main task is not to turn philosophers toward something utterly new, but to get them to recollect what
they already know.

What has prevented philosophers from giving friendship and aesthetic
appreciation their full due is a pair of errors that result from their im-
perfectly using the method of isolation upon them. The first error consists of confusing things good as means with things good as ends. The second, "more subtle" error consists of "ignoring the principle of organic
unities."[16] Moore considers freedom to provide an example of something
that has mistakenly been considered to be intrinsically valuable as a result of the first error. If freedom is a means to there being anything of
great intrinsic value in the world then even though it is not valuable in itself, it is not unreasonable to consider it so. Moore also provides an example of the second kind of error. Upon reflection, it is apparent that a
whole containing pleasure plus enjoyment has greater value (or disvalue)
than the whole consisting of the pleasure without the enjoyment. But, according to Moore, only the pleasure and not the enjoyment of it has (a
small amount of) value in itself.[17] Therefore, it is not unreasonable for
one who does not fully grasp the doctrine of organic unities to reach the
hedonistic conclusion that *all* of the value lies in the pleasure. According
to Moore, it should not be surprising that natural objects of cognition
are misidentified in these ways. Later in the chapter, he says that such
misidentifications are probably the single greatest cause of error in philosophy and psychology.[18]

So far, the mistake of identifying the wrong thing as valuable concerns
only the "place" of value and not its amount. A mistake about the amount
of value is committed after one concludes – correctly – that the smaller
entity just cannot hold all the value one originally found. But rather than
look for something else as the repository of value, one who has gotten
locked into a philosophical view will conclude, as world-weary hedonists
have always done, that there just is not as much value in the *world* as one
originally thought. It would be bad enough if this "shattering" of philosophers' "illusions" about the amount of value in the world did no more

---

[16] *Principia*, p. 187.   [17] Ibid., p. 188.   [18] Ibid., p. 191.

than leave them "sadder but wiser." But because the value they think themselves *mistakenly* to have found is actually in the world, they continue to encounter it without being able to acknowledge it. They thus become haunted by a value they think to have *vanished*. This deepens their sadness as they give way to Edenic nostalgia or hopeless hope about the world's remaking.

Happily, when the mistakes committed in the perfunctory casuistries of ordinary persons and practical reformers and thinkers do not stray very far from their right opinions about what things are good, they are unlikely to cause themselves any great anguish or the world any great harm. Reformers may improve the world without knowing any more about the great intrinsic goods than that getting rid of obvious evils makes more room for those goods. Some errors committed by reformers may even be beneficial to the world. If it is true that an increase in freedom often leads to an increase in the number of valuable things in the world, the mistaken thought that freedom is good as an end can be good as a means. When we turn to more distinctly philosophical errors, we may find later ones canceling out earlier ones. For instance, many who have become skeptical about the amount of value the world contains have taken that skepticism a step further and concluded that their prephilosophical conviction that value is objective was in error. Although the disavowal of the objective reality of value is likely to subject one's casuistry to a certain amount of whimsy, it also makes it possible for one to reorient her casuistry more closely with reality. By managing to believe at some level that value is purely a function of what one *likes*, and then by arguing that there are no logical limits on what one can like, one can conclude that rather than mere pleasure, say, what *oneself* likes is friendship and aesthetic appreciation. Thus by losing sight of the most fundamental truth of ethical theory does one return to the most important truths it serves.[19]

But not everyone is so fortunate who becomes a victim of the fact that the closer one looks, the worse one sees. Consider a philosopher at work on a treatise defending the view that things only become good or bad upon the decision of an omnipotent and inscrutable God. This view causes the writer a great deal of anguish, since he feels that neither he nor anyone else has any way of knowing what decisions God has made. He spends his morning writing with passionate conviction about our having to leap blindly into the abyss as we try to guess what things have been rendered good and bad. At noon, fully trusting nature, he leaves his study to go to lunch, whereupon he comes upon a child crying in great pain. Everything he has written that morning is like straw in the wind as he reacts in immediate sorrow to the badness of the child's suffering. Return-

---

[19] The distinction between fundamental and important truths is made by Butchvarov in *Skepticism in Ethics*, p. 1.

ing from lunch, he sees a child happily enveloped in the warmth of its parents' love. His contorted arguments are again as nothing in the face of the plain goodness of this scene. But it does not occur to him for even a moment that the thread of his morning's argument has been cut clean. Despite daily reminders, he is unable to bring his simple human knowledge to bear on his philosophical reflection. Notice how much at odds with the ideal of psychological integration this person must be. The more quarantined his philosophy is from the rest of his life, the better it is for him: better that one's thought remain distant from one's life than that it poison it.

According to Moore, a state of alienation this deep requires bewitchment by a *casuistic ideal*. Simply, an ideal is a philosophical conception of what the world is like when it is at its best. This description of them can make ideals seem quite harmless and in fact, they are an indispensable part of both practical and intellectual life. Any attempt at all to make something better appeals, however inarticulately, to an ideal. More fully worked out ideals serve as antidotes to complacency by helping us to test the limits of the world, by making it (a bit) more difficult for us to settle for its having less value than is possible. Ideals also play a crucial role in philosophy and other intellectual disciplines, where the goal is knowledge, not practice. To attain systematic knowledge in any field of inquiry, we must reach two goals lying in opposite directions from each other: We must develop an understanding of the unique nature of each of the different objects belonging to the field *and* we must also develop an understanding of the ways in which those objects fit together. An idealization enables us to remove a thing in thought from the surroundings that impinge on it. We are able thus to consider more deeply what there is in its nature that for better or worse has only been incompletely realized or realized not at all. But of course, things do not exist in isolation from each other. So what in thought we rend asunder, we must also join together. Idealizations provide the means by which to cut through the welter of phenomena and epiphenomena to locate the ultimate analytical and causal relations obtaining between such things as justice and happiness. Finally, idealizations give us the means to answer a question of the utmost importance – whether various things are related to each other only as separate things or whether they form organic unities whose value is greater or less than the value of them taken separately. Taken all together then, ideals are an essential component of any conception of value as a whole.

In the chapter's first section, Moore states that the different tasks philosophers must perform are distinguished by the three different meanings had by the question "What is ideal?" Two of these meanings give philosophers their holistic task. In its highest form, What is "the *best* state of things *conceivable*?," the question asks for a description of the *Ab-*

solute Good. Since a conception of Heaven presents this kind of ideal, this question brings us into the realm of religion. At a level below that one, the question asks for a description of the *Human* Good, "the best *possible* state of things in this world." Answering the question in this form involves the construction of political ideals. In its third manifestation, the question merely means "What things are intrinsically good to a great degree?" Moore considers it obvious that this version of the question, the humblest of the three, must be answered before attempts can be assayed on the other two. Although the doctrine of organic unities makes it possible for the valuable larger wholes not to have the goods from the third question as their parts, this is a possibility we can safely dismiss.[20] We must then be sure about what these smaller goods are before we decide what larger goods can be made out of them. It is a source of pride to philosophers and exasperation to nonphilosophers that philosophers tend to ignore details for the sake of the big picture. Moore insinuates that this exasperation is often justified. Misconceptions about the world and value arise and gain much more credence than they ever should because overly hasty philosophers bring to their study of the greatest goods a flawed understanding of the smaller goods.

Moore himself is quite hasty in discussing the exact way in which their idealizing brings philosophers to the depths of disappointment. Borrowing from Sidgwick, he suggests that philosophers conflate the different senses of possibility involved in the construction of ideals.[21] The general distinction by which to distinguish religious from political ideals is between that which is conceivable and that which is possible by the laws of nature. This distinction and another, between that which is possible and that which is probable, give philosophers all the rope they need to hang themselves.

Some things (barely) possible by the laws of nature, for example, that the average person be as altruistic as Mother Theresa, are yet so improbable as to be practically impossible. Although when philosophers construct political ideals they always suppose some things to be impossible by the laws of nature, they also "may suppose many things to be possible, which are in fact impossible."[22] Suppose then that they overestimate the extent to which average human beings can be altruistic. This may lead them to think that it is possible for a polity to be an instantiation of a kind of large-scale friendship whose value dwarfs the sum of the value of the much smaller friendships people actually have. The "light" this ideal sheds on actual friendships makes them more denigratory of actual friendships than they were after their original misidentification of friendship, as their overly generous sense of possibility has made their percep-

---

[20] *Principia,* pp. 184–5.   [21] *Methods,* pp. 18–22.   [22] *Principia,* p. 183.

tion of its actual constituents grow even faultier. They put into friendship things that do not really belong to it and also wildly overestimate the value of these putative constituents. If they forget that actual friendships may manifest great value even when their motivations are rather "selfish," they will denigrate "pathological" love for the sake of some kind of insufferably high-minded "practical" love. Their contact with reality reaches its most perilously tenuous state when they become convinced of their ability to conceive of things that literally, are inconceivable. This happens when they come to believe that a most valuable kind of relationship can obtain between human beings and a purely ethereal, "perfect" being. At that moment, their skepticism about what value *is* in the world is matched only by their credulousness about what value *could be* in it.

Because reality does not go away, not even philosophers can embrace an ideal completely. But their persistent encounters with reality become occasions to conclude that reality fails the test their ideals have set for it rather than the opposite. Since even a properly constructed ideal does not match reality *exactly* – for it would not then be an *ideal* – whatever gap philosophers espy between their ideals and their prephilosophical awareness of value in the world need not seem to threaten the ideal. Especially as it concerns value, it becomes easy enough to think that the point of an ideal is not to be a heuristic but rather a corrective to the views of reality we accept prephilosophically. Still, philosophers do feel some responsibility to bring reality back into sharper focus. Unfortunately, they do so by complicating their ideals with tail-catching details rather than by starting over with them. It takes great intelligence to follow all the details of a highly worked out ideal. The truth of the remark that some things are so foolish only intellectuals can believe them lies in the fact that only intellectuals can follow all the details. Many inaccuracies are tolerated and even celebrated in ideals because on the occasions when ideals do provide a perspective on reality, they can be so dazzling as to seem to light up *everything*. Finally then, in spite of the good intentions with which they have been constructed, ideals have been little more than monuments constructed by philosophers to create, perpetuate, and extend their disappointment.

Before philosophy can make its positive contribution to an understanding of the best the world has to offer, it must break this cycle of false observation and misguided expectation. Assuming once again the role of a revolutionary conservative, Moore must, in the name of common sense and humanity, topple these monuments. Only afterward can he provide the means to an understanding of the idealizing impulse that enables it not only to *not* be the thing we need to be delivered from, but that enables it to be something that makes an important contribution to human life. Let us follow him as he takes on the task of toppling religious monuments.

Critique of Religion

Although the tenor of Moore's thought from his 1901 paper "The Value of Religion" onward could reasonably be considered to be atheistic, he calls himself an agnostic there and elsewhere.[23] Perhaps he does not worry about the difference between the two positions because to do so would only serve to obscure the most important contention of his critique of religion: On the issues of what kinds of things have intrinsic value and whether the universe as a whole has value, the existence or nonexistence of God is utterly beside the point. Religious believers who come to accept this point will find themselves more at home in the world as they learn to enjoy its goodness more fully.[24]

In *Principia,* Moore takes up the task of explaining the course by which religion clouds our understanding of the things having intrinsic value. The "chief defect" of those who look heavenward to find intrinsic value "seems to consist in the fact that they omit many things of great positive value, although it is plain that this omission does *not* enhance the value of the whole." They look "for only the *best* of single things; neglecting the fact that a whole composed of two great goods, even though one of those be obviously inferior to the other, may yet be often seen to be decidedly superior to either by itself."[25] Presumably, the single thing of value religious ideologues look to is union or, if it does not sound too odd, friendship with God. Attempting to make an instance of friendship the sole good thing, they show their recognition that friendship is a great good. But they make serious mistakes in order to conclude that all other instances of friendship, and all other goods, are left lacking in the light of this one.

If we follow Moore from the "Value of Religion" and understand God to be a person "very greatly more powerful, more wise and better, than we ourselves," it is quite unlikely that a friendship with Him can be the only thing having intrinsic value.[26] As long as other people have some goodness, the friendships they engage in with *each other* are going to be good. Although it is possible that the attention given to a smaller friendship will harm one's friendship with God, what we know about human friendships suggests that there is a law of diminishing returns on even the greatest of friendships. No matter how valuable any single friendship is, it cannot manifest all the different kinds of valuable personal relationships one can enter into in the course of a lifetime. To focus solely on one's relationship with God is to deprive oneself of friendships that take place between equals and of the rich emotional unions that form among groups of friends or family members. It would even be to deprive oneself

---

[23] "An Autobiography," p. 11.   [24] "The Value of Religion," p. 120.
[25] *Principia,* p. 186.   [26] "The Value of Religion," p. 105.

of the touch of spice that is provided by the small exchange of pleas-
antries at the check-out line and water cooler. Moore says merely that a
single-minded devotion to one great good "does *not* enhance the value of
the whole," but it appears that the point can be put more strongly.[27] A
person who enjoys only one friendship, even if it is deep and abiding and
with someone of great goodness, lives less well than one who enjoys a
number of friendships. This discussion probably also provides the materials for a critique of the ideal of all-consuming romantic love, likely the
secular equivalent of this religious ideal.

Some religious apologists will reply that the nature of a relationship
with God is misunderstood if it is seen as being in opposition to human
relationships. It is rather that it is at least partly manifested through the
good relationships one has with other people – one experiences God and
other people in an indissoluble unity. But the attractiveness of this position begins to fade when it is remembered that it cannot allow that God
chooses to manifest Himself through friendships with other people *because* these friendships are good. That would amount to an admission that
they are valuable in themselves and not merely as a manifestation of
God's goodness. The thought the apologist must then try to make out is
that although it is not apparent on the surface, it is part of the nature of
a human friendship also to be a relation with God. If God were to remove
Himself from instances of human friendship then whatever the nature of
the things replacing them, they would not be valuable. Since this argument is a "metaphysical" attempt to give value to something temporal by
turning it into something super-temporal, it falls prey to the separation
problem discussed in Chapter 6. If the value of friendship is not separable from God, it will be difficult to hold off the fatalistic conclusion that
whatever is between one and God, whether friendship, enmity, or indifference, is valuable. If there is distinct value in its being *friendship* that attaches to God, the value of the friendship becomes separable from God
and then temporally bound, *human* friendships are not to be slighted.

Many religious apologists will respond that this line of criticism has
been based on too watery a conception of religious experience. If skepticism about friendship with God is well taken from *Moore's* perspective,
this is because the nature of God and the value of intercourse with Him
simply cannot be made sense of in the ordinary human terms in which
Moore seeks to understand it. All one can do who has had the ineffable,
uniquely valuable experience of God is to try to use whatever meager
terms are available to point others, however ineffectually, toward Him.
Moore does grant as a bare possibility that the Absolute Good lies beyond
ordinary human experience. But, since "We cannot judge of the comparative values of things, unless the things we judge are before our

---

[27] *Principia*, p. 185.

minds. . . . We cannot . . . be entitled to assert that anything, which we cannot imagine, would be better than some of the things which we can."[28] The gulf Moore is speaking to that is supposed to separate the beneficiary of religious experience from the rest of humanity is of a far more problematic order than the one that separates the most competent judges of human experience from the least competent. The least competent judge of human experience still has experiences of the same kind as the most competent: Moore's drunkard breaking crockery shares a drink with friends and spies beauty in the glistening of a glass. Despite his suggestion in Chapter 2 of *Principia* of radical discontinuities in the evolution of the human awareness of value, in this far more important and deeply felt chapter, Moore posits a smooth course of development for it. At all points on the course, we are all, at the deepest level, in agreement about what things are good. While it is true that some go farther on the course than others, see more deeply into the nature of the world's good things, we all remain on the same course.

There can be no real argument between those who are talking in completely different terms. The fact that the believer and the nonbeliever understand each other enough to recognize that they disagree about something suggests that the believer has really not left human experience behind. Moore offers an explanation why believers come to think they have transcended human experience when they have not: They overinflate by a mischaracterization of it, some ordinary experience of great value – the experience of beauty. As we shall see in the next chapter, although he grants that something about the experience of artistic beauty is not unreasonably thought of as "other-worldly," he thinks of it finally as fully characterizable in human, this-worldly terms.

Another point, which he makes in his own positive account of friendship, is the one definitively defeating the attempt to find value in a relation with a being such as God. Since God is incorporeal, any relation with Him, consisting of "the cognition of mental qualities *alone,* unaccompanied by *any* corporeal expression," could have little or no value.[29] Although it is mental and not physical qualities that make a person admirable, friendship, consisting of a complex interplay of perceptions between two or more persons, *requires that there be bodies.* Moore even suggests that because of their "mere" beauty, the appreciation of physical qualities alone has more value than the appreciation of mental qualities alone.[30] So in a style not unfairly described as abstract and ethereal, Moore revels in flesh and physicality. With less fire but also less bombast, Moore insists as firmly as Nietzsche that even if the thought of a purely spiritual realm is not chimerical, the thought that it is of inestimable, or *any,* value keeps us from appreciating what really is valuable. We find

---

[28] *Principia,* p. 185.   [29] *Principia,* p. 203.   [30] Ibid., p. 204.

value in a world in which the spiritual and the physical intermingle – *this* world.

Moore also provides the materials in *Principia* for a sketch of a philosophical-psychological case history of one very important kind of religious ideologue. Perhaps Augustine is an exemplar of this type. This history is of one who first succumbs to sexual hedonism and then in reaction to the immorality of that way of life, comes to look for value in a purely spiritual relationship with God. According to Moore, love is, depending on the appropriateness of the object to which it is directed, a part of both the greatest goods and the greatest evils.[31] The sexual hedonist distills from the great good of sexual-romantic friendship an object *too small* to be worthy of his love – sexual pleasure. Focusing exclusively on "cognitions of organic sensations and perceptions of states of the body" as the ones to love and "enjoying the same state of mind in other people," the hedonist engages in a spiritual dismemberment of himself and others.[32]

Because the hedonist asks one kind pleasure to carry a much greater burden than any pleasure possibly could, he must always be pushing the sexual act to its extremes in order to wring out the last possible bit of pleasure from it. At its farthest extreme, lasciviousness combines with another great evil, cruelty, the love of suffering and pain in others, to create the complex evil of sadomasochism. If the hedonist holds originally that a certain kind of organic *feeling* is all-important, as feelings of pleasure pale over time, he might well become indifferent about whether the feelings are of pleasure or pain, just as long as they are intense.[33] It may also be that sadism is the manifestation of a desire to take revenge upon one's partners or perhaps, in a paroxysm of unclear thinking, even sex itself, for failing to deliver on all they or it seemed at one time to promise. And if masochism reflects a sense of one's own unworthiness and a desire to be punished for it, or if it is somehow a reenactment of one's disappointment at the failure of sex to deliver on what one once took to be its promise, no circle could be more vicious.

At some point in this downward spiral, it might dawn on the hedonist that his love has been directed to the wrong sort of object and that he has been living very badly. Filled with horror at the way in which his exclusive concern with the feelings tied most closely to the physical has led him to denigrate the rest of the realm of the mental, he now overreacts and seeks to direct his love toward what is *purely* mental. But the reformed hedonist still looks for love in all the wrong places, as is shown by the fact that he can continue to use the same language as the practicing hedonist to describe his goal. He looks for some kind of *release*, which is finally a release

---

[31] Ibid., pp. 208–10.   [32] Ibid., p. 210.

[33] See *The Elements of Ethics*, pp. 183–4, for a discussion of intensity and value as it concerns pleasure.

from the contingencies and demands placed upon one by the fact of one's embodiment. It has become one of the age's soggiest clichés that the religious person hates and fears the body, and sex and its responsibilities of intimacy. But such hatred and fear can hardly go deeper than in one who thinks of the search for love "as the search for an orgasm more apocalyptic than the one which preceded it."[34] The use of such imagery to obliterate any suggestion of tenderness in sex must be born of the deepest feelings of physical and moral inadequacy. These feelings in turn must be tied to a passionate hatred of the body and a profound longing to escape from it.

The reformed hedonist now directs his love toward something that, even if it is "a mere creature of the imagination," *is* admirable, rather than something positively bad as before.[35] Therefore, he does make progress by looking for deliverance in religion rather than sex. Perhaps if he lives long enough to lose his loathing of the body for the degraded way in which he once tried to live entirely through its pleasures, he will deliver himself to the mean and direct his love toward those objects in which the body and the mind combine to form something worthy of his love. He might, that is, one day become capable of loving some of the people who live in *this* world.

[34] Norman Mailer, "The White Negro," p. 347.   [35] *Principia,* p. 200.

10

Cosmic Conservatism II

Art between Politics and Religion

It is the most important feature of Moore's account of the other of the world's great goods, aesthetic appreciation, that by it one achieves a level of detachment from the hurly-burly of the ordinary world that is not unreasonably considered "other-worldly." Moore's casuistry thus makes room for the kind of sensibility the religious believer rightly finds to be valuable but which, because of his thought that it requires the complete abandonment of the ordinary world, he cannot successfully articulate. But many will suspect that Moore must fail in his attempt to cultivate a sense of detachment that yet remains tethered to this world. By turning away from the ugly facts of politics and power, Moore makes his philosophy *escapist* and thereby seeks to avoid the burdens of responsibility that a transformative understanding of the world places on one.[1] Religion and politics thus provide the poles between which to place Moore's account of aesthetic appreciation. His claim at the beginning of "The Ideal" that religious and political exigencies are not to be allowed to intrude on the explication of the world's great goods provides us with the best way of understanding how he must proceed if his account of aesthetic appreciation is to be consistent with his cosmic conservatism: He must offer the possibility of an aesthetic sensibility that is neither escapist nor transformative.

The beginning of the disagreement between Moore and the politicized opponents we shall envisage for him concerns the extent to which the nature of artistic objects and ultimately, all objects, is determined by their history. While Moore's account limits the effects of their history on the nature of artistic objects, his opponents maintain that they are historical all the way down. And though they may reject the word, finding it to carry unpalatable theological overtones, these thinkers maintain a properly historicized understanding of the world to be redemptive of the evil it has so far contained. So as we watch Moore's account unfold against this one, we shall also see the way in which space is made within it for innocence as a permanent mode of understanding the world and the consequences, unseen by him, that this has for philosophy.

Any account of aesthetic appreciation must speak to the fact, noted in Chapter 2, that objects are artistic only if they are created in certain con-

---

[1] Abraham Edel, "The Logical Structure of Moore's Ethical Theory," p. 174.

texts. The same series of sounds that would comprise a piece of music if made in a certain way by a human being will not be music if made fortuitously by nature. Obviously then, its history has much to do with whether something is an artistic object and with what exactly its nature is. Whatever it finally makes of it, an adequate theory must take account of the crucial fact that from the perspective of the ordinary appreciator of art, its having a certain kind of history is what enables an object to *mean* or *represent* something. The more of its history that is involved in the determination of an object's meaning, however that notion be finally understood, the more encroached upon is the literalist side of Moore's thought. Since history does not lie on the surface, it becomes less plausible to maintain that a distinct kind of obtuseness leads philosophers to be skeptical of the "plain facts" of a situation, that it is perversity that encourages them to understand objects within larger contexts in which they turn out to be quite a bit more than what they originally seemed.

Let us consider a line of thought according to which the nature of artistic objects is determined by their history in such a way that *in the world as it is presently arranged,* acts considered by Moore to be intrinsically valuable acts of aesthetic appreciation, are not. According to this view, the objects Moore considers these acts to be directed toward are artificial and incomplete. Once some of its history is given a role in determining the meaning and hence the nature of an artistic object, the question must be faced whether there is reason not to include the *entirety* of its history in the determination of its nature. Let us consider Tchaikovsky's *Symphonie Pathetique,* said to be Lenin's favorite piece of music, as an example of such an object.[2] The history that would immediately appear to be most relevant in contributing to the determination of its nature has to do with a subset of the thoughts and feelings Tchaikovsky had while creating it; putting it rather circularly, they are the ones Tchaikovsky "meant" by it. But the thoughts and feelings Tchaikovsky had while writing the symphony form a vast and complex welter. They, in turn, connect to a vast welter of facts about who he was, what his position in his society was, what that society was like, what its relation to the rest of the world was, and so on. Even if Tchaikovsky did not "mean" all these things, is there not a very important sense according to which they are all expressed or represented by the *Symphonie?* To what principle can one appeal in order to distinguish in the welter between the things it represents *by nature* and the things it only *happens* to represent? If one accepts, as many have since at least the time of Plato, that the meaning of a piece just ain't in the head of the composer waiting to be read off by him, one's skepticism only grows about the possibility of our being able to find some narrowly circumscribed set of facts that give the piece its unique aesthetic character.

---

[2] Nina Gourfinkel, *Lenin* (New York: Grove Press, Inc., 1961), p. 135.

When the fact of class or other kinds of oppression as the dominant theme of history is introduced into the argument, the conclusion follows that the *Symphonie*'s being a particular manifestation of an oppressive social structure is more determinative of its nature than anything Tchaikovsky might have taken himself more narrowly to have meant by it. This puts his opponents in a position to invoke against Moore the principle that was invoked in his name against the sexual hedonist. An emotion that when directed toward an appropriate object is part of something good, is being directed toward an inappropriate object, and hence is part of something bad. To listen to and enjoy the *Symphonie* in a state of "pure" aesthetic detachment is to be ignorant of or is to refuse to take account of – is in some way to take advantage of – the suffering of others that it embodies. It is not then just that acts that are intrinsically good are instrumentally bad because of the way in which they keep people from engaging themselves fully in the task of transforming the world – they are actually intrinsically bad. Thus the distrust of music Lenin was said to have had can go very deep indeed.[3]

It is conceivable in some sense that the world not have had oppression as its most pervasive feature. Suppose in that case that someone had created for peoples' enjoyment a composition consisting of sounds identical to those found in the *Symphonie*. Because its history would give it a different meaning, it would be a different piece of music the appreciation of which would be good. Since the *Symphonie* is an object whose most brute properties are the same as ones the detached appreciation of which would be good, it is easy to conclude that listening to the *Symphonie* in a state of detachment is good. This helps explain both why some thinkers are haunted by a sense that value hovers above the world without touching down on it and why others are complacent in their belief that the world already manifests great value. The haunted find that those who already find the world valuable are subject to an illusion it is their job as philosophers to dispel. If in making their case, they fail to fulfill the prescription that philosophers not only understand the world but change it, perhaps they will at least cause some people who deserve to, to feel a bit uneasy in concert halls and museums.

Obviously, the objections Moore would make to this sort of view go very deep. One way he could begin is by claiming that his opponents' view about what contributes to the determination of the nature of these objects ignores the pivotal distinction he makes in *Principia* and "The Conception of Intrinsic Value" between conceivability and causal possibility.[4] Although given the world's initial conditions, it might not have been pos-

---

[3] Ibid.
[4] *Principia*, p. 29; "The Conception of Intrinsic Value," p. 267. This is the same distinction he appeals to in his delineation of casuistry's different tasks.

sible by the actual laws of nature for the *Symphonie* to have been composed in any way other than the one in which it was in fact composed, it is conceivable for it to have been. This is enough to distinguish the musical meaning of the *Symphonie* from the actual conditions of its making. Moore could continue by explaining that his critics' conflation of these two things has to do with their embracing the unacceptable version of the principle of organic unities he so scornfully dismisses in Chapter 1 of *Principia*.[5] As it is no part of the analysis of an arm that it is part of the body (because the part would then contain the whole of which it is a part), so is it no part of the analysis of a work of art that it is a part of a particular society with particular social arrangements. To maintain otherwise is to put oneself on the slippery slope to monism. When everything is made a "part" of everything else, there becomes just *one* object, the entire universe as it reaches backward and forward through all time. The smaller "objects" we pick out become more or less falsified abstractions of the entirety of Reality.

At the heart of what is being contended then is Moore's commonsense principle that reality does not come in a welter, but consists of discrete, naturally unified objects. To Moore's critic, to accept this principle is merely to enshrine our epistemic limitations within an *ideology of common sense*. Epistemological complacency both encourages and is encouraged by moral complacency. Those who allow themselves to think of what gives them pleasure as the diamond-hard bearers of intrinsic value convince themselves much too easily of the futility of extending their concern to larger social objects. They conclude much too quickly that they are living not only well but rightly, that they need not worry themselves overmuch about the suffering of others that is the accompaniment of their pleasure. In response to this criticism, Moore can concede, by calling upon the distinction between intrinsic and instrumental goodness, that it is a cause of sadness if the creation of symphony halls is at the expense of decent living quarters for many, and that the world would certainly be better if this were not so. Still, he would maintain that denying in the name of human solidarity that the music of the symphony hall is beautiful and listening to it is good makes that solidarity pointless. Ethical and political controversies about ends and means are radically misplaced when they are shifted to the metaphysical arena.

What is needed by Moore then is something that will enable him to treat the putative aboutness of a work of art in such a way as to make some of what it is "about" a part of its nature and some not. The bold course he characteristically takes is not unlike the one by which he treats the aboutness of thought in "The Nature of Judgment" and "The Refutation of Idealism" in his effort to prevent idealism from getting a foot in the

---

[5] *Principia*, p. 33. See also Chapter 2.

door. In fact, we can think of his work in aesthetics as an extension of that more fundamental work. Rather than hold that there is in thought some sort of ghostly representational intermediary between the thinker and the thing being represented, Moore holds that to have a thought is to be *directly* in contact with the thing the intermediary had been posited to represent. Thus the mind is provided with *immediate* access to what lies outside it merely by having a thought. Such a theory requires a commitment to a Meinongian view according to which the mind can be in direct contact with nonexistent objects. This commitment Moore unblushingly accepts. Remember that in "The Nature of Judgment," he says that the only difference between the horse one sees and the chimera one imagines is that the concepts constituting the horse stand in relation to the concept existence while those constituting the chimera do not.

The only way to get across a chasm is in a single leap and once one leaps, there is no sense going back. Having taken his leap, Moore makes a Meinongian element the centerpiece of a nonrepresentational theory of art. Rather than consider an art object to be an intermediary standing between the mind and some further thing it represents – which would lead to the fallacy of defining artistic beauty in terms of the truth of representation – he again eliminates the intermediary. The art object we directly cognize stands for nothing further, but is *itself* the source of all the beauty we espy. What distinguishes an art object from a non–art object is the fact that the art object directly *presents* to us an object – a world – that *does not exist*. What is valuable in an act of artistic appreciation is the direct contemplation of a beautiful *unreal* object, not the contemplation of a natural object in relation to something else it "stands for." Because of its unreality, an art object is complete and self-contained, with its nature and its beauty utterly independent of anything in the natural world. Since an act of aesthetic appreciation is of an object whose unreality places it outside history, the value of that act is no longer beholden to the history of that object's making. Thus the art object's unreality plays a crucial role in the articulation of cosmic conservatism against attempts at political-casuistic debunking, by giving us the means to achieve a level of remove from the world. We can justify our belief to have occasionally cognized intrinsic value without having to take on and justify *everything* in the world. The world provides occasions to enjoy that neither implicate us in all the miseries of history nor call upon us to redeem them.

But if Moore's account of art enables us to achieve a level of remove from the world, it also, paralleling his theory of thought, keeps us from feeling at too much of a remove from it. As a general matter, the elimination of any intermediary or barrier between thought and its object by itself goes no little distance toward addressing philosophy's endemic skepticism and sense of cosmic deracination – it is not with their shadows that we engage, but with the things themselves. If all we were directly

aware of when cognizing a work of art were a representation, we would
never be able to get beyond the representation to the thing being represented, as every attempt to reach the thing would set off a further series
of representations. As skepticism about our ability to gain knowledge of
the external world follows from the thought that the mind has no direct
access to it, so would skepticism about our ability to gain knowledge of
what works of art are beautiful follow from the admission that we lack direct access to the things they represent.

Of more immediate relevance to our discussion of Moore's cosmic conservatism is the way in which the recognition of art's unreality enables one
to do two things religious casuists cannot do: to give a full accounting of
the value had by states of contemplation and to enjoy them fully. Because
religious casuists commit themselves, in *some* sense, to the reality of the
greatest object of contemplation – God – they are likely to suffer an "unfortunate" case of "misdirected affection or admiration." As Moore notes,
"those . . . who have a strong respect for truth, are inclined to think that
a merely poetical contemplation of the Kingdom of Heaven *would* be superior to that of the religious believer, *if* it were the case that that the
Kingdom of Heaven does not and will not exist."[6]

To explain how the recognition of the art object's unreality provides the
means to the full enjoyment of art, we note the sense in which Moore is
more otherworldly than religious casuists. Agreeing with them that great
value is had by the contemplation of objects importantly different from
natural ones, he avoids the "metaphysical" mistake of maintaining that in
some sense, both kinds of objects are real. Religious casuists must try to
square their official view that both a natural and a "supernatural" world
are real with their unconscious recognition of the fact that only one of
them can be so. They do this by positing that the two worlds "partake of"
reality in different ways. Having then to worry the question of the relation
of these two different modes to reality, they are likely to come to the view
that one of them – the one more valuable – is also "more real." (They thus
commit the fallacy of defining reality terms of value.) But it is a very short
distance from the "more real" to the "only real," and so the tension must
always be to have the "more real" absorb the "less real." The objects of the
natural world are thus not understood in their own terms as objects capable of having value in themselves, but rather as objects whose only value
lies in their being manifestations and portents of the supernatural. (As art
objects are understood as manifestations and portents of larger social realities on the political-casuistic view we have considered.)

But no one can really deny the reality of what he confronts in every
waking moment. Thus we find Moore suggesting in a paper entitled "Art,
Morals, and Religion" that the religious person's claim to believe "in the

existence of the objects that he contemplates . . . is often, . . . a mere assertion; implying no dishonesty, of course, but distinguished from any belief, deserving to be taken seriously, in that it merely means that he is always ready in argument and in his thoughts, to affix to a given proposition
the predicate that it is true."[7] Although one might think that a ritual of
assertion this empty must be harmless, this is not so. Because we are complicated, it leads to the creation of complicated sets of false metabeliefs,
a general state of reflective befuddlement like the one suffered by all
those philosophers who believe themselves to be denying the uniqueness
of good. Those who suffer such a state have their contemplative states
rendered much less enjoyable, as they constantly worry about the truth
of the beliefs they *think* these states commit them to.

The simple solution to these difficulties lies in the frank acknowledgment of the unreality of the art objects we cognize. This immediately enables one to enjoy a work of art for its own sake without any worry about
its further significance. Tom Regan puts the point very nicely. The fully
self-aware contemplator of art:

does not suppose that he must assert the real existence of the characters depicted
in [a] novel in order to find them or the novel beautiful, and neither does the
appreciative listener or performer of . . . music believe he must assert that the
notes he hears or plays correspond to some "reality" beyond themselves. Art *just
is* what it is, and not another thing. Those who appreciate art are content to let
the matter stand there.[8]

The less direct benefit of this acknowledgment is that it frees one from the
religious worries that keep her from being fully engaged by the reality of
the *natural* world. With no need to worry about what their otherworldly
significance might be, one is able fully to enjoy the friendships and occasions to appreciate natural beauty that the natural world provides.[9]

But now we must confront a most important question: Can Moore's
theory of art really fit comfortably within a program of cosmic conservatism, or must it too be the manifestation of a feeling that the world as
it is, is in some way inadequate? If the only reason to contemplate unreal
objects is that real ones are unworthy, artistic contemplation becomes a
kind of *substitute* experience, a means of allaying our disappointment with
the actual world. In papers he wrote prior to *Principia*, Moore occasionally hints at such a thought. Admitting in the last paragraph of "The Value
of Religion" that the goodness of some real objects "is necessary for our
comfort," he assures us that the requisite goodness can be found in *people*. But he qualifies his optimism when he continues by saying that rather
than engage in a fruitless search for God, we ought to engage in friendships with people, "who though perhaps less good than we can imagine

[7] Quoted by Tom Regan in *Bloomsbury's Prophet*, p. 168.
    [8] Ibid.   [9] "The Value of Religion," p. 120.

God to be, are worthy of all the affections we can feel. . . ." It is not hard to find in this a suggestion that religious idols are expressions of self-reproach and religious rituals exercises by which we manage to give and receive more unreal love than it is possible to give and receive in reality. And when he says that the emotion enjoyed by the lover of art "need not lose *much* [emphasis added] of its force, because its object is not real," we might well think that he has not completely masked his own disappointment with the actual world.

In "Art, Morals, and Religion," Moore openly asserts that art engages in deception about the value the actual world contains. He writes of music that "it makes us believe, for the time being, that it is far more permanent and bulks far larger in the sum of things than it really does. It misrepresents the world as better than it is, as containing far more good of the same kind, than it really does." He also says, "Unless, then, we are willing to abandon the pursuit of Art, I think we must admit that it is necessary and right to deceive ourselves."[10] So it seems as if the only way in which the position of art lovers is an improvement on that of religious believers is that they only occasionally confuse their wish with reality. The view that we ought to continue in this course of self-deception also hints that there is nothing better to be had by taking up programs of political and social reform. Such fatalism is certainly pessimistic and perhaps even cowardly.

One might try to respond that the troubling parts of Moore's view on the superiority of art to the world are all presaged on the mistaken view he held prior to *Principia* that "nothing else" than that "which is good is a proper object of Art."[11] Once we grant what is obvious, that good art also trades in evil, we will realize that the real world need no longer come out second best to unreal ones. In fact, granting this point enables us to see how Moore more completely unfolds the dialectic of innocence. By providing a place where evil can be housed, art makes it possible for the actual world to be at its best when it is *wholly* good. Although he is generally skeptical of the claim that the virtues are intrinsically good, he does consider courage and compassion to be among a class of very valuable "mixed" goods, goods "absolutely dependent . . . upon [the] inclusion of something evil or ugly."[12] The fact that part of the Ideal is comprised of such goods might then appear to defeat his casuistry of innocence, making the best world one in which real evil is overcome or redeemed. But this is not so, as the evils we cognize in these acts may be the "purely imaginary" ones of tragic art.[13]

But in response to this argument, the critic will claim that making a place for evil in art only succeeds in shifting Moore's problem, that, in

[10] *Bloomsbury's Prophet*, pp. 166, 169.
[11] Ibid., p. 165.   [12] *Principia*, p. 219.   [13] Ibid.

198   G. E. MOORE'S ETHICAL THEORY

fact, it makes the articulation of a nonredemptive casuistry even more difficult for him. Although when stated baldly it sounds strange and troubling, we know it to be true that great art gives to the suffering and even to some of the evildoing we find in it, a purity and pitch they lack in actuality. Within the framework of Moore's theory of art, this would appear to give the unreal worlds of tragedy a grandeur in the light of which the actual world must appear paltry and wan. And if we compare *ourselves* to the unreal figures of the tragic stage, we cannot help but conclude that we "Shall never see so much, nor live so long." So whereas originally, the actual world looked inadequate in comparison to unreal, completely good worlds, it now appears inadequate in comparison to unreal worlds that contain, and perhaps even are, *evil*. The problem cannot be avoided by an argument that the value of tragedy lies in its being a purgative of some of our deepest impulses or in its enabling us to see that, appearances to the contrary, it is good that reality is not as pure or highly pitched as we can conceive it to be. The first of these arguments would make the appreciation of tragedy good only as a means, while the second would either do that or *redeem* the deep-seated tendency in human beings to see the world incorrectly by making it the source of great artistic beauty.

So far then, we have not seen a way for Moore to work out a casuistry in which the consciousness of intrinsic value does not give rise to a dialectic of alienation and redemption. Thus far, it appears to be Moore's insuperable problem that he requires there both to be and not to be a sharp divide between the actual and the ideal. Without such a divide, we can never be fully engaged in either realm; but with such a divide, the actual world appears not to be worth engaging in. The solution to his problem cannot be to effect the elimination of the impulse that gives rise to idealizations, even if such a thing were possible. For one, the ability to idealize is a prerequisite for our being able to effect an improvement in *anything*. As Plato never tired of pointing out, we need idealizations just to make better shoes and pruning shears. But the reason more relevant to this discussion has already been noted: the impulse to idealize is the gift by which we bring artistic beauty into being. So the only hope for Moore is to show how it is possible for there to be idealization without alienation.

Moore's Solution and Its Consequences

Once again, Moore steers a course at whose simplicity and "cleverness" we, but not he, can only marvel. Let us return to his brief introductory remarks at the beginning of "The Ideal." He acknowledges there, as he must, the best that is nomically possible and the best that is conceivable as necessary features of different kinds of ideals. He notes that the constructor of political ideals "may suppose many things to be possible, which are in fact impossible" and that those who construct religious ideals "may disregard *all* natural laws, however certainly established."[14] At first glance, the mere acknowledgment of these unrealistic notions of possibility stretches the gap between the ideal and the actual to a size large enough to hold an infinitude of disappointment with the way the world actually is. But without directly acknowledging the problem, Moore eliminates the inevitability of disappointment by articulating the ideal completely in terms of the *actual*. He thus shows to the disappointed that the best things we could possibly or even conceivably do are what we – sometimes – *already* do. This being so, we need never suffer the thought that the world is lacking something it can never have.

The "strategy" by which Moore defuses the dangers posed by the distinction between ideality and actuality, by which he makes it appear that there both is and is not a gap between the two, can be described in either of two ways: Either he keeps the gap between the ideal and the actual open, but makes it untroubling by placing the same things on either side of it, or he opens the gap only to close it *immediately* and leave no trace. It should be clear why it is important that Moore do all this with no fanfare, without even the whiff of a suggestion that he knows himself to be dealing with the crucial problem of his casuistry. For a moment at least, he makes it seem as if it is possible for innocence without knowing it to reassure itself against the possibility of its own loss. In that moment, Moore becomes the most antiprophetic of moral prophets: Our wisest seers and most impassioned critics tell us nothing but what every child knows as a matter of course. In order to know these things as deeply as it is possible to know them, it is not necessary for us to return to them from a period of self-imposed exile.

But however simple and beautiful we find Moore's negotiation of his problem to be, he has not yet found a safe place to land. The conception of the world in which the acknowledgment of a gap between the actual world and the ideal world does not give rise to disappointment is itself an ideal. Hence, by Moore's own lights, it is a conception of something *unreal*, is of a world that *does not exist*. If it is only in an unreal world that the gap between the ideal and the actual does not give rise to disappointment then in *this* world, there must be disappointment II. In actuality then, Moore's idealization of an innocent world makes this world a sadder place than it was before he staked his claim for its innocence. He raises our hopes, only to dash them, that what first appeared so fragile was actually strong enough.

There appear to be two courses available to Moore for dealing with this problem, one rather conventional in its implications for ethics and philosophy in general, and the other far more radical. The first is just to con-

---

[14] Ibid., p. 183.

cede the defeat of innocence. Because of the kind of beings we are, the acceptance of the objectivity of value cannot be a simple matter. It is an ineluctable part of our nature to problematize reality and with it, value; therefore, casuistry will have to be redemptive. Moore is right in thinking it to be the main task of ethics to speak to the spirit of resistance in all the ingenious forms in which it manifests itself. But since our creativity, like our perversity, is inexhaustible, there is nothing he or anyone else can do or say that will bring that spirit of resistance to a halt. Even if it were possible to do so, it would not be desirable, as without it we would lose the good by which we are redeemed, the ability to resist our original resistance and search, by searching ourselves, for a complete knowledge of good. This is to say that the recognition of the objectivity of good not only engenders resistance, but that taking the full measure of the objectivity of good *requires* resistance. Because we can only know as much about the world, and value, and ourselves as we have struggled against, it is by resistance that we both fall and are redeemed.

If we take this view of the matter, we are likely to find that Moore plays a very important historical role in ethics' dialectic of resistance and reconciliation. By finding a theme that ties together so many of the arguments of the resisters and a simple way of responding to them, he clears the way for new arguments and new responses. The historical irony Moore was subject to thus turns out only to appear to be cruel on the surface. The skepticism he engendered in his attempt to undermine skepticism will be or is already being redeemed in the next stage of ethical reflection. But Moore's historical achievement is not his only, or even perhaps his greatest one. It is in the spirit of resistance that it turn upon itself. It is thus in the spirit of philosophy that objectivist ethics not just answer the arguments of the resisters, but that it resist the original impulse to resist. With some part of ourselves, we do continue to honor and to try to hold on to innocence. Although it is nothing that can partly be held on to, Moore's "naïve" attempt to do so enables us to take the full measure of what we lose by our original resistance. If the value of a world redeemed is measured by what was lost in its coming to be, then Moore's vision of a beautiful world not needing redemption has enlarged our sense of the actual world's value.

The second, more radical, response to Moore's difficulty branches off into two different lines. If it is most in the spirit of his work to prevent certain kinds of skepticism from even getting a toehold in human thought, one of these lines is likely to be most in the spirit of his work, although this is not something that would have pleased him. We can begin to explore these lines by explaining and exploiting what until now has appeared to be a curious weakness of Moore's casuistry – his failure to make a place for knowledge, including philosophical knowledge, as a third great good. If it is a prerequisite of philosophical knowledge that it be systematic, that it be knowledge of something as a whole as opposed to piecemeal knowledge of this or that fact, then there can be no such thing as philosophical knowledge. The only world in which we could "discover" the systematic relations that would provide such knowledge is an ideal world we *create,* a world in which we *place* the relations we find. We thus put front and center at the beginning of Moore's great career in anti-skepticism the great issue he does not seem to have fully recognized. *Philosophy* itself, with the impossible demands it places on knowledge, is the source of skepticism.

The first way of dealing with this problem is to follow the thread in *Principia* that Wittgenstein can be seen to have picked up on and make it the goal of philosophy to annihilate itself in such a way that it never rises again.[15] (Upon the full recognition of the debilitating character of its spirit of skepticism, would philosophy's last murmur be one of regret that it ever was or one of gladness that it would never be again?) From this perspective, we again see *Principia,* which seems at first to be as straightforward as a battering ram, as a masterful work of indirection. By putting himself into a position where he does not see the paradox squarely confronting him – that innocence precludes *any* commerce with philosophy – Moore defeats skepticism momentarily and thereby gives to philosophy an *aphilosophical* conception of value it can peacefully take to its grave.

But a program of philosophical self-annihilation undertaken in an attempt to return us to a state of innocence must be born of a distinctly philosophical kind of self-consciousness. It is thus even more subject to undermining than a program that half-consciously seeks to preserve innocence. In this regard, we can again compare Moore to the far more self-conscious Wittgenstein. Wittgenstein claims it to be the goal of philosophy to discover that which would enable one to stop doing philosophy.[16] But he surely recognizes, after his failure to reach that goal in the *Tractatus,* that he will never be able to reach it. He knows better than anyone the impossibility of putting to rest skeptical-philosophical concerns by stratagems self-consciously designed in the light of them. Even as he attempts to bring his philosophizing to an end, he knows that he will be forever perched on his own shoulder, making the rejoinders and raising the questions that are both the signs of continuing unease and the spurs to further unease. Knowing too the power of the philosophical illusions from which he is trying to free himself, he knows that any glimpse of what it would be like to be free of illusion is likely to be just another illusion. Thus does the notion of innocence come under suspicion in Wittgenstein's work and thus is that work, in its recognition of the bottomlessness

---

[15] This is not to suggest that Wittgenstein was deeply directly influenced by *Principia.* But as Regan notes, p. 214, he did read it. And even though he derogates *Principia* to Russell, the line of thought he ruthlessly carries out is found in it.

[16] *Philosophical Investigations,* p. 51.

of the human capacity for self-deception, tragic in a way that, quite appropriately, Moore's is not. If we conclude, as we are likely to, that this gives Wittgenstein's work a dimension of greatness lacking in Moore's, we can only fully recognize that dimension in counterpoint to work such as Moore's. To appreciate the diabolical character of the labyrinths, it is necessary to have a vision of the world of sunlight they do not lead to.

The second response to Moore's problem, far more radical in its implications for philosophy, is to completely accept the implications of his views about the nature of ideals and grant that philosophy is entirely creative and not at all cognitive. The goal of philosophy is not to provide systematic knowledge of the actual world, but to create ideal worlds—philosophy aims for beauty, not truth. In the sentence immediately following the one in which he claims the goal of philosophy to be the discovery of that which enables one to stop doing it, Wittgenstein speaks of that discovery as "The one that gives philosophy peace, so that it is no longer tormented by questions which bring *itself* into question." This could be read as suggesting that peace can come to philosophy only upon the discovery of that impossible thing that stops the doing of it. But if philosophy's concern is solely with manifestations of beauty that are independent of reality, then the source of its torment, its fears about the tenuousness of its relation to reality, disappears. Philosophy can then either continue to be done without calling itself into question, or it can continue to question itself but with the questions no longer being the cause of torment. Since beauty provides its own justification, as long as its productions are beautiful, philosophy need no longer question itself. Or if it does continue to question itself, *that* will be justified as long as the results of the questioning are beautiful. On this conception of philosophy, we do not find so much that we have kicked away the ladder after finishing with it, but that we have used it to climb to a faraway place exactly like the place we left.

One might respond to this attempt to solve Moore's problem that since philosophy's obsession has been with knowledge that stands up to all attempts at refutation, it cannot be right to consider as philosophy something that abandons all concern for knowledge. It would be far more honest to speak about the *abandonment* of philosophy under this conception. But in response to that, one can say that this *is* the conception of philosophy that most exemplifies its spirit of invincible self-undercutting. When the spirit of skepticism is turned, as it must be, completely upon itself at the same time that it is turned on philosophical claims purporting to be about the world, what will be left are not claims that have withstood skepticism, but claims that have been *liberated* from it. The philosopher's dream has been to find presuppositions about the world that, by withstanding their own trial by fire, win immunity from all further trials. But the only way for any claim to withstand such a trial is for it to be a *postulation* rather than a hypothesis. Such a claim wins immunity by being

"about" what it creates. On this view, the lines of criticism that a philosophical conception implicitly contains, the ones it generates for itself,
are the means by which a community of philosophers is able to collabo-
rate on the creation of beauty. And the results of "external" criticisms of
a philosophical conception, if they are intelligible, serve to create new
conceptions and with them, new possibilities for beauty.

The possibility must be conceded, although it would be in spite of the
fact that great literature has been created by writers who reveled in their
creativity, that philosophy cannot survive the exposure of its nature as
purely creative. Philosophy might require, as Moore for a time thought
art did, a degree of self-deception. (It would be a nice irony to conclude
that for their peace of mind, the truth must be hidden from philosophers!) Although some would welcome the death of philosophy with
open arms, others just would have to resign themselves to the fact that
the creation of new kinds of beauty is often at the expense of old. Because
of the human impulse to preserve what is beautiful, they could also be
confident that the great philosophical works of the past will not be allowed to die completely. They will continue to be read and people will
continue to be amazed by them, just as they read and are amazed by such
distant artists as Homer. The great philosophical works may even manage
to be something more than museum pieces. Even if philosophical conceptions could only have been developed by those who saw themselves as
engaged in the deadly serious pursuit of truth, it is open to more self-
aware and playful writers to take them up in their own less serious works.
(If playfulness ran more deeply in the world, perhaps there would not be
real cops and real robbers. Still, children play cops and robbers.)

It may also be that the large-scale acceptance by philosophers of the
fact that they have been aiming at the creation of beauty rather than the
discovery of truth will lead to a great philosophical florescence. It is in
the spirit of this conception of philosophy not to consider that others or
even oneself ought to do philosophy only under this conception. (Artists
have shown throughout the ages that they can be equally absorbed in
what they do and do it equally well while having radically different conceptions of what they are doing.) So we may perhaps look forward to a
day when fewer thinkers are stifled by an unsuitable orthodoxy. There will
also be available to philosophers something that was not available to them
previously, a way of rescuing themselves if they get sucked in too deeply
by any variant on the ideology of truth they happen to work under, a way
to step outside that ideology and see it as based on make-believe. Thus
will Moore's work enable philosophers to avoid the trap of denying
beauty on theoretical grounds as it also enables them to avoid the trap of
denying good on theoretical grounds.

Although the rejection of the value of systematic knowledge seems at
first sight to deprive philosophers of what they have always considered

to be their goal, it will perhaps also restore to them what since Socrates
has usually been considered to be their most precious asset, their *self-*
knowledge. Philosophers will be freer now to recognize that since the self
is mercurial, knowledge of it must be piecemeal and tentative. Self-
knowledge follows self-creation, although one of the ways we create ourselves is by struggling to know ourselves. Our responses to beauty have
much to do with the selves we create and the selves we know.

At this point many readers who have been gritting their teeth for some
time are, in the name of Moore, finally going to shout "Enough." The
price being paid for holding off skepticism, namely, the complete irrele-
vance of philosophical thought to reality – in fact, the complete irrele-
vance of all systematic thought to reality – is simply too high. If idealizations aim only at beauty, then there are *no* truths more interesting than
the ones such as "Here is a hand" with which Moore fends off the skeptic. (And we are not very far from a view that sees the "assertion" of such
"truths" as these as merely a gesture in a peculiar ritual.) We thus find
ourselves with, on the one hand, thought that is incapable of going even
the tiniest distance beyond the hidebound conservatism and blind alle-
giance to common sense that Moore pledges in *The Elements of Ethics* and
on the other, with thought that is utterly anarchical. It is hard not to think
that Moore would have found such a predicament to be "monstrous." It
would be only the coldest of comforts to him to find that he was anticipating views of later philosophers who do not always credit him as an influence.

The question then is whether Moore has any materials with which to
close the gap between the two radically different kinds of thought without giving in to skepticism. In ethics, the need is to preserve the inviola-
bility of what we know good to be and what we know to be good. The usual
way to make the contrast between two kinds of things less stark is to place
other things between them. Our question then is whether it is possible to
construct a continuum on which to place objects the cognition of which
can be directed in varying degrees to both reality and unreality. If it is not
permissible within the terms of Moore's thought for any single object to
be partly real and partly unreal, is it permissible for what for convenience
sake is called a single object really to be a series of objects, some of which
are real and some of which are unreal? If so, it would then be possible for
different series of perceptual acts to partake of different degrees of actuality and ideality, for them to have different levels of awareness of, and
concern with, truth and beauty.

In order to get some sense of what is being suggested, let us start by
considering the strengths and weaknesses of Moore's theory of aesthetic
cognition as it concerns the relation of the value of an act of aesthetic appreciation to the history of the making of the object of that act. An obvious strength of Moore's theory is its ability to explain why people can be

deeply appreciative of art of whose conditions of creation they are completely ignorant. Even the readers of a realistic novel can be deeply
moved while remaining completely ignorant about whether or not the
novel accurately depicts the society it was inspired by. Still, it would be a
grave weakness of Moore's theory for it not to allow intrinsic value to attach to the historical knowledge of art. A dramatic way to display our
recognition of this fact is to examine our reaction to the pure aesthete's
account that the self-professed disciple of Moore, Clive Bell, offers in his
famous little book *Art*.[17] In this "free translation" of Moore's philosophical doctrines, Bell goes so far as to say that knowledge of an art object's
history gets in the way of an intrinsically valuable act of appreciation of
it.[18] He also concludes that literature's inability to escape as completely
as the plastic and musical arts do from the history that gives it "intellectual content" makes it intrinsically less valuable than they.[19]

Although it is true that appreciation often dies in pedantry, various
kinds of knowledge about the creation of a work of art can in many instances deepen our appreciation of it. Consider, for instance, how a
knowledge of the expressive range of the musical instruments that were
available to a composer may do this. While knowledge that the instruments were quite limited may not lead us to change our opinion about
the amount of beauty manifested by the composition, it may still lead to
our admiring it more than we did before we understood the obstacles its
composer had to face. We may conclude that the composer wrung about
as much beauty as it was possible to get from the available resources.
Such knowledge can also give us the means to a sounder judgment of the
strengths and weaknesses of the entire musical era in which the composer worked. Recalling the first example from the previous paragraph,
if a reader of a realistic novel were to find the portrayal of its society to
be historically inaccurate, a certain amount of disappointment with it
would not be inappropriate. Although the reader need not conclude
that the work is not as beautiful as he originally thought, he might well
conclude that the author did not achieve her aesthetic effects in the
fairest way possible.

No one will have trouble thinking of many other ways in which a knowledge of history complicates and deepens our aesthetic judgments. The
ease with which we can come up with examples shows that we make extremely complex aesthetic judgments as a matter of course. What we are
looking for then are series of awarenesses lying between the awareness of

---

[17] Clive Bell, *Art* (New York: Capricorn Books, 1958). Even if Bell's chapter "Art and Ethics"
had not explicitly credited *Principia,* the reader who was not asleep would be struck by
the commonality of the books' boldness and their grand, but careless, historical sweep.
[18] *Art,* p. 75. The description of Bell's book comes from Teddy Brunius, *G. E. Moore's Analysis of Beauty* (Uppsala: Almqvist and Wiksells, 1965), p. 9.
[19] *Art,* p. 110.

brute physical objects and the awareness of the purest unreal art objects that allow us to account for the complexity of the aesthetic-intellectual judgments we make. In the name of Moore, let us start by maintaining that there are the objects that enable a thought to be thoroughly concerned either with the real or the unreal. The one kind of object gives us a contact with reality that the skeptic cannot gainsay and the other a contact with beauty the skeptic also cannot gainsay.

At the end of series where the pure, unreal art object lies, we find what might be called *art-historical* objects. These objects consist of the various social and historical facts the art object reflects that we *need* not know about in order to be aesthetically moved by it. These facts can be ordered with their order determined by how directly or indirectly they are "represented" by the art object. For instance, the fact that a poet was suffering over a failed love affair while writing a certain lyric will lie more closely to the poem than facts about the political arrangements of his society; in another sort of poem, of course, the reverse will be true. Perhaps we will only infrequently find our aesthetic investigations taking up brute physical objects. Although a detailed analysis of a physical object that inspired a certain poem may help a critic to unravel some of the poem's details, the critic will move rather quickly from the actual object to the things the artist "found" reflected in it, or made it to symbolize. This is to say that the critic will move rather quickly from a consideration of the real physical object to a consideration of the unreal object created by the poem.

Although he does so in only the sketchiest sort of way, in Sections 115 and 116 of *Principia,* the sections in which he says most of what he has to say about the details of aesthetic cognition, Moore does provide materials for fleshing out his account along these lines. He first discusses an ambiguity in the term 'object' "which has probably been as responsible for as many enormous errors in philosophy and psychology as any other single cause." The ambiguity he notes is "between 'object' in the sense of the qualities actually before the mind, and 'object' in the sense of the whole thing which possesses the qualities actually before the mind." In Section 116, he discusses different kinds of aesthetic cognition and their relative merits as they are determined by the various relations they have to the truth and falsity of the judgments contained in them and their various relations to the existence and nonexistence of various objects detected by them. He notes, for instance, that despite the appearance of contradiction, it makes perfect sense to say that one sees a beautiful object without seeing its beauty. When such a thing happens, one cognizes the entire art object without singling out for special attention its beautiful qualities. An increase in one's historical knowledge of an object may certainly help point one toward its beautiful qualities. In this section, Moore also notes that one can cognize beauty in a work where there really is none. This happens either when one perceives an object to have a quality that really is beautiful but that is not in the object, or when one correctly perceives an object to have a quality and takes it to be beautiful when it is not. Moore calls the first kind of error an error in judgment and the second kind an error in taste. Perhaps we may wish to credit particularly interesting errors of judgment as actually creating new artistic objects.

With these few materials, we can begin to account for the ways in which judgments involving ideals become complexes concerned with truth as well as beauty. Some of these judgments will treat ideals as artifacts that reveal a great deal about those who create them. A historian who tackles a poem, for instance, will have as her original concern an object larger and more complex than the poem, namely, the poem in relation to the conditions of the society in which it was created. Her interest will be to uncover all the many things the poem reveals about its society. She might also consider objects larger than that, perhaps the relation of (a certain kind of) poetry in general to (a certain kind of) society in general. The more the investigator-interpreter becomes concerned with more general sorts of objects, the less is she a historian and the more is she a philosopher of history in the grand manner of Plato and Hegel. If our historian also concerns herself with the formulation of ideals to guide the way in which the study of such objects is to proceed, she will become a different kind of philosopher of history.

Some of the historian's interpretations about the poetic-social objects he studies will be true and others will be false. That is, he will find in these objects some qualities they have and some they do not have, and will also deny the objects to have some qualities they do in fact have. The value of the historian's interpretations will be partly a function of the truth and falsity of these judgments. Still, as there can be value in finding an object to have beauty it does not really have, so too can a historian's interpretation of an object have value by virtue of its being *interesting*, though false. The property of being interesting, although connected in some instances and ways to truth, is also connected to beauty. So we can acknowledge an aesthetic dimension to the evaluation of intellectual conceptions, including philosophical conceptions, but deny the evaluations to be purely aesthetic. The extremely rich vocabularies of evaluation developed over the ages suggest that there may be a great many other properties besides interestingness that are related to truth and beauty and therefore, also to good.

If we are to flesh out Moore's account along these lines, we will acknowledge what he does not, the great intrinsic goodness of knowledge. Moore's own view is that while knowledge has "little or no value by itself, [it] is an absolutely essential constituent in the highest goods, and contributes immensely to their value."[20] He maintains that instances of

[20] *Principia*, p. 199.

knowledge are good only when the known objects are beautiful or good. But he also maintains that a "true belief" in the reality of inferior objects can make the cognitions of them more valuable than ones in which the objects of cognition are superior, but in which "a true belief is wanting or a false belief present." It would seem then not to be stretching his theory too far to admit knowledge, even knowledge of *real* things positively ugly or bad, into the pantheon of intrinsic goods. Having accepted the property of being interesting as one related to both truth and beauty, we can allow what is obvious, that the knowledge of certain bad things is interesting and therefore good.

With these emendations to Moore's theory, we are also in a position to consider the ways in which thinkers who do not in general directly study ideals as artifacts make use of them in their intellectual work. Let us consider as an example the science of zoology. It is not expected that any animal correspond exactly to a zoological ideal. These ideals are unreal and may even be the object of pure aesthetic appreciation. (We might think of taxidermy as zoological sculpture.) But of course, this is not the primary purpose to which zoologists put these ideals. They use them for the purpose of gaining knowledge about objects actually in the world and rightly consider this knowledge to have intrinsic value, even if the objects lack beauty. (Of course, many of the objects do have beauty.) The ideals function somewhat in the manner of heuristic devices, helping zoologists to bring together many facts of varying degrees of generality about the objects of their interest. We may say then that even though it is no part of the intrinsic nature of an ideal to be a representation, these ideals can be *given* a representative function. We find then that scientific thinking also becomes concerned with series of complex objects that are partly unreal and partly real. And so is it also, as we found previously, that the contemplation of scientific theories has intrinsic value by virtue of the theories' being interesting.

Having suggested how Moore's theory can be fleshed out to include intrinsically valuable acts of cognition more directly concerned with truth than with beauty, we end by briefly considering whether on this version of it, it is capable of keeping skepticism and cosmic disappointment at bay. One might think that the series of objects we have been considering must be on slippery slopes. It might seem, that is, that for as long as the epistemic gap between actual and ideal objects is very small, then the well-taken doubts we will have about our ability to attain knowledge of actual objects through the use of ideal objects will, as a matter of psychological fact, cause us to lose confidence in our ability to know any actual objects directly. A fearful thought that might gain a footing now that the gap between our different kinds of access is seen to be less dramatic, is that even the seemingly most direct "knowledge" we have of actual objects involves falsifying idealizations to some degree.

Even if we cannot pinpoint the thought in which our loss of confidence originates, we might think that once we suffer that loss of confidence, the distance between thinking about the actual and thinking about the ideal is too small to leave us with any means of dealing with it. If that is so, we have reached a new turn in the road, one where it is again required that casuistry be redemptive. We would again be obligated to point to something that the inevitable loss of epistemic confidence gives rise to that is redemptive of the difficulties it creates for us. Almost certainly, we would try to redeem that loss of confidence by claiming that it is that which provides us with our primary motivation to create the complex, sophisticated ideals containing great beauty. To deal with the epistemic unease we suffer, we create those partly unreal worlds that make the real world so much richer and more beautiful than the world in which we originally found ourselves.

The first thing for Moore to do to fend off this sort of worry is to remind us of what he said so many times in his career: *Nothing* requires us to lose confidence in the things we *know*. Any argument concerning things we know with less than full certainty or things we do not know at all must leave the realm of certain knowledge inviolable or be known to be worthless. He might also argue, in the spirit of his placing beauty above truth, that the psychological theory it posits to explain the creation of beauty is in fundamental error. It simply is not the case that the creation of beautiful ideals is spurred primarily by feelings of epistemic or cosmic unease. Our creativity is deeper and purer than that; it is based on a natural sense of beauty that is one of our greatest gifts. The fact that we also use ideals to help us think about the actual world, to create problems about the world that we can then, in the name of truth, go about trying to solve, can be thought of as a *bonus*.

A final, simple thought can perhaps ease any remaining skeptical worries concerning the epistemic relation of ideals to the actual world. Even if we cannot know that anything our ideals tell us about the world is true, we do *know* that some of these ideals are *beautiful* – and in the presence of beauty we know skepticism to be empty. We know also that it is good to enjoy beauty with others, who in its light become our friends. And in this way we end with a Moore whose unironic humility is worthy of Socrates' ironic humility. However fearless and searching we be in our philosophical explorations, we must humbly admit to limitations in our ability to puzzle ourselves. Some things, most importantly some things about the value of love and beauty and truth, we do simply know.

Bibliography

Aristotle. *Nichomachean Ethics.* Martin Ostwald, trans. Library of Liberal Arts. New York: Bobbs-Merrill Inc., 1962.

Baldwin, Thomas. *G. E. Moore.* London and New York: Routledge, 1990.

———. Review of *Bloomsbury's Prophet,* Tom Regan, and *G. E. Moore: The Early Essays,* Tom Regan, ed. *Mind.* Vol. 97 (Jan. 1988), pp. 129–33.

———. "Ethical non-naturalism," in *Exercises in Analysis.* Ian Hacking, ed. Cambridge: Cambridge University Press, 1985.

Ball, Stephen W. "Reductionism in Ethics and Science: A Contemporary Look at G. E. Moore's Open Question Argument," *American Philosophical Quarterly.* Vol. 25 (July 1988), pp. 197–213.

Bell, Clive. *Art.* New York: Capricorn Books, 1958.

Broad, C. D. "Certain Features in Moore's Ethical Doctrines," in *The Philosophy of G. E. Moore.* Paul Arthur Schilpp, ed. Evanston and Chicago: Northwestern University Press, 1942, pp. 41–69.

Brunius, Teddy. *G. E. Moore's Analysis of Beauty.* Uppsala: Almqvist and Wiksells, 1965.

Butchvarov, Panayot. "The Demand for Justification in Ethics," *Journal of Philosophical Research.* Vol. XV (1989–90), pp. 1–15.

———. "The Limits of Ontological Analysis," in *The Ontological Turn.* Moltke Gram, ed. Iowa City: University of Iowa Press, 1974, pp. 3–18.

———. *Skepticism in Ethics.* Bloomington, Indiana: Indiana University Press, 1989.

———. "That Simple, Indefinable, Non-Natural Property *Good,*" *Review of Metaphysics.* Vol. XXXVI (Sept. 1982), pp. 51–75.

Darwall, Stephen, Gibbard, Allan, and Railton, Peter. "Toward *Fin de siècle* Ethics," *The Philosophical Review.* Vol. 101 (Jan. 1992), pp. 115, 191.

Edel, Abraham. "The Logical Structure of Moore's Ethical Theory," in *The Philosophy of G. E. Moore.* Paul Arthur Schilpp, ed. Evanston and Chicago: Northwestern University Press, 1942, pp. 135–76.

Field, G. C. "The Place of Definition in Ethics," in *Proceedings of the Aristotelian Society.* Vol. XXXII (1932), pp. 79–94.

———. *Moral Theory.* New York: E. P. Dutton and Co., 1921.

Foot, Philippa. "Morality as a System of Hypothetical Imperatives," *The Philosophical Review.* Vol. 81, No. 3 (July 1972). Reprinted in *Virtues and Vices.* Berkeley and Los Angeles: University of California Press, 1978, pp. 157–74.

————. "Goodness and Choice," *The Aristotelian Society Supplementary Volume* (1961). Reprinted in *Virtues and Vices*. Berkeley and Los Angeles: University of California Press, 1978, pp. 132–68.

Frankena, William. "The Naturalistic Fallacy," in *Readings in Ethical Theory*. Wilfrid Sellars and John Hospers, eds. New York: Appleton-Century-Crofts, Inc., 1952.

Fumerton, Richard A. *Reason and Morality*. Ithaca and London: Cornell University Press, 1990.

Gourfinkel, Nina. *Lenin*. New York: Grove Press, Inc., 1961.

Hampshire, Stuart. "Liberator Up to a Point." Review of *Bloomsbury's Prophet*. *New York Review of Books*. Vol. XXXIV, No. 15 (March 26, 1987), pp. 37–9.

Hill, John. *The Ethics of G. E. Moore: A New Interpretation*. Assen, The Netherlands: Van Gorcum & Comp. B. V., 1976.

Kant, Immanual. *Critique of Pure Reason*. Norman Kemp Smith, trans. London: MacMillan Press, 1978.

————. *Groundwork of the Metaphysics of Morals*. H. J. Paton, trans. New York: Harper and Row, 1953.

Keynes, John Maynard. "My Early Beliefs," in *Essays and Sketches in Biography*. New York: Meridian Books, 1956, pp. 236–56.

Langford, C. H. "Moore's Notion of Analysis," in *The Philosophy of G. E. Moore*. Paul Arthur Schilpp, ed. Evanston and Chicago: Northwestern University Press, 1942, pp. 319–342.

Levy, Paul. *Moore: G. E. Moore and the Cambridge Apostles*. New York: Holt, Rhinehart and Winston, 1979.

MacIntyre, Alasdair. *After Virtue*, 2nd ed. South Bend: University of Notre Dame Press, 1984.

Mailer, Norman. "The White Negro," in *Advertisements for Myself*. New York: G. P. Putnam and Sons, 1959, pp. 337–58.

Medlin, Brian. "Ultimate Principles and Ethical Egoism." *Australasian Journal of Philosophy*. Vol. 35 (1957), pp. 111–18.

Mill, John Stuart. *Utilitarianism*. Library of Liberal Arts. New York: Bobbs-Merrill, Inc., 1957.

Moore, George Edward. "Analysis," in *The Philosophy of G. E. Moore*. Paul Arthur Schilpp, ed. Evanston and Chicago: Northwestern University Press, 1942, pp. 660–7.

————. "An Autobiography," in *The Philosophy of G. E. Moore*. Paul Arthur Schilpp, ed. Evanston and Chicago: Northwestern University Press, 1942, pp. 1–41.

————. "The Conception of Intrinsic Value," in *Philosophical Studies*. Totowa, New Jersey: Littlefield, Adams & Co., 1965, pp. 253–76.

————. "A Defence of Common Sense," in *Philosophical Papers*. London: George Allen and Unwin Ltd., 1959, pp. 32–60

————. "Egoism," in *The Philosophy of G. E. Moore*. Paul Arthur Schilpp, ed. Evanston and Chicago: Northwestern University Press, 1942, pp. 611–15.

———. *The Elements of Ethics.* Tom Regan, ed. Philadelphia: Temple University Press, 1991.

———. *Ethics.* The Home University Library of Modern Knowledge. London: Oxford University Press, 1961.

———. "Identity," *Proceedings of the Aristotelian Society,* n.s.1 (London: 1900), pp. 103–27. Reprinted in *G. E. Moore: The Early Essays.* Tom Regan, ed. Philadelphia: Temple University Press, 1986, pp. 121–47.

———. "The Justification of Analysis," in *Lectures on Philosophy.* London: George Allen & Unwin Ltd., 1966, pp. 165–72.

———. "Meaning of "natural"," in *The Philosophy of G. E. Moore.* Paul Arthur Schilpp, ed. Evanston and Chicago: Northwestern University Press, 1942, pp. 581–92.

———. "The Nature of Judgment," *Mind,* n.s. 8 (April 1899), pp. 176–93. Reprinted in *G. E. Moore: The Early Essays.* Tom Regan, ed. Philadelphia: Temple University Press, 1986, pp. 59–81.

———. "Necessity," *Mind,* n.s. 9 (July 1900), pp. 289–304. Reprinted in *G. E. Moore: The Early Essays.* Tom Regan, ed. Philadelphia: Temple University Press, 1986, pp. 81–101.

———. "Preface to Second Edition of *Principia Ethica,*" *Principia Ethica: Revised Edition.* Thomas Baldwin, ed. London: Cambridge University Press, 1993, pp. 2–37.

———. *Principia Ethica.* London: Cambridge University Press, 1922.

———. "Proof of an External World," in *Philosophical Papers,* London: George Allen & Unwin Ltd., 1959, pp. 127–151.

———. "The Refutation of Idealism," *Mind,* n.s. Vol. XII (1903). Reprinted in *Philosophical Studies.* Totowa, New Jersey: Littlefield, Adams & co., 1965, pp. 1–30.

———. *Some Main Problems of Philosophy.* London: George Allen & Unwin Ltd., 1953.

———. "The Subject Matter of Psychology," *Proceedings of the Aristotelian Society* (London: 1911), pp. 36–62

———. "The Value of Religion," in *G. E. Moore: The Early Essays.* Tom Regan, ed. Philadelphia: Temple University Press, 1986, pp. 101–20.

———. "What is Analysis?" *Lectures on Philosophy,* pp. 153–65.

Plato. *Plato's Republic.* G. M. A. Grube, trans. Indianapolis: Hackett Publishing Co., 1974.

Prichard, H. A. "Does Moral Philosophy Rest on a Mistake?" *Moral Obligation.* Oxford: Oxford University Press, 1968, pp. 1–17.

Regan, Tom. *Bloomsbury's Prophet.* Philadelphia: Temple University Press, 1986.

Ross, W. D. *The Right and the Good.* Indianapolis: Hackett Publishing Co., 1988.

Russell, Bertrand. "My Mental Development," in *The Philosophy of Bertrand Russell*. Paul Arthur Schilpp, ed. La Salle, Illinois: Open Court, 1971.

Sidgwick, Henry. *The Methods of Ethics*. Chicago: University of Chicago Press, 1962.

Snare, Frank. "The Open Question as Linguistic Test." *Ratio*. Vol. XVII, (1975), pp. 123–9.

Stevenson, C. L. "The Emotive Meaning of Ethical Terms." *Mind*. Vol. 46, (1937), pp. 14–31.

Sylvester, Robert Peter. *The Moral Philosophy of G. E. Moore*. Philadelphia: Temple University Press, 1990.

Wittgenstein, Ludwig. *Philosophical Investigations*. G. E. M. Anscombe, trans. New York: The Macmillan Company, 1968.

———. *Tractatus Logico-Philosophicus*. D. F. Pears and B. F. McGuiness, trans. Great Britain: The Humanities Press, 1974.

Index

Wittgenstein, Ludwig, 2n, 6ff., 13, 75, 176, 201ff.

"The Value of Religion," 178, 185, 196, 197
verificationism, 12

virtues: as intrinsic parts of mixed goods, 197; value of, 81–2, 98, 151, 162–63

"The White Negro," 13n, 64, 189n
will to power, 84, 91